D1564875

At Home

Space, Place, and Society

John Rennie Short, Series Editor

At Home

An Anthropology of Domestic Space

Edited by Irene Cieraad

With a Foreword by John Rennie Short

Syracuse University Press

gift from Irene after Dec 1999 speaking engagement in Amsterdam

First Edition 1999

99 00 01 02 03 04   6 5 4 3 2 1

Chapter 4 contains material that was previously published in "Entrée, entrer. Approche
anthropologique d'un espace du logement," *Espaces et Societes* (1995) 78, no. 1:83–96. Chapter 8
contains material that was previously published in "Atmosphere at Home: A Qualitative
Approach," *Journal of Environmental Psychology* (1986) 6: 135–53. Permission to use
this material is gratefully acknowledged.

The paper used in this publication meets the minimum requirements
of American National Standard for Information Sciences—Permanence
of Paper for Printed Library Materials, ANSI Z39.48-1984.∞™

Library of Congress Cataloging-in-Publication Data

   At home : an anthropology of domestic space / edited by Irene Cieraad ;
with a foreword by John Rennie Short.
          p.   cm.   —   (Space, place, and society)
   Includes bibliographical references and index.
   ISBN 0-8156-0562-5 (cloth : alk. paper)
1. Human territoriality. 2. Home. 3. Spatial behavior. 4. Domestic relations.
I. Cieraad, Irene II. Series.
   GN491.7 .A7   1999
   304.2'3—dc21   98-31882

Manufactured in the United States of America

Contents

Contents

Illustrations

Foreword

John Rennie Short

I AM DELIGHTED to write a foreword for this edited volume. It touches a subject close to my heart; indeed all our hearts. Although it may come in all shapes and sizes, all manner of forms, the home is of huge social significance. We spend much of our lives in the home, our primary emotional connections are shaped in the domestic arena of the home; where we live and how we live are important determinants of our social position, physical health, and individual well-being. Home is a central element in our socialization into the world. The home is also a place of loathing and longing. George Bernard Shaw's flippant remark that a hotel is a refuge from home can be counterpoised to the deep feeling expressed in the spiritual refrain that a band of angels was "coming for to carry me home."

A strange paradox. Given the huge significance of the home, there is comparatively little work on its meaning. There is a lopsided understanding of the world; the domestic places of our lives are not given as much attention as the public spaces. We have much more work on the workplace than on the homeplace. This book corrects some of this imbalance and focuses attention on one of the most important places.

At Home is an anthropology of domestic space. Anthropology is often seen, both inside and outside the academy, as the academic discipline of "the other." Anthropologists are popularly seen as travelers, students of the exotic and the primitive. As the nineteenth century turned into the twentieth the savage other was replaced by the noble savage, and the western belief in progress was replaced by a sense of the fall from the golden age. In this book, the gaze is turned on the western home, on the urban rather than the rural, and on mass society rather than small communities. These papers focus on the home in the here and now. Rather than looking for the familiar in the exotic, they search for the exotic in the familiar. Objects that are taken for granted, like the window, the hall, exterior and interior decoration, and familiar activities like laundry and the family meal, are looked at anew.

At Home is also a human geography of the home. The volume resonates with the concern that space and place are more than just containers of social processes; they are the social processes. Many of the social sciences prioritize time rather than space. Marx and Darwin became the exemplars of social understanding with their emphasis on how things unfolded in time. It is just as important, however, to understand how things are constituted in space. The social organization of space tells us much about the structure and functioning of society.

The home is a key site in the social organization of space. It is where space becomes place, and where family relations and gendered and class identities are negotiated, contested, and transformed. The home is an active moment in both time and space in the creation of individual identity, social relations, and collective meaning. The home is an important site of ideological meanings, and a number of authors in this volume unpack these meanings.

Home is often idealized. What isn't? But it is idealized more often than other places. It is almost as if it has become one of the places where the songs of innocence are sung. Outside, the songs of experience are heard. No matter that home is a source of work, abuse, and exploitation as well as rest, love, and nourishment. In the early seventeenth century John Fletcher wrote, "Charity and beating begins at home." Domestic abuse and child abuse are nasty in themselves, but public outrage is often heightened by the fact that they take place in the home. It is like a murder in the cathedral; a sacred place defiled. It is no accident, I feel, that in recent years the home has been seen as a sanctuary just at a time when domestic tensions are increasing. We are losing our sense of the fairness of the polity but hanging on to the notion of a domestic harmony. The image of a serene home life haunts our collective and individual imaginations.

The home is a nodal point in a whole series of polarities: journey-arrival; rest-motion; sanctuary-outside; family-community; space-place; inside-outside; private-public; domestic-social; sparetime-worktime; feminine-masculine; heart-mind; Being-Becoming. These are not stable categories; they are both solidified and undermined as they play out their meaning and practice in and through the home.

The home is a place rife with ambiguities. Contrast the assertion that there is no going home to the poet Robert Frost's belief that home is the place where they have to take you in.

The home is a place of paradoxes. Reading this book will not help you resolve them, but it will enable you to understand them.

Contributors

Judy Attfield is course leader of the Master of Arts in Design History and Material Culture at Winchester School of Art, Southampton University, United Kingdom. She is author and coeditor with Pat Kirkham of *A View from the Interior: Women and Design* (1995, The Women's Press). She has published widely on twentieth-century design history and is currently compiling an anthology on utility design. Recent publications include (1996) "Barbie and Action Man, Adult Toys for Girls and Boys" in *The Gendered Object*, edited by Pat Kirkham, 80–89, Manchester University Press, and (1996) "'Give 'em Something Dark and Heavy': The Role of Design in the Material Culture of Popular British Furniture 1939–1965" in *Journal of Design History* 9, no. 3: 185–201.

Sophie Chevalier is a lecturer in social anthropology in the Department of Sociology and Anthropology at the University of Franche–Comté, Besançon, France. She specializes in material culture and consumer practices. During a two-year postdoctoral fellowship at the Department of Social Anthropology of the University of Cambridge she did comparative research on the furnishing practices in England and France. Her 1996 article "Transmettre son mobilier? Le cas contrasté de la France et de l'Angleterre" in *Ethnologie française* 26, no. 1: 115–28, summarizes the results of this research. She recently conducted anthropological research on material culture and consumer practices in Bulgaria.

Irene Cieraad is a cultural anthropologist and member of the interdisciplinary Belle van Zuylen Research Institute of the University of Amsterdam, the Netherlands. Her publications include a book (1988) and articles on cultural theory, popular culture, and imagery. In the early 1990s she coordinated an ethnographic research project on Dutch cultural identity, carried out by student ethnographers of the University of Amsterdam. Her research focus then shifted to material culture studies and in particular to the ethnographic study of the domestic environment. Some of her publications in this field are "The Material World of Five Dutch Households" (1993) and "A Celebration of Differences: An Analysis of the Decor of Boys' and Girls' Bedrooms" (1995).

Heidi de Mare is a senior lecturer in women's studies on the Faculty of Architecture at the University of Delft, the Netherlands. She teaches in the fields of art and architectural history, women's studies, and film theory. Her research focus is on seventeenth-century Dutch conceptions of architecture and gender. She is completing a book on the subject of the house in the works of Simon Stevin, Jacob Cats, and the paintings of Pieter de Hooch.

John A. Dolan is a principal lecturer in the School of Education and Social Science at the University of Derby, United Kingdom. He is head of the Learning Resources and Student Study Support Center, where his main responsibilities are in the field of staff development in teaching methods and learning cultures. He is also project director of a three-year study on "The Gendered Experience of Skilled Working, 1940–60," which draws from oral history research methodologies. He has published in both of these areas, as well as in the field of industry education.

Rudi Laermans is a senior lecturer in the Department of Sociology at the Catholic University of Louvain, Belgium. He has widely published on cultural and social theory. Most of his research has dealt with the sociogenesis of the contemporary body and consumer culture, and on individualization and modernization. Articles testifying to the results of this research were published in journals such as *Social Compass, Cultural Studies,* and *Theory, Culture, and Society.* More recently he has turned his passion for contemporary dance into a professional interest. His main project is an ethnographic study of the Belgian dance company Rosas, directed by Anna Teresa De Keersmaeker.

Ruth Madigan is a senior lecturer at the University of Glasgow, Scotland. She teaches in urban sociology and has a long-standing research interest in housing issues. Publications include (1990) "Gender and the Meaning of the Home" (with Moira Munro and Susan J. Smith) in *International Journal of Urban and Regional Research* 14, no. 4: 625–47, and (1991) "Gender, House, and 'Home': Social Meanings and Domestic Architecture in Britain" (with Moira Munro) in *Journal of Architectural and Planning Research* 8, no. 2: 116–32.

Carine Meulders is a sociologist of culture. Her research and publications bear upon the sociology of the body and the historical sociology of everyday life. As a researcher at the University of Louvain, Belgium, she conducted a study on the history of laundering, at the request of the corporation Procter and Gamble. Her book on this subject, *De tirannie van de vlek; wasrituelen sinds 1750 (The Tyranny of the Stain: Washing Rituals since 1750)*, was published in 1996. Recently she has studied the history of divorce, by tracing the tensions between everyday life and judicial norms.

Moira Munro was recently appointed professor in the School of Planning and Housing at Heriot-Watt University, United Kingdom. Along with her work on gender and the meaning of the home, largely undertaken with Ruth Madigan, she has wide-ranging interests in the economics of housing markets and the analysis of housing finance.

Paul Pennartz is an associate professor in the Department of Household and Consumer Studies at Wageningen Agricultural University, the Netherlands. He teaches environmental sociology, and his research pertains to cognition and the built environment. Publications include (1989) "Semiotic Theory and Environmental Evaluation" in *Symbolic Interaction* 12, no. 2: 231–50, and (1990) "Adults, Adolescents, and Architects: Differences in Perception of the Urban Environment" (with M. G. Elsinga) in *Environment and Behavior* 22, no. 5: 675–714.

Tim Putnam is professor of history of material culture at Middlesex University in London. He has directed (with Charles Newton) a number of research projects and a national collaborative exhibition project on home arrangement, and edited the accompanying book, *Household Choices* (1990). He also works on the museology of industrial heritage and is coauthor with J. Alfrey of *The Industrial Heritage* (1992). Putnam is a founding editor of the *Journal of Design History* and of Routledge's series on *Cultural Futures.*

Céline Rosselin is a doctoral candidate at the Sorbonne University of Paris and at the associated Research Institute of Material Culture Studies. She has published (1994) "La matérialité de l'objet et l'approche dynamique-instrumentale" in *Le paradox de la marchandise authentique,* edited by Jean-Pierre Warnier, 147–77, and (forthcoming) "Les métiers du meuble au pied du mur: entre partimonialisation et obsolescence planifiée" in a volume edited by Warnier.

Elizabeth Shove is deputy director of the Center for the Study of Environmental Change and director of the Space and Society Research Unit at the University of Lancaster, United Kingdom. She is a sociologist who has conducted research in areas relating to energy, the built environment, science and technology, and research policy.

At Home

1

Introduction
Anthropology at Home

Irene Cieraad

THE REASONS for the characteristics of our domestic surroundings seem self-evident, preventing us from asking such obvious questions as: Why do we cover our interior walls and windows? Why is it that we seldom put a bed in the kitchen? Why store dirty laundry in hidden corners? Answers solely referring to aesthetics, status, privacy, or hygiene are not completely satisfactory. What do we express in our decorating and segregating practices in the domestic space? The focus of this book is on Western domestic space, a field of study in which several disciplines have been involved since the postwar period. For example, there is a vast amount of Anglo-American literature on the history of domestic architecture by architectural, art, and social historians (Clark 1986; Daunton 1983; Foy and Schlereth 1992; Handlin 1979; Hayden 1981, 1984; Motz and Browne 1988; Muthesius 1982; Rybczynski 1987; Schlereth 1982; Stamp and Goulancourt 1986; Swenarton 1981; Wright 1980, 1981).

Analyses and research concentrating on contemporary domestic architecture are for the most part written by housing sociologists and human geographers. In general, however, these disciplines focus on quantitative analyses of housing conditions and interior decoration as indexes of social class, ethnicity, and status (Chapman 1955; Felson 1976; Fox 1985; Halle 1993; Saunders 1990; Warner 1960; Zukin 1982). Qualitative research on contemporary Western domestic space is scarce, and interpretations of domestic practices are even more exceptional. The few publications that touch upon these subjects derive from diverse domains of research, such as ethnology, material culture studies, consumer studies, and environmental psychology.

These publications often reflect national research traditions. For example, in present-day French social sciences there is a keen interest in the material aspects of daily life, mixing an ethnological tradition of material culture studies with modern French sociology of lifestyle and consumption (Baudrillard 1981; Bourdieu 1984; Pellegrino 1994; Segalen and Le Wita 1993; Warnier 1994). The same holds true for the

Scandinavian studies (Frykman and Löfgren 1987; Gullestad 1984); the British studies of contemporary material culture deal with the "muted" experiences of consumers, notably women (Allan and Crow 1989; Attfield and Kirkham 1989; Douglas and Isherwood 1979; Matrix 1984; Miller 1987; Putnam and Newton 1990; Roberts 1991), a focus that seems to be related to the postwar tradition of oral history and working-class studies in British sociology.

Most American studies concerned with contemporary Western domestic space, however, are rooted in psychology, in particular in environmental psychology.[1] The crucial theme in these studies revolves around housing and identity (Altman and Gauvain 1981; Cooper 1974; Csikszentmihalyi and Rochberg-Halton 1981; Duncan 1981; Duncan and Duncan 1976; Kron 1983; Lawrence 1987; Porteous 1976; Sadalla et al. 1987). A powerful mix of strains from diverse research backgrounds, ranging from psychology, sociology, and anthropology to material culture studies, is exemplified in American consumer studies (Dittmar 1992; Gould and Schiffer 1981; McCracken 1988, 1989).

But why is an anthropological approach in the study of Western domestic space still missing? This is even more curious considering the fact that there is an established research tradition in the anthropological discipline focusing on "the house," that is to say, on the tribal house or on exotic domestic spaces. In this tradition the internal structure of the tribal house is symbolically interpreted as a visual model of the tribe's or the group's cosmology and social hierarchy (Cunningham 1973; Douglas 1972; Fortes 1949; Kent 1990). One of the most prominent social hierarchies is the gender division reflected in the spatial structure of most tribal houses, in exotic domestic spaces, and even in the floor plans of nineteenth-century houses (Ardener 1981; Spain 1992). However, a silent opinion among symbolic-oriented anthropologists, trapped as they are in the old evolutionistic link between symbolism and primitivism, is that Western people lost this precious and authentic symbolic drive somewhere in the course of the civilizing process. Nineteenth-century industrialization and urbanism are generally considered to have dealt deathblows to residual popular symbolism in the West (Cieraad 1991a).

However, we still express ourselves symbolically in the spatial arrangements and decorations of our houses and the surrounding public space (Cieraad 1991b, 1993). When invited to show that anthropology can make a contribution in the interpretation of Western domestic space, I called for papers on that topic and on related issues such as domestic practices and domestic objects. My call resulted in specimens from all disciplines and research traditions involved in the study of domestic space

---

1. The American psychological tradition has an Italian counterpart. See Rullo's (1987) bibliography on psychological research.

in the West. As might be expected, anthropologists were not overrepresented. Nonetheless, I aimed to select articles contributing to the development of an anthropology of domestic space. In such a study the key word is "meaning"; the inquiry engenders questions on the construction of meaning, on the interpretation of meaning and imagery, and on the relationship between meaning and practice.

For the last two decades global themes have dominated the anthropological discipline, even though anthropology's history is for the most part written along regional or colonial lines. Reintroducing a spatial category such as "domestic space," in combination with a regional focus on the West, may seem a regressive act.[2] However, an anthropology of domestic space is by definition rooted in the West. The concept of domestic space and its conceptual counterpart, "public space," evolved in a Western historical setting of rising urbanism, tracing back to seventeenth-century Europe.[3] In this context historians like Simon Schama (1987) claim a pivotal role for the seventeenth-century Dutch Republic with its flourishing merchants' towns.

The concept of domestic space introduces not only an inevitable historical dimension, but also a temporal dimension often clad in nostalgic images. The notion of domesticity is one of the most powerful images related to domestic space. It is the intertwining of the notion of domestic space and the image of domesticity that is examined in chapter 2, "Domesticity in Dispute: A Reconsideration of Sources." The author of the chapter, Heidi de Mare, a Dutch architectural historian, contests the fixed borders historians attributed to Dutch seventeenth-century domestic space. Although the front door marked the jurisdictional boundary between the sovereign domestic space of the burgher and the town's jurisdiction, it did not yet parallel the behavioral and emotional boundary between public and private space we are familiar with today.

Likewise the image of primordial Dutch domesticity is mistaken, according to de Mare. This image was created in the nineteenth century, at the time of an almost international glorification of the arts and works of the Dutch seventeenth century. In the eyes of nineteenth-century beholders the lifelike portrayal of Dutch domestic scenes reflected the nostalgic domesticity and peaceful family life they longed for. This image of domesticity has haunted us ever since.

In chapter 3, "Dutch Windows: Female Virtue and Female Vice," I illustrate the historical process of the fixing of the borders of domestic space. The female predica-

2. In his introduction to *Anthropology at Home* Messerschmidt (1981) legitimizes conducting anthropological fieldwork in one's home country, referring to changes in the North American academic environment, from difficulties in funding research abroad to the lost monopoly on exotic research "paradises." The anthropology of domestic space can become a native research paradise illustrating the exotic in the familiar.

3. See Coontz (1988) on the origins of private life in the United States.

ment, or the "domestication of women," is tied to the solidifying borders of Western domestic space. For example, in the course of the eighteenth century the wives of Dutch burghers lost their controlling position as border guards in the "front house," a liminal zone between the domestic space of the home and the public space of the street.[4] The progressive retreat of upper-class women from the border and especially from the most fragile part of that border—the window—culminated in the nineteenth-century domestication of women.

This process was typical for the West in general, but again the case of seventeenth-century Holland adds a particular element to the history of women's domestication, namely the curious symbolic link between the female hymen and the window pane. The honor of the house and the honor of the females inhabiting the house were metaphorically related by linking both fragile borders. This symbolism, although long forgotten, is still enacted in current Dutch female behavior toward the window. Cleaning the window was once an exclusively female affair, as decorating the window still is. Present-day Dutch window prostitution is the most notorious example of this forgotten symbolic link.

The issue of forgotten symbolism brings to the fore the fact that meaning and meaning construction are not necessarily conscious affairs, but are essentially related to and sustained in practice.[5] Meaning dissolves when it is not enacted time and again. The recurrent practices in which meanings are imbued and coined are designated in the anthropological vocabulary as "rituals." The religious and primitive overtones of the term seem to inhibit its application in situations we encounter day by day. When anthropologists apply the term to everyday situations in the West they do it jokingly by "tribalizing" their subjects, such as calling Americans "the Nacirema" (Miner 1956) or describing England as "Native Land" (Barley 1989).

However, chapter 4, "The Ins and Outs of the Hall: A Parisian Example," written by Céline Rosselin, a French anthropologist, is a serious attempt at describing an everyday ritual of passage. She illustrates how a visitor's entering and leaving a Parisian apartment follows a ritual procedure akin to the ceremonial rites of passage in traditional societies as once described by Van Gennep ([1909] 1981). She points out that domestic borders are not just materialized in brick and mortar, but are also confirmed and expressed in the residents' behavior toward visitors. This chapter illustrates not only international differences in the demarcations of domestic space, but also regional differences between urban and rural areas. Urban France is known for its fortified houses and apartment buildings; there are many barriers to cross be-

---

4. This situation is quite similar to the traditional American front porch, as described by Beckham (1988).

5. Cohen (1986) discusses the meaning and interpretation of symbols and symbolic marking in the West, especially the "unconsciousness" of symbolism.

fore entering a French living room. Rosselin describes how occupants of one-room apartments who lacked the extra physical barrier of a hallway felt the urge to improvise one.

To the American Susan Carlisle (1982) these fortified French houses mirror the formal social behavior of the French in general. By relating physical barriers upon entering a house to the experienced psychic barriers in social contact, Carlisle runs the danger of reading an interpretation straight from the static material structure of the house. Therefore, it is important to remind ourselves that, although the material structure of houses might not have changed for decades or even a century, the inhabitants' behavior did change over the decades, as did the meaning related to the material structure.

An intended, although not always consciously defined, change of meaning is exemplified in chapter 5, "'I've Always Fancied Owning Me Own Lion': Ideological Motivations in External House Decoration by Recent Homeowners," written by the British sociologist John Dolan. He describes how in the 1980s the "right to buy" housing policy of Britain's Conservative Prime Minister Margaret Thatcher stimulated renters to buy their rental homes from the local authorities. Those who did so immediately tried to differentiate their facades from their neighbors'. By relating types of alterations and facade decorations to Thatcher's conservative rhetoric, Dolan constructs a typology of these homeowners. Through political symbolism, the alterations and decorations express the national divide between owners and renters. Nostalgic imagery so widely used when domestic space is concerned is translated into political iconography when related to Thatcher's stress on Britain's glorious past.[6]

Britain exemplifies the intertwining of politics and housing characteristic of industrialized countries with a vibrant past of labor and social reform movements.[7] The public or social housing policies of governments materialized their often censorious concerns for the well-being of their citizens, making domestic space a locus of primal political reform (Swenarton 1981). From this perspective the nation's well-being and future depended on prevailing domestic standards in raising its future citizens and in organizing the household, the state's microcosm (Crow 1989).

In chapter 6, "Bringing Modernity Home: Open Plan in the British Domestic Interior," Judy Attfield, a British design historian, analyzes the postwar housing politics

6. It is worth comparing Dolan's British ideological interpretation of recent home ownership (chapter 5) with Rakoff's (1977) American ideological interpretation. Rakoff exemplifies the American psychological research tradition by showing how the ideological contradictions are mirrored in the psyche of American homeowners (see also Cohn 1979).

7. The housing situation in the Soviet Union was a supreme example of the relationship between politics and housing (Boym 1994).

of implementing social reform by the introduction of "open plan" in urban and domestic architecture. New towns mainly consisting of family houses were built to house working-class families from dilapidated inner-city areas. The open-plan living room reflected first and foremost its designers' interpretation of a new and modern way of life in which social borders and hierarchies were denied. This interpretation would soon clash with the inhabitants' interpretation of their new residential environment and open-living arrangement.

In this so-called failure of modernity debate, Attfield takes sides with the "muted" inhabitants by letting them speak for themselves. The inhabitants' alterations of the open plan into two separate rooms—the designers' proof of their failed intentions—or the inhabitants' old-fashioned style and arrangement of furniture, so despised by designers, are different but legitimate interpretations of modernity, according to Attfield. She catches the power of individual consumers in the word "appropriation," a concept coined by the British anthropologist Daniel Miller (1990) in opposition to the powerless, mass-related concept of "alienation" in traditional Marxist rhetoric.

These opposing concepts are central to chapter 7, "The French Two-Home Project: Materialization of Family Identity," written by Sophie Chevalier, a French anthropologist. She personifies the recent Anglo-Gallic mix of Miller's interpretation of material culture with a solid background in French ethnology. This mix results in a comparison of property attitudes of "muted" consumers, so-called alienated urbanites living in tower blocks in a Parisian suburb, with property attitudes within the traditional Maori society of New Zealand. By describing and analyzing the attitudes of the mainly working-class residents, not only toward their flats' interior decoration but also toward their two-home projects—having a second family residence in the country—Chevalier illustrates striking similarities in the way meaningful universes are constructed by modern consumers and tribal people alike.[8] Most of all, she discredits the tacit opinion among symbolic-oriented anthropologists that Western people have lost their symbolic drive and are forced to live in an alienated, disenchanted world.

Interviews with residents and notably their discourses on interior decoration direct our attention to the narrated dimension in the construction of meaning. Discourses are also practices—narrative practices—in which meanings are constructed, reaffirmed, activated, and reactivated over and again. However, the recorded meanings of objects may differ from the meanings enacted in dealings with objects. Since actual behavior has more credits than discourse in the traditional anthropological paradigm, there is a hierarchy of trustworthiness involved. This hierarchy at pres-

---

8. Olson's (1985) research on communication and artifacts, and especially the expression of family relations in objects, confirms Chevalier's findings for the United States.

ent may be contested, for it was once created to support the scientific claims of the new ethnographic method of participant observation in tribal societies. Participant observation of tribal life and dealings had to compensate for the anthropologists' poor command of the language of the societies involved.

Semantics is the subject of chapter 8, "Home: The Experience of Atmosphere." It is written by Paul Pennartz, a Dutch environmental sociologist dedicated to the American tradition of environmental psychology. By carefully scrutinizing the residents' answers to such questions as "When and where do you think it is most pleasant in the house?" he reveals important consistencies in their experiences of pleasantness in the home. Although spatial characteristics of the home environment may contribute, they are not as decisive as sociopsychological elements.

This chapter on atmosphere in the home confirms the emotionalization of domestic space and conspires to support the myth of two worlds apart, the public and the private—worlds that since the nineteenth century have been divided along emotional, moral, and economic lines; sculptured to opposing design patterns; and most frequently referred to as "work" and "home" (Cieraad 1991a; Nippert-Eng 1996). One of the most crucial consistencies in the experiences of the residents was their reference to home as a place to relax from work, thus confirming the liminal professional category of housewives whose work is in the home.

Chapter 9, "Negotiating Space in the Family Home," written by the British sociologists Moira Munro and Ruth Madigan, deals with another aspect of housewives' liminal position. The same myth of two worlds apart endowed the private space of the home with its exclusive aura of privacy. Privacy came to be synonymous with the home and its inhabitants—the family—and this self-evidential link inhibited critical questions such as "Whose privacy is warranted in the home?" In retrospect, privacy was a supreme home condition to be created by the then-bourgeois housewives to help their husbands recuperate from work. This patriarchal condition became ingrained in the hierarchical organization of domestic space, separating males from females, junior family members from senior members, and domestic inferiors from their superiors. By assigning every room its own function, an optimum amount of privacy was warranted for the head of the household (Spain 1992, 111–40). Even the very confined domestic spaces of the lower classes were hierarchically organized.

Nowadays, especially for those forced to live in cramped houses, privacy is an issue for negotiation between family members. Munro and Madigan illustrate the liminal position of today's housewives when privacy is concerned. Although housewives do not claim a room of their own, they have created their own privacy conditions in an effective combination of space and time zoning. However, not only is the private space of the modern home often effectively zoned for space and time, but the public space is also zoned in this way. The nineteenth-century split between public

Irene Cieraad

and private space was foremost a split enacted in gender behavior (McDowell 1983a). The rules of decency allowed upper-class women and children to be in public by day, not by night, and only in restricted, "safe," and "clean" territories.

The late nineteenth-century discovery of bacteria and other germs reinforced the dangerous image of public space by "infecting" these places with permanent impurity and fear of contamination. This very notion of public impurity was a major impetus in "The Domestication of Laundering," the topic of chapter 10, written by Rudi Laermans and Carine Meulders, two Belgian sociologists. The "outdoor" history of domestic laundering describes a spatial shift contrary to most household practices. Traditionally, washing was a communal affair in which women gathered around village washing places or in urban washhouses. Later, in reaction to the contamination of public places, all "hygienic" practices from washing to bathing had to be performed in the home. The domestic space was proclaimed to be the only safe and clean environment, guaranteed by the new professional reputation of housewives as "germ busters."

Laermans and Meulders are influenced by the works of the late Norbert Elias on the history of European civilization.[9] Shifting boundaries, not only spatial, but also social and emotional ones, are crucial elements in Elias's interpretation of Europe's history of civilization and state formation ([1939] 1978, [1939] 1982). The civic code of, for instance, immaculate white collars—once the courtier's distinction—dispersed to ever-widening social circles, urging ever more frequent washing of linen. The dispersing of courtly civilization was counterbalanced by centralizing forces in Europe's state formation, tying local communities to central bureaucracies. By taking Elias's point of view the authors implicitly discredit the cherished myth of two worlds apart, as is exemplified by the subterranean centralizing force of the technical infrastructure connecting individual households to the state's public facilities.

Chapter 11, "Constructing Home: A Crossroads of Choices," written by British housing sociologist Elizabeth Shove, is another example of crosscutting the two worlds. Though from a different theoretical perspective, Shove illustrates the intertwinement of choices of providers and consumers. The two separate worlds of economics meet in a joint construction project called "home." Providers of houses and furniture seem to determine what customers can buy, but they legitimize their choices by referring to their market knowledge of what customers want or, more accurately, their knowledge of what sold before. However, as it is far more difficult for house builders than for furniture retailers to know their target group, house builders avoid the financial risks involved in experimenting with new designs and turn to the proven

9. Historic approaches also from a neo-Marxist perspective flourished in postwar continental European sociology.

8

traditional patterns. This market policy seems to be responsible for the traditional outlook of Britain's postwar private housing stock, although it does not explain the striking national differences, for example, between European countries in the most popular types of private house.[10] It illustrates that, even when decisions are made within the same economic constraints, the outcome is likely to be more culturally than economically determined.

Shove, however, does distinguish between two patterns of choice relating to different market sections of customers—the "better-" and the "worse-off" sections—who describe their respective choices in emotional or pragmatic terms. This contrast mirrors class-related taste patterns as described by the French sociologist Bourdieu (1984). British pragmatism, unlike its French counterpart, seems to be strongly influenced by a design ideal of the postwar domestic reform movement in which decor's constituting elements needed to match, especially with relation to color and material.

Domestic reform movements, like "ideal homes" in Britain, were upper-class initiatives most dominant in the postwar period (Morley 1990).[11] Their all-modern design programs were directed at traditional, and often working-class, predilections of massive reproduction furniture, clashing patterns, and nonfunctional items and layout of the furniture. Traditional predilections were described by the reform movements as "emotional," in contrast to the rational and functional design the movements favored. Ironically, the present taste of the "better-off" section does not stress matching combinations or functional design and layout, but stresses a unique and "daring" combination of heterogeneous furniture elements all favored for their authentic individual merits. The emotional aesthetics of postmodern eclecticism simply overruled the rational and pragmatic aesthetics of the univocal modern scheme. This development illustrates in my opinion a remarkable change in the discourse of "legitimate" taste—from rational to emotional—half a century after the most influential domestic reform movements.

10. The bungalow is one of the very few examples of house types that are globally favored (King 1984).

11. The Swedish reform movement was called More Beautiful Everyday Living (Löfgren 1993b), and the Dutch was called Good Living (Van Moorsel 1992). Cohen (1984) describes the early domestic reform attempts targeting the American working-class interior. Zeldenrust-Noordanus (1956) comes forward with a psychological explanation for the dislike of modern design among the lower classes: The fragility and openness of modern furniture conflicts with their psychological need for security expressed in massive bulky furniture and a need for the comfortable enclosure of an easy chair. These needs stem from their precarious occupational position, according to Zeldenrust. Greenhalgh (1990) gives an overview of modern design movements in Europe and North America.

Women's superior knowledge of taste and color, once propagated in nineteenth-century advice books on home management for bourgeois women, also proves to be an established fact within these pragmatic, "worse-off" circles. This model of gendered expertise, now termed "conventional," contrasts with the advocated model of mutual respect of the partner's preferences in the "better-off" category, according to Shove.[12] It illustrates not only the long-term effects of nineteenth-century home-advice books, but also a gender shift in "legitimate" homemaking responsibilities, a century after the home-advice books made homemaking into a supremely female task.

This century's transformations in domestic architecture and domestic living are the subject of chapter 12, "'Postmodern' Home Life," written by Tim Putnam, a British historian of material culture. He describes how the modern house constructed according to functional principles became a technical terminal tied to a vast network of sewers, mains, cables, and lines. Despite the myth of two worlds apart, home life and life chances came to depend more and more on public systems, including those of education and occupation. However, the resistance to the very idea of intertwinement grew stronger too, as is witnessed in the denial of "public" destinies of class and gender, and in the glorification of individual choice.

The modern trend toward personalizing may have been stimulated, if not broached, by "public" powers in the guise of education, media, marketing, or politics, but the home has become its prime locus of expression. It is self-evident that children need rooms of their own, just as it is commonly approved that adolescents want to have a place of their own before settling down (Cieraad 1994, 1995). However, setting up a shared household means more than mutual tuning of individual projects in an ongoing process of negotiation, as illustrated by Putnam.

The home's aura of sharing and communality is likely to conflict with individual projects of household members. Technical systems in the home, like television sets and telephones, stimulate individual use, but their use is also the topic of many heated family debates. The electronics industry has responded to these domestic conflicts by promoting more individual devices and headphones and by integrating a muting switch into their designs.

As negotiations, according to Putnam, have become the supreme characteristics of postmodern democratic family life, the tilting ground has shifted from the master bedroom to the postmodern living kitchen. The new focus of family life, being at once a newly acquired zone of personalization in design and a celebration court of shar-

12. A high degree of personalization in Shove's "better-off" section corresponds to the findings of Italian research on living room styles in relation to occupational status and income (Amaturo et al. 1987).

ing, exemplifies the contradictions of "postmodern" home life. Functional kitchen design, once hailed for its modernity, is now considered impersonal and outdated, needing a more personal, romantic, or even a more glamorous touch. In not only bringing family members together for the sharing of a meal, but also revealing plain domestic labor, the postmodern kitchen has become the battleground of domestic responsibilities.

People seem to live a home life full of illusions, contradictions, and myths.[13] Personalization not only impinges on the family illusion of sharing, but it also disguises shared lifestyles. The democratic family ideal of negotiation may be a cover-up of traditional gender roles, in the same way that the augmentative gender differences between boys' and girls' decors seem to contradict the professed equal rights of the sexes (Cieraad 1995).

Even though the "cocooning" trend is waning, the home is still the focal point of most people's lives. Research data indicate that youngsters dream of becoming homeowners (Cieraad 1994). However, despite the emotional and huge financial investments in the home, there has never been a period in Western urban history when people spent so few hours at home. The urban and suburban quarters with predominantly dual-income households are often deserted during the day.

Still we cling so much to the illusion of two worlds apart that maintaining it seems to warrant large investments. Perhaps, because having a home and a job is not as certain as it was forty years ago, losing both has become a "postmodern" nightmare, represented by growing numbers of homeless people in the streets. Home as the emotionalization of domestic space is more than ever a core symbol in Western culture, one that derives its meaning not only from its opposite, the public space, but also from the practices performed on it and in it (Saunders and Williams 1988). These practices may be related to its material structure, like decorating, renovating, and moving house, or to domestic activities like cooking, cleaning, raising children, or gardening, or to the psychological and narrated practices of remembering and dreaming. The home images and house dreams of the homeless illustrate more than anything else the illusions and myths we cherish (Moore 1994).

The contributions to this book are univocal in their claim on the meaning and importance of the home in the West. It is not by chance that most of the research, al-

13. Contradiction is the proper representation of modernity, according to Miller, linking his account to Schama's description of seventeenth-century Holland: "The core dilemma of modernity lies in the consequences of the new temporality: that is, a distinct sense of present, future and past, which leads to an increasing concern with the knowledge of self-construction of the criteria by which we live. Schama certainly echoes these concerns in seventeenth-century Amsterdam, a people constantly alert to the fragility of their fortune" (1994, 79).

though from different perspectives, focuses on the transition or the relationship between the domestic and the public space, that being the crucial split in Western culture. The topics range from the fixing of the borders of domestic space to interpretations of attitudes toward the window, toward facade decorations, and toward visitors entering and leaving the house. These topics deal not only with spatial transgression of domestic activities and the mixing of economic spheres, but also with the home's separate spatial identities.

This volume on the topic of domestic space brings together research traditions that have never been mingled before: art history, social history, women's studies, design history, architectural history, cultural anthropology, ethnology, sociology, housing sociology, environmental psychology, material culture studies, and consumer studies. Having made the anthropological approach and its search for meaning exemplary, I hope to push the development of a new and broaching research tradition: an anthropology of domestic space. It will be a native research paradise illustrating the exotic in the familiar.

2

Domesticity in Dispute
A Reconsideration of Sources

Heidi de Mare

LITERATURE that examines the way people lived in the past depicts the seventeenth-century Dutch interior as the cradle of domesticity. The architect Witold Rybczynski in his book *Home: A Short History of an Idea* (1986) devotes a chapter to seventeenth-century Dutch bourgeois culture. In his view the features characterizing everyday life during this period are "family, intimacy, and a devotion to the home" (1986, 75). The literary scholar Mario Praz remarks on seventeenth-century Dutch interiors that "their sobriety is not without a sense of ease and warm bourgeois intimacy" (1994, 102). Similarly the historian Simon Schama writes that "the Dutch had elaborated their domesticity so far that they were able to indulge the almost universal craving for *gezelligheid* (coziness or comfort) without, as they supposed, incurring the odium of luxury" (1979, 117).

The assertions made by these authors are often illustrated in paintings of seventeenth-century Dutch interiors. An air of domesticity pervades "an idyllic, peaceful scene" by Emanuel de Witte or "the still atmosphere of the room" in works by Johannes Vermeer (Rybczynski 1987, 68, 71). The paintings by Pieter de Hooch of light, uncluttered rooms are a "celebration of domesticity" and represent "middle-class home life" (Sutton 1984, LIV). Even the chaotic group scenes in untidy, overcrowded rooms, as depicted by Jan Steen, are regarded as "wonderful scenes of domestic life" (Rybczynski 1987, 67), or as an allusion to the "ideal ordering of the family home" by turning it upside down (Schama 1987, 391). The popularity of these "paintings of domestic subjects," as summed up recently by the art historian Wayne Franits, lies in "a peculiar charm and modesty as they provide a vision of the centrality of domestic life in a long-vanished, democratic society" (1993, 1).

It is striking in this connection to note that "domesticity" is interpreted by most authors as the expression of something else. The paintings are said to portray the increasing emphasis on privacy in the middle-class family, resulting in a clear dividing line between the intimate, cozy, secure indoor world of the home and the public, perilous world outside (Schama 1987, 382–93). Scenes of mothers and children are said to indicate that a more affectionate relationship was emerging between parents and children, with the nuclear family constituting the focus of domesticity (Rybczynski 1987, 59–60). The neat, uncluttered interiors by Pieter de Hooch reflect the disciplined organization of Dutch households, while the untidy rooms depicted by Jan Steen are an expression of the very antithesis. Objects of many kinds portrayed in the paintings, from brooms to water pumps, emphasize the interest in household matters. The authors also refer to other manifestations of the same intimate, domestic atmosphere. It is to be found in books, for example, the much-read work by Jacob Cats containing his advice on marriage (Schama 1987; Franits 1993), and it is also reflected in the narrow Dutch houses of the period (Rybczynski 1987, 55–56).

However, every author gives a second interpretation: Schama stresses the metaphorical relationship between cleansing the house and the general craving for moral purity. Rybczynski emphasizes the role of the housewife and her maid in the practical organization of the household. Like Franits, he sees women's devotion to the home as a sign of the final feminization of the domestic sphere and as a typical characteristic of Dutch domesticity.

Many of these elements can indeed be found in writings and paintings from the seventeenth century. The actual concept of "domesticity," however, rarely occurs in those works; the same is true of related sentiments such as "coziness," "intimacy," "snugness," "privacy," "comfort," and "home." The all-embracing concept of domesticity proves to be a creation not of the seventeenth century but of the nineteenth century. It was during this latter period that domestic, bourgeois family life became a nucleus around which the nation was formed (Schuurman 1989). These sentiments were then projected into the past and applied to seventeenth-century paintings, books, and houses (Schotel 1867; Grijzenhout and Van Veen 1992). Thus was born the wide-ranging, homogeneous concept of domesticity.

During the nineteenth century the myth of seventeenth-century Dutch domesticity was also exported to other countries, especially to the United States, as a result of the sale of seventeenth-century interiors (Broos 1990; Hollander 1991). This explains how the myth came to be spread worldwide and why it is still being echoed in the work of Franits, Praz, Rybczynski, and Schama. Such a concept of domesticity has had a powerful influence; it still manifests itself in prevailing ideas on how to create a "cozy" interior.

My investigation of the house in seventeenth-century Holland reveals a different, more heterogeneous picture. Around 1600, for example, the engineer Simon Stevin wrote a treatise on the burgher house as a sovereign space. In 1625 the poet-statesman Jacob Cats described the physical arrangement in the house, a matter of honor for both man and woman. Finally the painters Pieter de Hooch and Jan Steen experimented with pictorial codes, producing different "house" scenes on a flat plane. All three lines of approach are of a conceptual nature; fundamentally, therefore, they form part of a wider conceptual universe, one that takes shape in the Dutch Republic over a period lasting roughly a century and a half.

It is striking that the intense interest in the house is in all instances directed at physical aspects: the space, the objects in the house, and the pictorial representation. The purpose of this chapter is to examine three of the ways in which this physical house came into being in seventeenth-century Holland.

Sovereign Space: Simon Stevin's House

Around the year 1649 the engineer Simon Stevin wrote an architectural treatise devoted to the town and the burgher house, the first treatise on this theme ever to be published in the Dutch language (Stevin 1590). His work falls within a tradition of architectural treatises dating back to the Italian Renaissance in which the town was an important component (Taverne 1984; Van den Heuvel 1995). So far, however, little research has been carried out into those aspects of the work that reflect a growing interest in the house. This interest manifested itself from the fifteenth and sixteenth centuries onwards, both in the practical field and in theoretical treatises such as those of Sebastiano Serlio (Goldthwaite 1972; Rosenfeld 1978).

Stevin considers various types of burghers, including persons of independent means, artisans, public servants, merchants, and innkeepers. Unlike Serlio, however, he provides but one drawing—of a house suitable for all types of burghers (illus. 2.1). Stevin's drawing, therefore, is not a design for a real three-dimensional building. In contrast, it is a diagram serving as a memory system stored with various kinds of architectural knowledge (de Mare 1998).

Stevin's aim is to create new spaces, spaces that are cut out of and rigorously cut off from the town. Defining the boundary by erecting a wall is a first step toward the creation of such spaces. With this purpose in mind, Stevin lays great stress on the robust construction of the roof and walls, so that there are no leaks or drafts. Understandably in this connection he attaches great importance to the transitions between the indoor and the outdoor world. The newly gained space must be well demarcated in relation to the town. He therefore puts extra locks on the front door and places bars and blinds on the windows, in order to safeguard the space (de Mare 1993, 1997a).

There are numerous spaces in the house. Stevin arranges five large rooms on each of the three floors. Following tradition, both the internal positioning of the rooms and their relative sizes are independent of their function (Tzonis 1972; de Mare 1992). The configuration of walls in the floor plan is first and foremost a matter of geom-

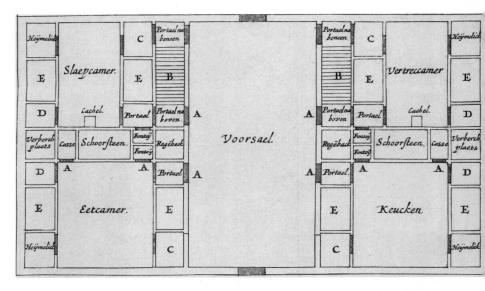

2.1. Simon Stevin, floor plan in Hendrick Stevin, *Materiae Politicae*, Leyden, 1649. Engraving, 9×6.5 in. Courtesy of the Royal Library, The Hague, the Netherlands.

etry.[1] At the same time the walls create the individual rooms. Here too doors (indicated by shades) and hallways (named *Portael*) make each room in the house a separate entity.

All rooms in the house have to be kept free of smoke. For this purpose Stevin advocates having a chimney (*Schoorsteen*) that will draw well. Another problem is the smell. The bad habit of burning food scraps is one cause of the smell. The sanitary arrangements are another. Despite this drawback, Stevin is of the opinion that sanitary facilities should be indoors—not only because it is inconvenient to have to go out of the house in order to answer a call of nature but also because the house has to be hermetically closed at night. Each room in the house has a water closet (*Heymelick*) as a demarcated space. There are two windows in the outside wall that can be opened to relieve the smell. The water closet is fitted with a seat that is covered with a lid. Rainwater is used for flushing and there is a drain going deep into the ground.

Rainwater is in fact piped into every room (*Fontey*). There is a connection to the water butt, where rainwater is collected and subsequently purified. This means it is not necessary to go outdoors to fetch water. The kitchen (*Keucken*) also has two

1. The configuration of symmetrical lines forming the basis for Stevin's house plan is primarily founded on what is nowadays known as the "Golden Section" (de Mare 1992).

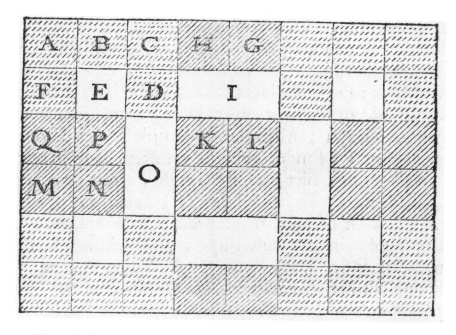

2.2. Simon Stevin, one of the five plans of housing blocks for burghers in Hendrick Stevin, *Materiae Politicae*, Leyden, 1649. Engraving, 2.2 × 2.8 in. Courtesy of the Royal Library, The Hague, the Netherlands.

pumps, one with purified rainwater for "cooking peas," the other with water from the well. The latter water is unpurified and is used for washing the dishes (de Mare 1994b).

In these internal spaces, in the same way as there is outdoors, there must be a profusion of direct daylight. Each room, including the stairs and the water closet, has at least one window. At the same time outsiders should not be able to see in. Stevin therefore raises the ground floor slightly so that nobody can see inside the house from the street. He also prescribes blind walls facing the adjacent house in the courtyard (illus 2.2). The result is a block of houses forming a coherent whole but strictly separated from one another. The surface area of each house in the smallest block covers six squares, with the variants ABCDEF, HGIKL, and MNOPQ. The shaded squares indicate the rooms and the unshaded squares the courtyard.

The nature of activities to take place in a given room is determined solely by the specific objects and furniture placed in it. Put a dining table in the room and it becomes a dining room (*Eetcamer*); a bed makes it into the conjugal bedroom (*Slaepcamer*). The smaller rooms, indicated in the drawing (illus. 2.1) as C, D, and E, can be used in different ways. C can be a writing room acting as an extension of the office (*Vertreccamer*), but in combination with the kitchen (*Keucken*) it can also be a scullery. D can be used for storing fuel or oddments, and E can contain a closed-in bed or function as a cupboard.

The use of the rooms is regulated by means of the keys in the possession of the master and mistress of the house. Thirty of these keys fit general locks. In addition, the husband and wife each have six keys for places and cupboards to which only they have access. The husband has the keys to the chests containing valuables and important papers, while only the wife has access to the linen cupboard, wardrobe, and her own jewel chest.

Finally Stevin gives each member of the family a room, so that they do not get in each other's way (de Mare 1994a). The hall (*Voorsael*) is the central location where the family gathers and where strangers are received. Only a door separates the hall from the street, making it a transitional space leading from the public space to all the other rooms in the house.

Stevin's prime objective is to create sovereign spaces, both in terms of the house, which he separates from urban space, and in terms of the separate rooms in the house. The rooms are self-contained: they can be locked; they are provided with an adequate amount of direct sunlight; they have permanently purified rainwater, clean air—owing to the removal of smoke and smell—and a place for the disposal of excrement. Above all, Stevin wishes the interior space to have positive qualities in relation to the town.

Honorable Order: Jacob Cats's "Marriage"

In studies of Dutch domestic life in the seventeenth century, a much cited source is the work of the poet-statesman Jacob Cats, in particular his book on marriage ([1625] 1655). His book forms part of a moralistic tradition of Christian-humanist writings having as their theme the virtues required of women (Carter 1974; Leuker 1991). Rarely is his work used as a means of gaining insight into domestic space, space in which everything has its proper position, space that can be a source of honor in everyday life.

The interior is like a stage on which Cats erects his own structure, the "business of the house." He builds his construction layer by layer. Cats writes that laying down rules for objects, activities, and manners may seem futile compared with affairs of state, but for life in the house and for the family these matters are of vital importance. All elements should be in harmony, for even a large clock will stop if the smallest cog suddenly goes its own way.

The first rule applying to the business of the house is to decide on and adhere to the arrangement of things in the house. In order to ensure that objects do not get lost, each one, after use, should be put back or hung up again in the same place. Cats also gives items of furniture—previously "movables"—a fixed position in the house. As well as having a fixed place for objects that need to be readily at hand, routines are needed that will keep them in good order. This means constant maintenance and supervision, both of the objects and of the rooms. Floors need to be mopped, cupboards polished, beds made, dishes washed, and linen bleached. Everything should be clean and tidy and ready for use.

The doings of the occupants of the house are embedded in this firm foundation. The objects and the activities related to the objects all have their own special locations. The place where books should be read and letters should be written is in the office and not in the bedroom. There should be no dozing off by the fireside, only in the bedroom. There is also a right time for everything to be done. Cats draws up a daily routine to this end, with seven hours for sleeping, eight hours for work, four hours for religion, three hours for helping others and the upbringing of children, and two hours for diversion.

A formal regime also governs individual behavior, especially that between men and women. Like a Hollywood film director, Cats gives instructions for the way men and women are to behave in moments of high tension. He intervenes whenever peace in the house is threatened. In a quarrel he urges the husband to use his hand not in order to beat his wife but to caress her. He should pull her toward him and kiss her on the mouth. The wife should throw her arms around her husband's neck and embrace him until his anger subsides.

Cats does not simply give a list of objects, activities, and forms of behavior. He also interprets these things in terms of honor and disgrace, involving a spatial aspect.[2] Cats considers not only the street but also the interior as public spaces. In both locations there is a risk of disgrace being brought on the house. The occupants may be talked about outside the house if their clothing is too showy or too slovenly or if they are indiscreet about things going on in the house.

Inside the house excessive cleaning, dining too lavishly, or quarreling too much mean loss of face in front of servants, children, or guests. Such persons may make the disgrace public. Both inside and outside the house, the occupants should treat one another with respect, so that the honor of the house is upheld. Only the conjugal bedroom is not a public place. There husband and wife can say what they really think; the truth must never be made public, however.

Cats is concerned with the demarcation between the street and the house and also with the demarcation between public space and inner self. Doors and windows are a threat to honor, as objects and persons can pass through them (de Mare 1993, 1997a). Tongue and hand are also a threat to honor, as they may express eruptions of the

2. These terms have a history of their own (Van Oostrom 1992).

inner self. In order to maintain the honor of the house, both types of demarcation lines must be kept under control. Thus Cats's view of an honorable house is one in which peace and order reign.

Both spouses play their parts in founding and maintaining an honorable house and passing it on to others. The fact that the house can be built at all is first and foremost due to the husband. He is the one who earns the money that is needed in order to set up home. It is a disgrace if he cannot afford the furniture required or if he cannot offer his wife enough space for her to move freely.

According to Cats the mistress of the house is the shining light around which the honorable business of the house revolves. He calls her "the best piece of furniture." Her task in life is to keep the house in order; her practical knowledge will ensure that the household runs smoothly. Only through her good care can the home and family be kept together in peace and harmony, and the business of the household be honorable. All women of pre- and postmarital status, from virgin, bride, mother, to widow, derive their dignity from their function in the house. Whores and adulteresses have forfeited their honor.

Cats's main concern is to arrange the "business of the house" in an honorable fashion. He does so by providing order for the objects that enter the house and also by directing the way the members of the family behave toward one another. To him honor and disgrace are a code that extends the significance of the house beyond its physical boundaries. This code is, moreover, a public matter, not a private one.

Apprehensible Planes: The Paintings of Jan Steen and Pieter de Hooch

The paintings of Jan Steen and Pieter de Hooch are often interpreted as representations of two types of seventeenth-century households. Steen (illus. 2.3–2.6) illustrates the untidy, disorganized, informal household, and de Hooch (illus. 2.7–2.10) shows the ideal, ordered, organized household. Some authors see the paintings as a kind of mirror held to people of the times (Damsma 1993, 33); others consider them to be "carriers of cultural significance" (Franits 1993, 1). In either case the emphasis on the social group is a legacy left by nineteenth-century art historians (de Mare 1997b).

Instead of reading the paintings as illustrations of the real world, my approach is to consider the visual organization of information relating to the theme of the house.[3] In my analysis I distinguish four signifying levels: the characters, the objects, the space, and the method of visualization. Comparison of these four levels in paintings by Steen and de Hooch pinpoints just what the difference is between them.

3. Domestic scenes and the depiction of everyday matters have a long tradition in, among others, the Flemish and Italian schools of painting. Well into the sixteenth century, such scenes often formed part of religious presentations.

2.3. Jan Steen, *The Dissolute Household,* ca. 1668. Oil on canvas, 31.6×35 in. Courtesy of the Wellington Museum, London.

If we start with the first level, we see that Steen's paintings are often filled with a whole range of stereotypes: the high-spirited lovers, the old man and woman, the sleeping mother, and any number of naughty children. Animals are also depicted: a parrot, monkey, cat, dog, pig, or duck.[4] In contrast, de Hooch's paintings rarely show more than a few figures together at any one time. Most show a housewife with a maid and one or two children. Any male figures are either just leaving or just arriving. Sometimes a dog or cat is depicted.

There are other marked differences between the characters portrayed by de Hooch and Steen: their attitudes, their gestures, and the way they look at each other. De

4. Iconological studies construe these figures as representations of proverbs or as references to human vices and virtues (Haak 1984; Sutton 1984).

2.4. Jan Steen, *The Merry Family,* 1668. Oil on canvas, 110.5×141 cm. Courtesy of the Rijksmuseum, Amsterdam.

2.5. Jan Steen, *The Way You Hear It Is the Way You Sing It,* ca. 1665. Oil on canvas, 134×163 cm. Courtesy of the Mauritshuis, The Hague, the Netherlands.

2.6. Jan Steen, *Beware of Luxury*, 1663. Oil on canvas, 105×145 cm. Courtesy of the Kunsthistorisches Museum, Gemäldegalerie, Vienna.

Hooch's figures sit up straight on their chairs or stand upright in a relatively empty space. They have turned away from the spectator and seem to be absorbed in their domestic activities: delousing a child, putting away the linen, or giving a child something to drink. Steen's characters, on the other hand, often look the spectator in the eye, while sprawling at the table or gesturing broadly in the already overcrowded space.

The second signifying level is that of the objects. Here too the differences are immediately obvious. Steen always shows an abundance of objects. He uses the table, the floor, the ceiling, and the wall as a background on which to place tableware, pots and pans, musical instruments, a clock, a birdcage, or a wall plate containing some aphorism. Food is also much in evidence: bread of many different kinds, biscuits, fruit, mussels, and eggs. Steen's figures often sit around a table placed in the middle of the room. Sometimes the scene is completed by a bedstead, cupboard, or fireplace. De Hooch's interiors contain few items of furniture. His canvases show only a single chair, a table, and perhaps a cupboard against the wall. Objects such as a basket, a tray, a warming pan, or a jug are ready for use. A single painting adorns the wall.

2.7. Pieter de Hooch, *Man Handing a Letter to a Woman in the Front Hall of a House*, 1670. Oil on canvas, 68×59 cm. Courtesy of the Rijksmuseum, Amsterdam.

2.8. Pieter de Hooch, *A Mother's Task,* ca. 1658–60. Oil on canvas, 52.5×61 cm. Courtesy of the Rijksmuseum, Amsterdam.

The third signifying level I consider is the organization of architectural space. Steen's paintings usually show one room. Two or three walls are shown; often there is no ceiling. A window or door merely suggests a space outside the room. De Hooch, on the other hand, shows glimpses of several rooms. The street and also the facades on the other side of the street can be seen through an open door or window. A ceiling and a spiral staircase even suggest several floors in the house.

Both Steen and de Hooch use perspective to create a three-dimensional space. De Hooch's paintings in particular are known for the sophisticated use of perspective. Steen's space, in comparison, receives only summary treatment. Without the figures little remains, apart from a few items of decor in the form of a cupboard and a few walls.

Light too is used to suggest space. The light falling on de Hooch's paintings through windows and doors gives shape to the space, creates depth, throws figures

2.9. Pieter de Hooch, *Interior with Women beside a Linen Chest,* 1663. Oil on canvas, 70×75.5 cm. Courtesy of the Rijksmuseum, Amsterdam.

into relief, casts shadows on walls, and makes the tiled floors shine. Every single tile has a different shape, color, and shine. The interplay of light and shade, the reflections in the mirror or on the wall—all this helps to create a three-dimensional effect. Shadows can also be seen in paintings by Steen, but the light comes not from a painted window but from the front. More than de Hooch, Steen uses light to make substances physically different.

The fourth and last level concerns the pictorial codes of seventeenth-century Dutch genre painting. Pictorial codes are prevailing views on the ordering and placing of pictorial elements on the canvas. A seventeenth-century painting is not so much a window on the world as a system of lines determining where objects and figures are to be placed on the flat plane (Alpers 1983; de Mare 1997b; Wheelock 1995). By an economical use of perspective in the same plane de Hooch creates several

2.10. Pieter de Hooch, *Woman with a Child in a Pantry,* ca. 1658. Oil on canvas, 65×60.5 cm. Courtesy of the Rijksmuseum, Amsterdam.

spaces inside and outside the house, thus enabling various objects and figures to be shown at one and the same time. De Hooch's differentiated internal space functions as a background against which to place objects and characters. He achieves variation by constantly returning to the same themes.

In Steen's paintings it is not the three-dimensional effect but primarily the flat plane that governs the placing of objects and figures on the canvas. As a result Steen displays as many things as possible within the same frame. He generally uses an indoor space as a flat plane. "Floors," "walls," and even the "ceiling" are strewn with various items: food, pots and pans on the floor, a dog on the table, or a basket containing beggars' staffs hanging from the ceiling.

Moreover, he often shows a particular object from different angles. Thus he paints not one biscuit or one playing card, but a whole series. Taken together they form a sequence that, if it were a film, would show how the object rolls and finally comes to rest, shattered or in a heap. Figures too are depicted by Steen in attitudes that set them in motion: turning away, sprawling on a chair, bending over, and gesticulating.

By twentieth-century standards things are not in the right place, and we experience this as untidy. References to untidy and chaotic households as being "households of Jan Steen" have become proverbial in the Dutch language. This view, however, is based on the idea that the painting is a representation of objective reality; it ignores the fact that Steen uses the pictorial code in his own special way.

De Hooch and Steen use the same pictorial codes. The purpose of the paintings by both artists is to depict the house, in the broadest sense of the word, time and time again. The differences in their work are fewer than would appear at first sight. Both show human figures, rooms in the house, and household activities and objects, representing them in all their richness of color, texture, and variations, in their volume and movement. Both invite the eye to examine the images, to wander around them, to follow the areas of light and shade, to understand the facial expressions of the characters as they look at one another, to be confronted with the direct nature of things (Hollander 1991).

The essential difference is the *manner in which* de Hooch and Steen have depicted their theme. De Hooch's main emphasis is on the three-dimensional effect within the house. His paintings form a series, with a slight displacement of details in each painting (Sutton 1984). De Hooch confronts the eye with the order of things in space, thus creating what can be regarded as an overall three-dimensional view (Hollander 1991, 136).

Steen, on the other hand, is more concerned with the plane; the various elements within the house can all be seen at a single glance. His canvases are condensations; they show as many things as possible at the same time and the same place. A comic confrontation is created by this juxtaposition of contrasting elements all forming part of the life of the house; it illustrates what happens when times and places are confused (Hollander 1991, 126). Should a mother not sleep? Of course she should, but in the bedroom and not in the midst of her family or when guests are around.

Thus, what seems "wrong" with Steen's "households" is basically not to be seen as the depiction of an asocial type of family; similarly de Hooch's paintings do not show what is considered to be the ideal situation. We see here two interpretations of the same pictorial code, with both artists striving to portray the house, in all its dimensions, on a flat plane. They solve the problem of time in two different ways: de Hooch by painting a whole series of different interiors, Steen by capturing, over and over again, all possibilities in the same painting.

Thanks to de Hooch and Steen, and also to the many others who painted scenes of indoor life in seventeenth-century Holland, the house has been portrayed a countless number of times. The theme each time is the house and its relationship to the town, with constant variations. The colors, the light, and the areas of shade build up a picture of the house in all its visible details: the objects and characters to be found in it, their shape, the tactile impression. By dint of frequent repetition the house in seventeenth-century Holland has become an image imprinted on the mind's eye.

Conclusion

It has been shown that during the seventeenth century the house was the focus of interest in at least three domains—those of architecture, literature, and painting. In architecture the main aim was that the space of the house should have positive qualities in relation to the town; moralistic literature is concerned with the ordered, honorable, public business of the house; painting strives to depict the house in all its material detail.

The "house," as described by Stevin and Cats and painted by de Hooch and Steen, is the house of the burgher. The burgher is not to be thought of as a member of a sociological category, representing a sort of middle class between the nobility and the ordinary people. In early modern Europe the burgher represents a historical category that takes its identity from the walled town, the stronghold (*Burcht*) (Lukacs 1970). The inhabitants, the burghers, are offered a safe, dignified, peaceful existence in exchange for their compliance with laws and obligations.

Stevin adopts the same term but identifies the burgher in particular as someone who appropriates his own walled territory ([1590] 1939). The house in which the burgher is lord and master is his own property. He can impose his own laws there, as long as they are not at odds with the higher laws of town or state. Cats uses a formula that is very similar. He compares the house to a kingdom, where husband and wife hold sway, keep order, and uphold honor. De Hooch and Steen, and many other painters, depict these burghers in their houses of many different types and sizes.

Thus the house in the seventeenth century is found to be a complex metaphor for a new civil status and dignity. The house proves to be the means par excellence by which the existence of the new burghers can be conceived and represented. The fact that this occurs within the traditions of architecture, literature, and painting means that the new civil order was embedded in much of the cultural production of the period.

From the material that I have studied, a picture emerges of the house of the burgher, the house on which he bases his identity. In the seventeenth century the house is primarily an external matter. It is concerned with material possessions, how to use them and how to represent them. The house is seen as a fine building, stocked with furniture, in which people comport themselves honorably and respectfully. Later, after this seventeenth-century external world had been internalized, the house was accorded the attributes of nineteenth-century "domesticity," and civil dignity became petty bourgeoisie.

The image emerging from the three sources is at odds with prevailing ideas claiming that domesticity originated in the Netherlands during the seventeenth century. Schama does indeed stress that the domain of the house was of great importance to the burgher and his place in the Dutch Republic. Nonetheless the "house" he depicts is primarily a moral house. As the abode of virtues it is strictly demarcated from the chaotic, dangerous world outside (Schama 1987, 388–89).

Rybczynski does indeed describe the domain of the house in a positive fashion, emphasizing the work of the housewife herself in creating a special interior space. Nonetheless the "house" he depicts is principally governed by "a set of felt emotions" that existed "in the imagination of their owners" (1987, 75).

Once again, Franits does indeed see the house as the place where, both in literature and in painting, an infinite number of female characters are portrayed. In his view, however, the "house" and the woman inside it principally shed light on "the subordinate position of women in Dutch society, a position oriented to the home in obedience to husbands who had more 'significant' public careers" (1993, 197).

The contrasts between the private and the public domain and the related *emotional* aspects are not of the seventeenth century. On the contrary, what is important during this period is the *spatial* separation between the indoor and outdoor world, coinciding with the legal demarcation. But *inside* the house public codes prevail. Paintings too illustrate the public nature of life in the house. Seventeenth-century sources have little to say about any emotional annexation of the home: "domestic feelings" are, as it were, fallow ground—they are not to be "talked about" until a later era. Not till the nineteenth century did the inner emotional world become extended, taking over the space within the four walls of the house and dominating concepts of the "home" until far into the twentieth century.

Translation: Hazel Wachters-Patmore

3

Dutch Windows
Female Virtue and Female Vice

Irene Cieraad

FOREIGNERS visiting the Netherlands often wonder how to interpret the open coverings used in Dutch windows. Especially in the evenings, when curtains are not closed, these lighted showcases may appall visitors, who often regard the uncovered Dutch windows with a somewhat hostile curiosity: It seems a strange habit of exposing not only one's interior, but also one's intimate family life, to the eyes of passersby (Baker 1983; Capek 1934; Kruizinga 1962; Sadooghi 1989; Skelton 1971; Vera 1989). In the straight tourist view there is something sexual about this "showcase mentality" in its resemblance to the notorious window prostitution in Dutch cities.[1]

In both the evenings and daytime there is much to see when strolling the sidewalks, passing along the diversely decorated front windows of Dutch family houses. The decoration of the window is a silent statement to the outside world of the lifestyle the household is cherishing or striving for. Window decoration, in combination with glimpses of the interior decoration, enables Dutch women to guess lifestyle and household composition. Decorating the window and judging the window decoration of others are essentially a woman's affair.

The relationship between windows and women has a long and fascinating tradition in Dutch social history. For example, many Dutch seventeenth-century paintings of home interiors show a woman sitting at the window. In the eighteenth and nineteenth century, however, the picturing of Dutch women at the window becomes very rare and runs contrary to the dominant northern European tradition in the portrayal of women in the interior (Thornton 1985). Following the French fashion, Dutch windows became more and more veiled by layers of curtains. As a result nineteenth-

---

1. Window prostitution is allowed in certain areas in Dutch cities. The prostitute, scarcely dressed, sits at the window of what appears to be a sitting room and gives inviting looks to male passersby. The red light in the room is a definite indication that the woman is a prostitute.

century Dutch living rooms looked like dark caves, functioning as secluded territories for respectable housewives.

The opening up starts slowly in the beginning of this century and reaches its climax in the postwar showcase mentality witnessed by open curtains not only by day but also in the evening. The development of Dutch window prostitution is concomitant to this process of opening up in family homes, but in its sheer exhibitionism it is an excess of the postwar showcase mentality.

In this chapter I will explain what seems to be specifically Dutch in the relationship between women and windows. I lean heavily on the work of Mary Douglas (1979), who pays attention to the symbolism of borders and border markers. Following her symbolic approach, windows can be interpreted as transparent borderlines between the inside and the outside, between the domestic interior and the outside world of the street and the neighborhood.

The Gendered Borderline

In her study of cognitive classifications in several cultures the English social anthropologist Mary Douglas (1979) draws attention to the ways in which these classifications are materialized and obeyed in daily life. Borderlines of any sort, physical or symbolic, are manifestations of cognitive classifications. The nature of these borderlines, be they solid or permeable, and the way they are transgressed and maintained, whether revered by meticulous cleaning or neglected, are indications of the importance of the classifications involved. From this point of view, the Dutch window is a symbolic borderline of special cultural importance.

Its particularity is underlined by its multifarious meanings. The window indicates, first of all, the rather general classification of social reality in a public male-oriented space and a private female-oriented space. The special character of the window as a borderline has not only to do with its fragility in contrast to the solidness of the walls, but also with its relationship to the other opening in the facade: the door. Finally, the most dominant temporal classification of day and night is signaled by an uncovering or a covering of the window.

The ritual character of the window is revealed by its treatment, notably by the way it is guarded, cleaned, and decorated. Douglas pays special attention to the role of the border guards, maintainers, or cleaners, and to who is allowed to transgress and who is not (1979, 35, 68, 114). In the case of the Dutch window, women play a pivotal role in guarding, cleaning, and decorating. A window may not be the most convenient way to transgress, but window climbing by male suitors was an old Dutch courting tradition. Border transgressing in the case of the window, however, is predominantly of a monitorial and controlling nature; more often than not, these activities are of the female kind.

The history of female involvement in Dutch window arrangements will be discussed under two headings. "Window architecture" focuses on the female proximity to this borderline, and "window decoration and cleaning" addresses the female involvement in decorating and cleaning the window.

Window Architecture

The streetscape of a seventeenth-century Dutch town showed rows of rather narrow, tall brick facades with stepped gables. Each story had at least two windows flanked with shutters. A window cross divided the window into two fixed upper parts and two lower parts that could be opened and winged inside. Exterior wooden shutters covered the lower parts of the window at night and sometimes by day.

The upper parts of the window, however, lacked exterior shutters and were the main entrances of daylight in the house (Zantkuijl 1993, 211). A painted ornament on the upper windowpanes, often the family coat of arms, connected family honor with the windowpanes. Deliberately breaking or blotching a family's windowpane is still considered a violation of the inhabitants' integrity.

Seventeenth-century painters like Pieter de Hooch and Gabriel Metsu often portrayed a woman seated at the window of a room facing the street (illus. 3.1). She is reading a letter or engaged in domestic or maternal duties, while a sweeping maid or a child keeps her company (Franits 1993). Often an open door included in the picture offers the spectator a view of the street and the canal. The high hall-like room, the so-called front house, in which these women are portrayed was not a secluded territory but was open to visitors and street vendors. With her chair on a heightened stage the housewife secured her guarding position at the often open window, while monitoring life in the street and supervising the open entrance door (de Mare 1993). Family activities, however, centered around the hearth in separate, low-ceilinged rooms, situated above one another at the back of the house (Levie and Zantkuijl n.d., 79–80).

The discomfort of the cold and the draft to which the women in the front house were exposed probably initiated in the course of the century a restructuring of the interior. In the large and high front house a separate, heightened side room was constructed (Levie and Zantkuijl n.d., 81). When the housewife was seated at the window of this side room, her supervision of the entrance door became rather difficult, if not impossible.

At the end of the seventeenth century a new type of front window developed: a large sash window with a sliding lower part. In architectural literature this type of window is called a "Dutch window" (Muthesius 1910, 191; Rybczynski 1987, 57). Its name is not surprising, for the frequency with which this window was used in the Netherlands at the end of the seventeenth century must have been amazing

3.1. Gabriel Metsu, *Woman Reading a Letter,* ca. 1663. Reproduction, oil on panel, 52.5×40.2 cm. Courtesy of the National Gallery of Ireland.

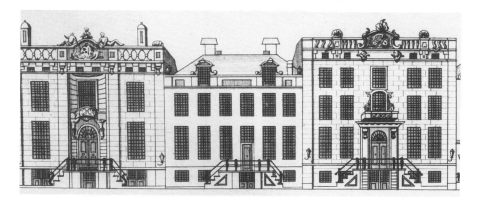

3.2. Caspar Philips Jacobszoon, enlarged detail, *Herengracht 539–543, Het Grachtenboek,* ca. 1767. Courtesy of the Amsterdam Municipal Archives.

to foreign visitors. These shutterless windows gave the houses' facades an air of transparency.

The size of the windows, as well as the size of the front door, grew. The result was a more prominent and sculptured front door in one piece. The facade's air of openness and transparency contrasted markedly with the usually closed front door. The habit of leaving the front door open during the daytime, as had been the case with the old-fashioned parted front door, grew obsolete.

The more prominent front door gave entrance to a central corridor, flanked by side rooms with windows facing the street. This corridor leading to the garden at the back of the house marks a gradual shift in the inhabitants' attention, as it turned away from the public space of the street to the back of the house and notably to the garden, a favorite family retreat in the eighteenth century.

Engravings of eighteenth-century canal houses show large, palacelike facades with giant sash windows and raised doorsteps leading to majestic front doors (illus. 3.2). Although these impressive, huge sash windows seem to negate the borderline between the public and private territory, it is the difference in levels between the public and private space created by a raised ground floor that marks a development toward further distancing between public and private territory.

The front living rooms could have been excellent control towers for the monitoring of street life, but the available controllers, the upper-class mistresses of the house, retreated from the window in the course of the eighteenth century. They left most of the actual controlling to their maids, who answered the doors and enjoyed leaning out of the windows of the upper floors. By the end of the century the "window attitude" of women marked their status. Upper-class women were not to be seen at the front window or to be seated in an open window, acts from which lower-class women were not yet restrained.

The large eighteenth-century sash windows totally disappeared from the Dutch urban architecture of the nineteenth century. This disappearance occurred not only because of the short period of French reign and its introduction of the window tax, but also because the tastes and preferences of the urban elite remained French-oriented throughout the nineteenth century.[2] The window tax legislation considered the number of windows facing the street to be a sign of the homeowner's prosperity. Houses built in the nineteenth century still bear the traces of this tax measure; windows plastered to reduce the tax burden are still visible (De Vrankrijker 1969, 62–64).

At the end of the nineteenth century the front windows in the upper-class town houses were still larger than those of the middle and lower classes, and positioned higher. These differences faded in the course of the twentieth century. The status-bound size of the intermediary space of the front garden, however, remedied the fading of the unleveled public-private boundary.

The construction of huge sash windows grew obsolete, but sash windows of a reduced size became characteristic of nineteenth-century apartment buildings built for the middle and lower classes (Prak 1991). Brick facades of long rows of terraced houses, often more than three stories high, formed the streetscapes of the nineteenth-century working-class districts in Dutch cities.

The distancing between the public and the private was the focus of the civilizing movement initiated by the Dutch elite in the second half of the nineteenth century. The practice of working-class women leaning out of the window while monitoring street life and having loud conversations by shouting to one another was condemned fiercely. The goal of domestication of working-class women and privatization of working-class family life required the retreat of working-class women from the window. In the same vein the outdoor family life of the working class had to change into an indoor, domestic family life.

Documented by late-nineteenth-century travelers to the Netherlands are the so-called spying mirrors fixed at the window frames of the apartments of the middle and lower classes (De Amicis [1876] 1990, 43, 50, 178, 209; Koumans 1930, 60). Spying mirrors were used to monitor street life secretly and avoid the ostentatious and shame-

2. The English window tax was calculated according to the size of the window. At the end of the nineteenth century it was abolished for reasons of public health. Until that time the English poor lived in damp and dark places with no or only very small windows (De Vrankrijker 1969).

3.3. Marc Kolthoff, A prostitute sitting at the window, ca. 1934. Photograph.
Courtesy of Kees Kolthoff.

ful act of leaning out of the window. The monitoring demanded, however, that a person occupy a fixed position in the vicinity of the window with the spying mirror in
view. This position was considered to be harmless for disabled and elderly people,
but improper for decent women, girls, and housewives.

A new phenomenon in Dutch domestic architecture of the 1920s was the construction of a bay window. Ironically, by its outward construction the bay window fa-
cilitated the monitoring of street life. The pretense of carefully inspecting the potted
plants in the windowsill gave housewives an excuse for a prolonged stay in the window's vicinity.

For women in the prewar period the window indicated a dangerous borderline between honor and shame. The repression of public prostitution initiated a cautious
start of window prostitution in the 1930s; prostitutes seated at the window invited
men in by knocking on the windowpane (illus. 3.3).

After World War II the Netherlands, like many other European countries, was confronted with an enormous shortage in housing. Most of the newly built blocks of flats were prefabricated constructions with large window frames as prefab facades (illus. 3.4). The abundant application of window glass became the very symbol of modernity (de Jonge 1960, 67; Van de Ven 1981, 79).

The postwar architects dedicated to the egalitarian, functional principles of modern living considered the extensive glass window to be an annulment of the borderline between the public space of the community and the private space of the individual family. However, the lack of privacy in these modern "glass houses" clashed with the still dominant family ideals of domesticity and intimacy fostered by social reformers and traditional architects (Van Moorsel 1987; Van Setten 1986, 63).

Pursuing their revolutionary ideas, the modernists even dissolved the age-old unity of front window and front door, which resulted in blocks of flats and family houses with entrance doors facing the street and "front" windows facing a public lawn or a back garden, as in the case of family houses. Vegetation and green zones seemed to conspire in their suggestion of a natural borderline between the public and the private, guaranteeing at least a minimal degree of privacy.

3.4. Photographer unknown, Blocks of flats with large window frames as prefab facades, Amsterdam, Burg. de Vlugtlaan, ca. 1956. Photograph. Courtesy of the Amsterdam Municipal Archives.

In a new type of family house, mainly built in Dutch commuters' villages in the 1960s and early 1970s, the living room became a through lounge fitted with extensive glass windows in both the front and the back of the house, resulting in total transparency. The tremendous popularity of the through lounge also affected the owners of prewar houses. They broke away the sliding doors to create the same effect. Likewise authentic stained glass windows were removed and replaced by large modern glass windows. This development signaled the pinnacle of Dutch showcase mentality by its daily and nightly show of family life and interior decoration.

The Dutch oil crisis[3] in 1973 put a temporary halt to the application of large glass windows in domestic architecture (de Weert 1981, 51). Energy saving became more important, at first for economic reasons, but then for ecological reasons, and the size of the windows in newly built houses shrank drastically in the late 1970s. However, subsequent government subsidies for double-glazed windows rescued the postwar architectural tradition of extensive glass windows as a symbol of progress and modernity (de Weert 1981, 62–64).

Postwar domestic architecture mirrored in its large glass windows and glass doors the spirit of the time. Modernity was hailed for its honesty and openness in matters of life, notably sexual matters. In the same period of sexual liberation, Dutch window prostitution developed its notorious exhibitionistic character. The prostitute's act of standing or sitting close to the window demonstrates the violation of the female boundary between honor and shame.

Window Decoration and Cleaning

In most of the Dutch interior paintings of the seventeenth century a woman by her presence "decorates" the window. Seated at the window, she is engaged in reading or sewing. This kind of activity seems to warrant her presence in the vicinity of the window. In addition to a functional explanation, there is a symbolic interpretation of this vicinity. The postwar iconographic tradition in art history has demonstrated the legions of symbolic references in the seemingly very realistic portrayal of domestic scenes in Dutch seventeenth-century paintings (Franits 1993, 11).

On superficial observation Gabriel Metsu's painting *Woman Reading a Letter* (see illus. 3.1) is simply the portrayal of a woman seated at the window while reading a letter, handed to her by her maid, who still holds the envelope in her left hand while lifting with her right hand the curtain covering a painting depicting a ship on a heavy sea. The presence of the dog, the shoe, the laundry basket, and the mirror on the wall

---

3. The Dutch foreign minister's protective attitude toward Israel displeased the Arab oil-producing countries and resulted in a temporary stop of the oil supply.

seem to underline the realistic, lifelike portrayal. A symbolic reading of this painting, however, creates an alternative perspective on the scene and sheds light on the symbolic meaning, not only of the domestic attributes, but on that of the window, the windowpane, and the use of curtains.

The hazards of love are the central theme of the painting, indicated by the partly revealed painting of a ship at heavy sea, which suggests the commotions and emotions of love. Therefore the letter the woman is reading has to be a love letter (Robinson 1974). The sunlight shining through the windowpane sets the letter in a bright light, indicating the focus of the scene. The mirror above the woman's head reflects not by chance the latch of the closed windows.

Window symbolism in European art is rooted in Christianity (Gottlieb 1981, 65–286). A seventeenth-century panegyric on the Virgin Mary illustrates the Immaculate Conception of the Holy Virgin by the symbolism of the divine, male light shining through the clear, female windowpane without breaking it (illus. 3.5). The act of the putto, who tries to veil the window by pulling the curtain, is condemned in this panegyric and interpreted as a devilish defilement of the Virgin Mary (De Leenheer 1681, 22–23). The unbroken windowpane transmitting the bright sunlight symbolizes the virginal hymen, the very symbol of maidenhood (Gottlieb 1981, 69, 289). The reflected latch of the closed window in Metsu's painting reinforces this image of virginity. Open windows and broken panes, on the contrary, are depicted in paintings of married or deflowered women.

In the panegyric, the curtain symbolizes a devilish darkening of the divine light and alludes to the defloration of the Virgin. It is precisely as an allusion to defloration that curtains are portrayed in seventeenth-century paintings. Courting and erotic scenes are often indicated by a large number of heavily pleated and semilifted curtains. This is not surprising, for curtains were also used to surround bedsteads (Thornton 1978, 145).[4]

The seventeenth-century habit of veiling oil paintings by curtains is functionally explained by referring to sunlight protection. A symbolic explanation, however, refers to the resemblance of the frame of the painting to the frame of the window (Gottlieb 1981, 76). A semiveiled painting is frequently depicted in canvases portraying women engaged in courting, symbolized by musical instruments, and also in paintings hailing women or couples with a quiver full of children (De Jongh 1986, ills. 50, 60, 69, 78). Most indicative for the relationship between semiveiled paintings and the presence of fertile women is the absence of a painting curtain in the twin painting of

---

4. A strip of pleated curtain also surrounded the mantelpiece. The functional explanation refers to a protection against draft and soot from the chimney. A symbolic explanation, however, stresses the known female character of the hearth as another connection between inside and outside, with references to the inner chimney as the vagina.

EMBLEMA SEXTUM.

MANENT ILLÆSA.

3.5. Sixth emblem to J. de Leenheer, *Maria, virgo, mystica sub solis imagine. Emblematice expressa. Opusculum votivum.* Antwerp, 1681. Steel engraving, 10.4×17 cm. Courtesy of the Library of the Univ. of Amsterdam.

3.6. Gabriel Metsu, *Man Writing a Letter,* ca. 1663. Reproduction, oil on panel, 52.5×40.2 cm. Courtesy of the National Gallery of Ireland.

Woman Reading a Letter, titled *Man Writing a Letter,* one of the few examples of a young man seated at the window (illus. 3.6).

Dutch seventeenth-century painting is full of symbolic references to the primary classifications of social reality as a male-oriented public and a female-oriented private, domestic territory (Franits 1993). Shoes, like the ones on the man's feet, symbolize their usefulness in the public space of the street (see illus. 3.6). However, a slipper that is flung about, like the one in the woman's portrait, is a negation of the shoe's use in public space and therefore a symbol of private, domestic territory. The same holds true for the hat on the man's chair: in its uselessness in the private space it is the only symbol of the man's prospective role as husband and master of the house. The laundry basket in the woman's portrait is a reference to domestic chores, just as the globe in the man's portrait is a reference to the world outside.

However, the cleaning of the boundary between the domestic and the public worlds was an exclusively female activity in the seventeenth century, preferably performed by maids. Dirt and defilement are, in a symbolic interpretation, matters out of place, violating boundaries and classifications (Douglas 1979, 35). That is why the handling of dirt and the act of cleaning are dangerous and defiling border activities, preferably done by subordinates and in the Dutch case by female inferiors. Maids not only washed the windowpanes and scrubbed the window frame, the bricks of the facade, and the steps to the front door; they are also portrayed sweeping the front house.

Popular Dutch cartoons in the seventeenth century on the topic of the abhorred reversal of gender roles depict among other ridiculous situations a man washing the window (Schama 1987, 446). This may be surprising, for professional window and facade cleaning is nowadays an exclusively male activity, even more so considering the fact that seventeenth-century window cleaning was one of the first "mechanized" domestic activities. The huge windows were cleaned with the help of an instrument, a pump in a large bucket of water. As a handle was pulled up and down, the water was pumped up and splashed high against the windowpanes. This instrument was used until the end of the nineteenth century and then disappeared from the domestic scene.

The housewife's presence at the front window and the cleansing activities of her maid marked symbolically the borderline between domestic territory and that of public street life, even though the windows and doors to the street were opened wide. This, however, was the situation only in daytime; at night, the outer shutters closed off the lower parts of the window and the door was shut. The curtains covering the window on the inside solidified the nightly borderline between public and private as did the shutters on the outside.

At night a decent Dutch household of that time turned its house into a fortress, unlike the seventeenth-century brothels, which were indicated by an open door and a lantern lighting the entrance to the back of the house. Sometimes a maid seated in the front house guarded the open door of the brothel (t'Amsterdamsch Hoerdom 1684).

The fortresslike character of a seventeenth-century house at night disappeared in the next century. The huge eighteenth-century sash windows of the patricians' houses lacked outer shutters. The nightly solidifying of the boundary between public and private space shifted from the exterior to the interior. Large inner shutters covered these huge windows at night and were hidden by long curtains. In daytime the shutters were folded back, and the curtains were drawn aside.

The eighteenth-century Dutch elite, being strongly influenced by the French style in interior decoration, fancied French draperies and net curtains (Thornton 1985, 62, 162). The ease with which the French fashion spread to the middle classes is illustrated in a drawing by Cornelis Troost dated 1739, showing a middle-class woman seated at a small sash window veiled by a transparent muslin net curtain (illus. 3.7). Close observation of Troost's drawing suggests two layers of curtain; the muslin curtain is partly covered by a silk curtain, which is drawn aside. Other new and fancy elements, like a lace window screen and a pelmet, a boxlike fitting to hide the curtain rod, are also depicted.

Troost's portrayal of a woman at the window,[5] signed 1739, bears resemblance to Metsu's painting, which is dated about 1663, with its similar setting of a woman seated on a heightened stage and its similar pictorial symbolism. The empty birdcage refers to woman's premarital status, as does the single rose in the vase. The visible tip of a slipper she is wearing contrasts with the foot warmer depicted next to it. It suggests her liminal status: one shoed foot in the public space and the other on the foot warmer in the domestic space. The sewing gear hanging on her skirt refers to female and domestic qualities. Her suitor, the top-hatted and shoed man, presents in his outfit the public space. Finally, the context of the situation is also determined by a painting depicted in the back: the portrait of the religious leader of the Mennonites.

But what about the window and curtain symbolism? The vine tendril visible through the windowpane is a biblical symbol for fertility and propagation. It is important to note that in this case the tendril is situated outside, for in the case of family portraits with little children, the tendril grows through the sash window into the room (Gottlieb 1981, 251). The symbolic relationship between the windowpane and the hymen is perfectly illustrated by this penetrating vine tendril. The muslin curtain and the window screen only partly cover the window without obstructing the di-

---

5. The drawing represents a scene of a popular theater play, *Jan Klaasz, of gewaande dienstmaagd,* in which a clumsy suitor proposes. It has, however, the same relation to everyday life as Gabriel Metsu's painting: a mixture of realism and symbolism (Niemeyer 1973, 53).

3.7. Cornelis Troost, *Déclaration d'amour de René à Sarotte* (Scene from the play *Jan Klaasz, of gewaande dienstmaagd*), 1739. Drawing. Courtesy of Musée des Arts Décoratifs, Paris.

vine light shining through the upper part. The modest passion of the woman is not symbolized by a draped or lifted curtain but by her heavy, pleated skirt.

The situation depicted in the drawing by Troost, in which a virtuous young woman is seated at the window on a heightened stage, would, however, become a rare phenomenon at the end of the eighteenth century, even though the net curtains or a window screen would have prevented the woman from being seen by passersby. The gradual withdrawal of upper-class and middle-class women from the window heralded the accelerating process of domestication of women in the nineteenth century. The veiling of the eighteenth-century window stressed the borderline at daytime, as the closed front door did, and in fact belied the facade's air of transparency.

Nowadays it is hard to believe that the famous Dutch passion for potted plants in the windowsill is not an age-old tradition, but had a slow start in the last quarter of the nineteenth century. The symbolism of window-penetrating vine tendrils was shunned by the upper classes, who preferred a solitary potted plant on a pedestal behind the window pane. Perhaps it was for symbolic reasons that the popular way of placing potted plants at the outside of the window frame was considered to be vulgar.

The overall impression of Dutch living rooms throughout the nineteenth century, from those of the well-to-do to those of the poor, was that they were crammed, dark, and gloomy: a marked contrast with the light-soaked living rooms of the patricians in the former period. The size of the windows, but more so the kind of curtains, betrayed the status of the inhabitants. The more layers of curtain there were, the more voluptuous the draperies, and the more expensive the material and the trimmings, the wealthier were the inhabitants. Because of their shape, the draperies of the upper classes were mockingly named "knickers curtains." The sexual connotation of this nickname confirms the tradition of curtain symbolism.

Curtain symbolism was very much alive in the nineteenth century, as is illustrated by Italian visitor De Amicis's description upon entering a public coffeehouse at dusk ([1876] 1990, 60). Men were sitting at the windows of this coffeehouse while talking and smoking. A thick curtain in the middle of the room divided the place into a twilit zone in the front and a fully lighted zone in the back. Like the nineteenth-century construction of a spying mirror, the habit of sitting in the twilight was another way of secretly monitoring street life. Not daylight but outer darkness transgresses the borderline and penetrates the private space.[6] Devilish darkness endangers female in-

---

6. The reverse situation, the complete shutting out of daylight, is a traditional Dutch mourning ritual. In the house of mourning even the net curtains and other embellishments were removed. Wrapping oneself in darkness by shutting out the life-bringing daylight of a "male" deity, and by removing the secular, vain, and "female" window decoration, are symbolic acts of the highest degree (de Jager 1981, 78).

tegrity as was illustrated by the seventeenth-century emblem. In the same vein, De Amicis casts serious doubt on the reputation of the only woman he discerned in the twilight: "a lady who shuns the light" (60).

Unhampered by this rigid judgment, the habit of sitting in the twilight remained very popular among the lower classes, men and women alike. The naming of a special dim lamp accommodating the stay in a dark room, called a "twilight lamp," is the best indicator of the habit's popularity. Although the habit grew obsolete in the course of the twentieth century, most Dutch households have several twilight lamps installed in their living rooms for their contribution to a cozy atmosphere.

The writings of nineteenth-century foreign visitors are also very informative on Dutch window decoration and window cleaning. Like their seventeenth- and eighteenth-century predecessors they were amazed about the scrupulous cleaning of the facade, the windows, and the pavement by Dutch women. However, a silent revolution in window cleaning took place at the end of the century, when for the first time professional male window cleaners offered their services. In letters of recommendation to potential clients, these professional cleaners emphasized the welfare of maids: they could be protected from the hazards of cleaning high windows and the obstructions caused by window decoration when they were hanging out of windows to clean them.

The shunning of the window by upper-class women and the gradual process of restraining maids from cleaning the public side of the window are vital elements in the completion of female domestication. The nineteenth-century reinvention of exterior shutter blinds or "modern" wooden roller blinds, paralleled by the use of a mass of draperies on the inside, confirmed the solidification of the window as the borderline between private and public space. The solidification seemed to justify the appearance of male window cleaners.

Resemblance of the practice to the old courting tradition of window climbing by suitors did not seem to have bothered the window cleaner's upper-class clients: outward chastity had reached the point of sheer sterility. Decades later, however, the window cleaner was a favorite topic of naughty jokes, alluding to lusty women and sexual intercourse or, to put it in more general terms, the violation of female integrity.

At the turn of the century the French craze in interior decoration suddenly waned and the style orientation of the Dutch upper class turned northward. Massive draperies quickly disappeared and simplicity was hailed. This sudden change has to be linked to the evolving women's liberation movement and the plea for female rights in the public domain. The concomitant reform movement tried to free women from another form of textile oppression: the enslaving bonds of dress. Both movements had only an upper-class appeal.

In the 1920s the upper classes decorated their windows on both sides with long, simply pleated strips of net curtain, complemented by a small pleated strip at the top of the window. The cover curtains were of the same simple arrangement, without the top covering of a pelmet box (Clarijs 1941, 158–60). No wonder the Czech writer Karel Capek, who visited Holland in the 1930s, was astonished by the scarcely covered windows: "Every passerby is able to judge (at daytime, i.c.) the material status of the household and the exemplary domestic family life by simply looking at the Dutch windows" (1934, 75).

During the German occupation of the Netherlands in the 1940s, the authorities ordered a total blinding of the windows in the evening and at night. The forced blinding during the war is often mentioned as the reason that in the postwar period curtains were no longer closed in the evenings (Vera 1989). However, the effect of numerous nightly showcases of the interior, exposed by lighted front windows, was first perceived in the 1950s in suburbs filled with newly built blocks of flats. If the openness of windows had been a passionate reaction to the forced blinding, it would have happened straight after the war and not five years later.

Adversaries linked the rising showcase mentality to the commercial effect of lighted shopwindows. A sociologist called it "the conformation to the controlling and commercial mechanisms of mass culture" (Van Braam 1966, 18–21). On the whole it seemed to be an upper-class reaction to a lower-class, or in any case popular, habit of publicly exposing one's domestic life—one very similar to the nineteenth-century upper-class reaction to the public, street life orientation of the working class.

A national survey in 1964 indicated that a large majority of the urbanites (65 percent) did not close their curtains in the evening, in contrast to 50 percent of the rural population (Nederlandse 1966, 83). Two decades later these percentages shifted markedly. In 1984 the group of urban nonclosers declined sharply, to 46 percent, but the rural group of nonclosers rose slightly, to 52 percent (Nederlandse 1984, 183).

A symbolic interpretation of this nightly showcase mentality has to concentrate on the treatment of the borderline between public and private space at night. In the postwar suburban situation of well-lighted streets, the lighting of twilight lamps in the room did not prevent the monitoring of street life. In dark, rural surroundings, however, the effect was the reverse. Monitoring was virtually impossible because of the reflections of the lighted lamps on the black, mirroring windowpanes. The suburban two-way screen imitates the unobstructed, fluid borderline as witnessed during the day. These circumstances may explain the primal suburban base of the showcase mentality. The progressive postwar urbanization of the Dutch countryside can account for its rising popularity two decades later.

Uncovered windows in the evenings came under attack during the oil crisis of 1973. In an emotional televised speech Prime Minister den Uyl begged the Dutch people to close their curtains in the evenings to save gas and oil. Stimulated by double-glazing and other energy-saving measures in the 1970s and 1980s, most of the Dutch recaptured their habit of leaving the curtains open. Rising crime rates in the 1980s resulted again in government summonses to close the curtains.

Although the curtains in most homes were not closed during the 1960s, they remained indispensably decorative parts of the Dutch interior. The 1960s also heralded a color revolution in net curtains among the younger generation: crude and brightly colored strips of net textile replaced the "dull" white net curtains. This trend was followed by the vegetation trend in the 1970s, when huge green-leafed potted plants filled the windows and ousted the net curtains. A vast number of potted plants, not of the flowering kind, was indicative of an intellectual or an ecologically motivated lifestyle. Although, on one hand, the symbolism of the penetrating tendril must have faded, there is, on the other hand, a definite link with the concomitant "sexual revolution" that advocated premarital intercourse.

The vegetation trend of the 1970s was paralleled by the artistic and rustic trend, when handicraft and country objects embellished windows and filled windowsills in a carefully designed arrangement. By imitating eighteenth-century sash windows, the suburban woman even tried to give her all-glass windows a nostalgic outlook. For the same reason there was a revival of scrolled wooden window screens. Caring for the plants, creation of the handicraft objects, and the choice of rustic elements have been exclusively female activities.

The window-filling trends among the young upper-middle classes turned white net curtains into old-fashioned forms of window decoration. However, among the lower classes there was a revival of "knickers curtains"—draperies that seemed to illustrate a nostalgic longing of working-class women for an upper-class outlook. The combination of draperies with a symmetric arrangement of flowering plants in the windowsill still today betrays a senior household of a lower-class background.

On the eve of the 1980s the young urban generation took the lead in a revolutionary abolishment of female-associated window decoration. They abdicated not only all types of curtains, but also the potted plants and the rustic objects in the windowsill. Instead they fancied horizontal aluminum blinds in black or white (Cieraad 1988, 133–34). In their cool and businesslike outlook and in their basic material, the blinds blatantly denied the age-old female qualities of textile window decoration. The permanently blinded windows had a definite male aura, symbolizing social distancing on the verge of inhospitability.

The same need for privacy stimulated in the suburbs another type of permanent blinds: vertical white strips of coated textile interconnected by tiny chains. The blinds can be drawn aside like curtains, and the degree of privacy can be regulated by the positioning of the strips. They even leave some space on the windowsill for female decoration: a few small potted plants or modern statuettes of white porcelain. These vertical blinds create an image of the modern Dutch household, in which the wife of the family combines her domestic duties with a part-time job. It is as if the blinds' combination of female and male characteristics—not only half curtain and half blinds, but also coated textile in combination with tiny metal chains—symbolizes the liminal position of housewives in the Netherlands: one foot in the male-oriented public space and the other still planted firmly in the private space of the house.[7]

With the growing labor participation of Dutch women, their symbolic role as guards of the border between the inside and the outside will fade away. This is best illustrated by the waning popularity of window cleaning among women (Neder-landse 1984, 150). The frequency of window cleaning is also inversely related to the amount of a woman's education (de Weert 1981, 45). However, the popularity of the services of the professional male window cleaner is still modest. As would be expected, they are most popular among upper-class women and among working married women (de Weert 1981, 45).

The revival of draperies and nostalgic window decoration in the 1990s seems to be a temporary halt in the process, dictated by the new cocooning kind of domesticity. It is paralleled by the nightly closing off of the window to safeguard oneself in times of rising crime. The present situation is best described as a mixture of the trends of the past two decades. The exception is the front windows of migrant households, which are closed off with traditional white net curtains or draperies.

Conclusion

The symbolic interpretation of the historical relationship between Dutch women and Dutch windows stresses the coinciding of two important borderlines: a physical one and a societal one. The hymen as the historically vital physical borderline of the woman coincides with the windowpane as the vital societal borderline between pub-lic and private space. The conditions of both fragile borderlines are symbolically re-lated, as was illustrated by examples of seventeenth-century Dutch paintings of the interiors of homes. The sexual status of the portrayed women was indicated not only by the condition of the windowpane or by its veiling with a curtain, but also by the locking or unlocking of the window.

The symbolic intertwining of female and domestic integrity from the seventeenth century onward had an enormous effect on the amount of window decoration and on the guarding and cleaning of front windows. The concomitant process of do-mestication of women resulted in a solidifying of the fragile borderline of the win-dow by more and more layers of curtain. By physically retreating from the window,

7. The Netherlands still has, compared to other European countries, the lowest percentage of women participating in wage work.

the nineteenth-century upper-class woman stressed its dangerous character as a fragile borderline between female virtue and female vice. By the end of the nineteenth century even the cleaning of the window lost its solely female appeal, with the introduction of male window cleaners.

The process of the domestication of women started, however, in the upper class and only slowly affected women of the lower classes. Therefore the relationship of lower-class women to their windows differed considerably. Their proximity to the window and to the public domain became an issue in the nineteenth-century civilizing movement of the upper classes. The construction of spying mirrors and sitting in the twilight were ways in which the lower classes tried to circumvent the civilizing pressure.

The changing stress on the borderline, in the seventeenth century on the outside of windows and from the eighteenth century onward on the inside, does have symbolic meaning. The closed outer shutters at night in the seventeenth century reconstruct, as it were, the walls of the house and make it into a fortress. The shutters symbolically underline the period's sharp classificatory differences between day and night, between being open and being closed in the relationship between public street life and private family life.

The diminishing solidness of the exterior covering at night from the eighteenth century onward demonstrates a gradual weakening of this classificatory difference between night and day as regards feelings of safety. But the nineteenth-century interior fortification by massive draperies of net curtain covering the windows in daytime demonstrates, on the contrary, the secluded position of upper- and middle-class women in daily life. The dedomestication of upper-class women at the end of the century, in line with the women's liberation movement, is paralleled by the gradual unveiling of upper- and middle-class windows at the beginning of the twentieth century.

In the postwar openness of the Dutch window, by day and night, two traditions meet: the working-class tradition of the nightly negation of the boundary between public and private space joined the upper-class tradition of the negation in daytime. The showcase mentality is in its complete nightly openness a virtual symbolic negation of the difference between night and day, rooted in the working-class tradition of sitting in the twilight. The openness is not only a glorification of modernity and prosperity, but also of open-mindedness and sexual liberation. In its fading of the boundary between public and private domains, the showcase mentality is also a symbolic expression of the entrance of women into the public domain.

However, the window is still a favorite zone of female expression, and in its decoration it is a painting of class history and professed lifestyle. The latest type of window decoration, the vertical blinds, illustrates in its combination of male and female qualities the present liminal position of Dutch women: both inwardly and outwardly oriented. The neglect of window cleaning among young women seems to be a true omen of a changed attitude.

The dedomestication of women has initiated a female approach to the window, but the present notorious Dutch window prostitution signals the alarming limits of female proximity and presence. Not just rising crime rates, but also female fear of rape, initiated the recent trend toward closing off in the evening. The symbolic relationship between Dutch windows and Dutch women, though weakened, is still a matter of female virtue and female vice.

4

The Ins and Outs of the Hall
A Parisian Example

Céline Rosselin

Strong will and patience are essential requirements for a visitor who wishes to get through the front door of a Parisian apartment building. At the building's main entrance, the visitor must dial a code to open the door. The residents have to reveal this code to their invited guests. Once the door has been opened by the magic buzz, one might end up in a hall leading to different apartments. Often a visitor will also meet with the female caretaker of the building, the concierge. "May I help you?" she asks as a response to an indecisive look. If there is no concierge, as is increasingly the case, the interphone will put visitors directly in touch with their host, who will invite them in. The sound of the elevator, the clicks of approaching footsteps, the knock at the door, or the ring of the bell signals the arrival of the visitor at the apartment door. The apartment door is the last boundary to cross before one gets inside the flat itself. This description clearly shows that the apartment door is one among several thresholds dividing people's private world from the public world.

The concept of the threshold is a prime concept in traditional anthropology. It is connected with the work of famous French and British scholars, such as the seminal work of the Frenchman Arnold Van Gennep ([1909] 1981) and his British followers Mary Douglas (1979) and Victor Turner (1969). According to Van Gennep, society is like a house with rooms and corridors. Thresholds symbolize beginnings of new statuses. The "dangerous" act of crossing the threshold is for that reason controlled by ritual, similar to the popular ritual performed by the bridegroom who carries his bride over the threshold of their first home together.

However, it is not only in matrimonial ritual, but also in daily rituals of reception, that the threshold of the front door, being the borderline between the private and the public space, is of special importance. Van Gennep refers to this threshold as a *zone*

This chapter is a reworked version of "Entrée, entrer. Approche anthropologique d'un espace du logement," published in 1995 in *Espaces et Sociétés* 78, no. 1: 83–96.

Céline Rosselin

de marge, a marginal or liminal zone that separates and links two distinct territories. Consequently, it represents an ambiguous, neutralizing space. The "dangerous" passage through a marginal zone means a temporary ambiguity involving a transition of statuses that is ritually controlled.

The borders of the marginal zone are not necessarily marked, but are acknowledged by a mutual and tacit agreement, by a social and cultural consensus (Hall 1966; Rapoport 1969). For example, in rural areas in France the contrast between the private and the public space is less outspoken than it is in the cities. Farmhouses lack a hallway, and consequently visitors step straight into the main room. On the contrary, in cities, this contrast is more marked: the hall, as a marginal zone, enables a gradual transition.

This study of the entrance hall in modern Parisian apartments describes everyday phenomena of ritualization in contemporary Western urban areas. It illustrates how not only the architecture and the decoration of the hall, but also the ritualized behavior that takes place in it, conspire in a forced neutrality, temporality, and ambiguity akin to marginal zones.

The Hall in Architecture

In Western domestic architecture the hall was originally designed to be the main room of the house and the showcase of the residents' wealth. However, in nineteenth-century apartment buildings for the middle classes the size of the hall was reduced and its function changed into a distributing one: giving entrance to the various rooms of the apartment. The changed morphology of the hall is not a result simply of the formal separation of rooms, but more so of the nineteenth-century, urban split between the private and the public domains. The hall became the intermediate zone to protect the privacy of the residents (Eleb-Vidal and Debarre-Blanchard 1989, 1995). Nowadays, the hall is defined as an adjacent space to the entrance door; beyond this zone, the visitor is no longer in the hall and is already in another area, either an intermediary zone or a proper room, usually the living room.

However, modern architects, in restricting the hall to its traditional distribution function, omitted the hall in the design of one-room apartments. The need for a hall as a transitional zone is illustrated by the opinions and actions of residents living in modern French one-room apartments. One resident expresses her embarrassment: "This apartment is not very convenient because there is no hall and visitors are getting straight into my room!" Residents create substitute halls; a couple in their fifties created a space behind the door by the placement of a wardrobe with a coat rack fixed on the side. Similarly, a young student has put a carpet of one square meter on the floor, where guests have to leave their shoes. This carpet represents his imaginary hall.

Objects that can usually be found in a hall are also located in this area and contribute to the re-creation of the missing room.

Architects often forget that the hall plays a more important role than just distribution. It is not only an entrance room to welcome visitors, but also a protective and neutralizing zone to prevent or ease transition from the public to the private world. Once in the hall, the visitor is not outside the apartment yet not inside it. Located on the edge of the private and public, the inside and the outside, the exterior and the interior, the familiar and the foreign, the hall neutralizes the qualitative aspects of both domains. Not only does the spatial layout of the hall as a marginal zone contribute to its neutrality, but also its decoration and the performed rituals of reception do so.

Protection and Identification

Being a threshold, a marginal zone, the hall is the space where controls, such as the identification of visitors, take place. At the same time this space requires extra protection. The objects used to identify a visitor are closely linked to the necessity of preserving and protecting the residents' privacy against outside intrusion. For example, the judas, the peephole that takes its name from the traitor of Christ, allows, like the *moucharabieh* in Arab countries, a resident to see without being seen and to identify a visitor before opening the door. The apartment door is the first line of defense, sometimes signaled by a barking dog or the sound of an alarm. The protection of the home can take on a more symbolic aspect and even become religious. For example, it is quite common to find in the halls of older people small wooden frames holding mottoes written on copper plates. They often invoke God's protection of the place with sentences such as "God bless you" or "God protect your home." A similar role is played by the mezuza, a small case with parchment inscribed with religious text placed on the door frames of Jewish homes located in Le Marais, a quarter in the center of Paris.

It is not exactly in the hall itself that the action, the first contact between people from the inside and those from the outside, starts. The first role-playing game starts either over the interphone or just behind the door: on the one side, people have to identify the visitor, and on the other side, the visitor has to announce himself or herself. The negotiation stage starts at this point, when everyone takes up a set role: the visitor is often in an inferior situation, whereas the resident may decide whether to open the door to let the visitor in, or to leave him on the threshold of the door. Anthropologists have shown that a foreigner who tries to integrate into a society is in a similar position.

Once the door has been opened by one of the residents, it takes a few seconds to identify or recognize the visitor. This waiting time is justified by the liminal characteristic of the hall as a threshold. The hall is a limit threshold: the last one for the public world and the first one for the private world. As a threshold, it plays a selective role, and consequently not everyone can succeed in crossing it and being let in at any time. As pointed out by Françoise Paul-Lévy and Marion Segaud (1983, 64), each threshold plays a specific role in the selection process.

During this first stage, the resident will decide whether the visitor can be let in. Strictly speaking, it is the first face-to-face contact. In the face-to-face encounter studies in Western societies, a minimum distance is necessary to avoid a feeling of intrusion. When someone reaches the door, he or she often takes a step backwards, which also enables the resident to see the visitor in full size. The face-to-face meeting can be the beginning of an interactive ritual that can go on in the hall but may also be the first and last contact between people if the visitor is not let in.

If the resident and the visitor have never met, the identification procedure might be even more complex. In our society, this procedure is defined according to one's social status with respect to the visitor (either known or unknown) and with rules of politeness. If the visitor is a complete stranger, this step will be very conventional, that is to say, very close to an ideal pattern. Only when the visitor is a close friend is he or she allowed to violate the conventional rules by deviant behavior, such as hiding or making faces.

The situation of identification and negotiation is necessarily temporary and depends on the preexisting relationship between people or on a first impression when people do not know each other. The question of who opens to whom also depends on social rules and safety precautions: men more often reply to unexpected visits and women to planned ones. When people are coming for dinner at the home of a couple, the man is usually in charge of welcoming the guests, and the woman is in the kitchen finishing the preparation of the meal. However, social rules of welcoming forbid children to open the door to guests.

When the resident invites the visitor in, he or she enters the house in one big step so as to revere the *Dieu du seuil,* the God of the threshold, as was mentioned by Gaston Bachelard (1957). Van Gennep ([1909] 1981) also described such practices, such as newlyweds who are not supposed to step on the threshold when entering their new house. This ritualized passage recalls what has been said before about the marginal, the dangerous, and even the sacred aspect of the hall as a threshold. Finally, it is the host's decision to close the door when the visitor has stepped in. This action also illustrates the repartition of the roles to each protagonist in the next stage.

Neutrality and Purification

Once the visitor has been allowed into the house, the hierarchy of the roles tends to disappear. Now the hall is a place for mutual identification where the objects play an important role as much for the visitor as for the host. For the visitor, the objects give information about the number of people living in the apartment and on their activities. For example, the number of shoes, slippers, or cloth pads used to walk on a freshly waxed wooden floor is a good indication of the number of people living there and which residents are at home during the visit. Similarly, the presence of children is indicated by drawings put on the entrance door or the hall walls, by a pram left outside or inside the flat, or by a parent's note saying, "The child is sleeping; please do not ring the bell." Some objects give indications of the residents' outside activities, like sports equipment, travel photos, or posters from museums.

For a host it is very important to have a nicely decorated hall to give the best impression to visitors. Most hall decorations, however, preserve some neutrality: a neutral wallpaper or plain white paint is often preferred to colorful patterns. On the one hand, this neutrality can be interpreted as a way to allow your guests to take possession of the space: they will hang their coats there and leave their umbrellas to dry— objects that represent a foreign intrusion. On the other hand, neutrality prevents the visitor from gaining an all-too-personal impression, and in doing so it protects the privacy of the inhabitants. The resident often justifies the neutrality of the hall by its functionality. In fact, the entrance is neutral not because it is functional but because the residents wish it to be as neutral as possible.

The hall conversation, like the hall decoration, is also quite neutral and limited to greetings and polite phrases: "Hello" or "How are you?" At this stage, a formal language is used because private or personal conversations are not allowed. The formal aspect of this dialogue aims at saving face and putting people at ease, as pointed out by Erving Goffman (1967, 11). Consequently, the answer to "How are you?" is usually "Well. Thank you." During this encounter, people are checking that their respective status has not changed since the last visit.

The hierarchy of roles decreases not only through the exchange of greetings, but also through hugs and handshakes. These gestures epitomize the acceptance of a contract or an agreement on both sides, most clearly illustrated by the shaking of hands to confirm a business deal or by the kiss sealing a wedding ceremony. The representation of this contract between visitor and resident depends on their relationship and on the time elapsed since their last encounter.

Another way of balancing positions is the presentation of a gift by the visitor: flowers, sweets, or a dessert, which are "bartered" against the invitation to come into the apartment. Gift exchange belongs to the logic of social transactions as described by Marcel Mauss ([1923] 1990) and involves a sequence of obligations and expectations: gift giving, accepting, and returning. The host has the obligation not only to accept the visitor's gift, but also to give a present at a return visit.

As a marginal zone, the hall is also a purification area. According to Mary Douglas (1979) marginal zones are intrinsically dangerous because of their ambiguous, in-between character. Some objects in the hall play a part in the rituals of purification, in order to neutralize the danger of ambiguity and impurity. For example, there are often two floor mats: the first one can be found in front of the entrance door, and the second one in the hall itself. People wipe their shoes on the first and take them off on the second one. Shoes and other objects defiled by the public space, like coats, hats, umbrellas, shopping bags, and leisure equipment, are often left behind in the hall. Looking in the hall's mirror and correcting one's appearance either before leaving the house or before entering the living room are also purifying acts. Neutrality and purity are both conditions for transition.

Transition and Temporality

The transitional character of the hall, the area where people are not meant to stay, gives a special temporality to the actions performed there. For example, the look in the hall's mirror has to be cursory, in contrast to the more intimate and elaborate inspection of one's appearance in the mirror of the bathroom or the bedroom. The greeting and welcoming of guests are also dictated by temporality, for they are progressive stages in the transition process. They are followed by the invitation to take off the coat and by preparation of the guest for the final stage: the entrance into the more intimate space of the apartment. In this final stage the conversation also switches from formal language to more personal topics.

Entering and leaving, especially by visitors, can be interpreted as so-called rituals of passage, which involve not only a progressive spatial transition but also a change of status. Generally speaking, the hall allows the transition from one status to another. Office clerks become parents at home, students become sons or daughters of residents, the stranger becomes acquainted. Changes of status can also go the other way around. For example, if a friend leaves you after an argument he can become an enemy who is not welcome anymore. The transitional aspect is reinforced by framed mottoes that decorate the hall: "A friend is always most welcome at our table" or "Friendship is a flower which can be shared when blossoming." These mottoes kindly welcome the guest who changes from stranger into friend.

Thanks to the change of status, the leaving of a visitor is not ruled by such strict behavior. Indeed, the conversation will be more spontaneous, less conventional, and after visitor and guest have spent some time talking in the hall, it might continue on the staircase when showing the visitor out. Getting the coats, saying good-bye, launching new invitations, and putting an end to the conversation are now submitted to a much less rigid ritualization (wine might also contribute to a more relaxed atmosphere!). The initial role playing might even be reversed: the resident decided to let the visitor in, but the visitor might decide when he or she wants to leave. After saying good-bye, the guest might even take the initiative in opening the apartment door, as the residents do not want their visitor to believe that they are pushing him or her out. The transitional space of the hall is also a space of reversals, as Gaston Bachelard (1957) defined the entrance door, through its opening and closing functions, as twice symbolical in linking the two worlds.

Conclusion

The descriptions of objects, actions, and words exchanged between the protagonists of the interaction ritual show that the hall is a threshold, an in-between of two other worlds: interior versus exterior, private versus public, and intimate versus foreign. As a marginal zone, the hall does not belong to either of these categories but plays a spatial role in both of them. Kenneth Ames underlines this when writing about halls in Victorian America: "For it was a space which was neither wholly interior nor exterior but a sheltered testing zone which some passed through easy and others never went beyond" (1984, 221). The hall does have a role of protection: it physically and symbolically protects the private and the domestic world. It also has a level of intimacy while allowing for the process of identification, neutralization, and purification.

The hall is not a univocal space: it is a space where the reversal between interior and exterior, private and public, and opening and closing are always possible. Consequently, this space holds a variety of behaviors and actions that tend subtly to a transition, a change of status. The objects put in the hall refer back to the representations that derive from this zone and to its role.

This study was aimed at putting into question the architectural approach to domestic space in Western societies. However, an anthropology of the domestic space cannot be established solely from the observation of architectural data, the objects as such, or the interviews with the residents. Only the study of the interaction between the domestic space, the occupants, and the objects that surround them will reveal the mechanisms of creating a meaningful universe.

5

"I've Always Fancied Owning Me Own Lion"
Ideological Motivations in External House Decoration by Recent Homeowners

John A. Dolan

THERE ARE, perhaps, few stronger pieces of nostalgic iconography than the dark-timbered, white wattle and daub English country cottage. Love it or hate it, the sight of such a house is not easily ignored (illus. 5.1 and 5.2). Neither, for that matter, is a house with a shallow, horseshoe-shaped, cobbled drive, with ornamental globes on each of its four guardian gateposts, and a Victorian streetlamp standing centurion by the front door. No matter what your architectural preference, houses that proclaim themselves like these demand viewing attention—especially when they are found just a short distance from each other, and in the middle of a sprawling, former local authority housing estate dating from the late 1940s. Such housing estates were residential districts of only rental homes, planned and owned by local councils to provide low-cost housing.

We all live in an everyday world in which houses—their costs, their supply, their locations—fascinate us, and we all accept the fact that the purchase of a house will probably represent the greatest expenditure (and become the most valued asset) incurred by an adult in contemporary British society. Certainly, homeownership was a dominant theme within the domestic political agenda of the former Conservative government, emphasized by the White Paper on Housing published in June 1995.[1] Yet

1. The daunting reality of "negative equity" now means that up to a million British householders have mortgages higher than the reduced value of their homes. Despite this, a social survey conducted jointly by Market and Opinion Research International Ltd. (MORI) and the housing charity Shelter reported in December 1993 that 78 percent of adults in Britain want to own their own home. Home improvement (DIY) remains the most popular pastime among British males over age twenty-five.

5.1. An imitation of the dark-timbered, white wattle and daub English country cottage, 1995. Photograph by John A. Dolan.

5.2. Heritage idyll with vestigial, heraldic features, 1995. Photograph by John A. Dolan.

deliberate changes to external house appearance such as these inevitably prompt certain questions.

What, for example, motivates a householder to seek such a radically distinguishing identity for her or his property? Why would one do this when, at the same time, choosing to remain sited in one's traditional neighborhood? How do such changes become reconciled to one's continuing location within the enduring collectivity of "the estate"?

Raymond Williams (1977) has suggested that any emerging social group must struggle to assert its identity against the articulations and priorities of a dominant culture that disregards the concerns of the emerging group. If this is so, then the members of any such emergent group have to attempt to articulate some sense of themselves by employing available systems of signification, which can give some expression to their needs and—crucially, for Williams—their feelings. While Williams is essentially concerned with the relationship between social identities and language, his ideas also offer theoretical illumination of the choices that individuals make about the external decoration of their homes, because such architectural and decorative features are themselves part of a symbolic codification having meaning and intelligibility.

In addition to these ideas of Williams, there have been some North American studies of the cultural significance of transient features of exterior domestic decoration, most notably on "yard landscapes" and their furnishings (Harris 1990; Synnott 1990). These studies have developed useful ideas about personal landscape creation, management, and embedded cultural values. Other studies produced in the United States (Nasar 1989a; Sadalla and Sheets 1993; Sadalla et al. 1987) argue that, by their expressions of housing preferences in terms of styles and construction materials, individuals communicate substantial symbolic information about themselves as social agents. Significantly for present purposes, Sadalla and Sheets (1993) conclude that "linkages between materials symbolism and homeowner were found to depend on the homeowner being perceived as *actively choosing* the materials" (my emphasis).

The oppositional dichotomy, "homeowner" and "tenant," is one of the dominant polarities in our culture, with the latter being subordinate to the former in terms of material structures of power and resources. Former tenants who have bought their houses from the local authority can be understood as forming an emerging group that needs to express the difference between its members and those who remain in the subordinate grouping to which they, too, so recently belonged. Decisions about altering the external appearance of the house have the potential to be symbolic statements about the individual homeowner's struggle to express a "new" identity centered on the literal threshold between the "private" and the "public"; on the boundary between the personal and affective interior, on the one hand, and the social and instrumental exterior, on the other.

These ideas begin to have congruence with elements in the debate on the nature of social stratification, most notably those concerned with status. Status is often understood in respect to its ascribed and collective, and its achieved and individual, aspects. Macdonald (1989), for example, discusses the linkage between architectural decisions and the pursuit of status inherent within the "professional project." He argues that such a project is characteristic of "professional bodies," such as the Law Society, the Royal College of Surgeons, and the Institute of Chartered Accountants in England and Wales. His descriptive survey of the headquarters buildings chosen by these and other bodies leads Macdonald to suggest that aspects of achieved status have expression in the context of collectivities, which themselves are "an important part of the status system" (57). The scale, appearance, site, and neighborhood location of the headquarters building bestow a complementary spatial prestige to the social status already sought by the organization itself, and symbolize the crucial public attributes of "respectability" and "trustworthiness" (55).

It has been possible since 1980 for tenants of local authority houses in England and Wales to buy their homes from the authority at a discounted price. This legislative scheme was part of Prime Minister Margaret Thatcher's political project to turn Britain into a "property-owning democracy," during her administration, 1979 to 1990. Her project appears to have been a success, at least on some measures, albeit at the cost of the public sector and specifically the local authority housing provision (Stewart and Burridge 1989). Between 1980 and 1990 some 1.25 million former local authority homes have been sold to tenants under the "right to buy" legislation (Whitehead 1990).

Crucial to the success of the Thatcherite project was its emphasis on an insisted-upon linkage among "freedom," the "ownership" of property, and the exercise of "property rights." In its turn, this ideological coupling of essentially competing notions was legitimated by the claim that it was part of the national past and central to a distinctive national identity. In her now notorious, self-validatory *Newsweek* interview, "Don't Undo What I Have Done" (reprinted in the *Guardian* 1992), Thatcher gave her estimate of the success of this project: "Our task as Conservatives was to uncover . . . this remarkable character. We didn't discover it. We knew it was there, we had great faith that although it had been smothered and strangled, if we got the laws right again, the spirit of enterprise would re-emerge. People had become accustomed to having no responsibility. . . . I set out to destroy socialism because I felt it was at odds with the character of the people. . . . We reclaimed our heritage." In a strange way, these claims made by Thatcher in her political exile echo the despairing reaction of Tom Nairn (1983) to the populist and popular support for the Falklands War of a decade earlier: "The real England is irredeemably Tory."

However, having now bought his or her freehold, the newly enfranchised home-owner is presented with the sometimes unexpected dilemmas of unaccustomed personal "freedoms." What color to paint windows and doors; indeed, whether to keep such fixtures and fittings? Leaded panes or wooden shutters? A flat-roofed open porch, or classical capitals and pediment? Whether to leave one's newly acquired market asset looking like many other houses in close proximity, or to seek to distinguish it in some way, was never an issue when the Local Authority Housing Department arbitrated all such matters, usually resolving them by the egalitarian expedient of patterned uniformities.

The shift from "tenant" to "owner" potentially produces a disturbance of the former, centered identity of the householder. She or he now enters into a period of cultural disorientation. It is during this period that the effort to articulate a new identity might occasionally give rise to (arguably) aesthetically illiterate statements, such as those of the "country cottage" and the "elegant town house."

These are neither isolated nor indiscriminate examples. The manner in which such questions of external decoration have been answered by former tenants seems to go beyond mere whimsy, and instead to offer indications about the extent to which Thatcherite political priorities have, literally, contoured that most immediate and material of cognitive landscapes—the house plot, which is called home—while transforming it into an ideological castle. Thatcherism's emphasis on market forces and on the commodification of personal choices and experience would seem to mean that a new reality of neighborly competition has replaced any cozy notion of "imitation" so prevalent among past romancers of community study (see, among many others, Townsend 1977).

The Study

This chapter examines some of these theoretical and experimental ideas by means of a critical case study carried out in the field. Inevitably, such a qualitative study of this sort is exposed to problems of reliability and validity. However, its findings and conclusions are offered as only provisional statements of how the relationship between homeowners' architectural choices and tenets of dominant ideology might best be understood. In large part, these rest on the interpretation of features of style as symbolic expressions, supported by photographic evidence, and with some quotations provided in selected instances as evidence for the self-conscious intentions of particular homeowners.

Investigation of a large local authority housing estate, a residential district of rental homes, on the edge of an English Midlands city offers a good opportunity to identify expressions of determinations about private landscapes. Further, such identifications can prompt attempts to extrapolate the deeper meanings embedded in such apparently personal decisions. In the past decade or so, more than half of the total housing stock on the estate has been sold, the bulk to sitting tenants. It is, then, suitable territory on which to examine the extent to which new recruits to Thatcherism's property-owning democracy might give outward expression to that set of ideological premises on which the social revolution of Thatcherism was based.

The estate lies on the northern boundary of the city and was planned and built during the late 1940s and early 1950s. At that time, its housing stock was vaunted in the local press as being state-of-the-art with respect to features of its design and construction. The housing stock itself consisted mainly of semidetached, or short-run, terraced houses. The estate was landscaped with open green spaces and few boundary markers, and would become, it was locally hoped and expected, a model of postbellum community. A report in the local press in 1948, for instance, confidently claims that the estate will become a "little township on its own," a prospect perhaps still awaited by some who live there, though possibly yet in the process of being realized.

Many neighborhood amenities promised in the 1940s, such as youth clubs, public baths, and a health center, were never constructed. Through the 1960s and 1970s, the estate became locally notorious for its high levels of youth-associated vandalism and petty offenses; its open spaces and often shared house frontages came to be dominated by wandering gangs of aimless youths and served as the spoiling grounds for packs of dogs. This is, of course, a characteristic of incomplete development and consequent disadvantage all too typically experienced on many of the planned local authority estates of the period, and critically commented upon by some who have studied post-1945 housing policy in Britain (McKenna 1991). However, and at least to an outsider, all of this hardly amounts to a recommendation for home purchase on the estate.

A Typology of Estate Homeowners

Two of the essential tenets of Thatcherism are an emphasis on national heritage coupled, rather perversely, with a celebration of the individual, chiefly in a politically determined role of consumer. Among those who have bought their houses on the estate, these values find most obvious material expression within a group I term "the transformers."

The Transformers

The owners of the English country cottage, and of the grand town house referred to in my opening, both clearly belong here. Each has transformed a semidetached property into an image of the British past, denying the period of municipal provision and ownership, despite the fact that the adjoining properties in both instances continue to look like what they remain and have always been: council houses.

A yet more individual transformation is seen in the semidetached house that now has the appearance of a Spanish hacienda. With its scalloped, whitewashed walls and facade, complete with textured, "exposed" brickwork, the house appears as a sort of icon of Britain's favorite foreign holiday destination.

I spoke to the woman who lives here about the intentions behind the transformation that she and her husband have wrought on the property: "We saw them [houses with the appearance they have sought to ape] when we went on holiday abroad, to the Costa del Sol, and we've always liked them, so when we had the chance we thought, right, let's have one here. It's something a bit different."

It is this last motivation, the concern *to distinguish* her house from the very many of identical appearance on the estate, that differentiates the determination of transformers from the more understated, sentimental, and private nostalgia of naming one's semidetached house after the place of honeymoon or favored holiday resort. The latter practice, of naming a house by fixing a nameplate to the facade, is common in British suburbs (that is, housing speculatively built and privately owned from the very start).

The Privatizers

Though, in a sense, Thatcherism remains essentially an ideological project concerned with the shared invention of a national past, one part of which is the *commodification of individual choice,* its most compelling component is the arrogation of personal consumption to an equation with freedom.[2] The emphasis on privatization, including the enforced freeing of former state-owned industries and provisions by offering their equities in the capital marketplace, is its clearest political statement of this priority. Of course, the "right to buy" legislation had its origin in this wider purpose. Among those who bought their estate houses is a recognizable group whom I term "the privatizers."

This group would seem to represent the majority of those who have exercised their right to buy, and they appear to have two distinguishing totem architectural expressions: the enclosed glazed porch, and the front boundary fence or wall (illus. 5.3). The erection of an enclosed porch seems to be the preferred means by which the privatizer marks off the newly acquired property from those of his neighbors that remain in the ownership and control of the local authority. At its simplest, the porch is rendered merely as a shallow extension at the front door, with a single window. In some instances, however, this matures into an elaborate structure, almost aping the con-

2. It might be remembered, too, that Thatcher's own choice of house style, when she bought a new private home in 1985, was a fiercely antimodernist, subclassical, yet newly constructed home in Dulwich Gate, South London.

servatories more associated with suburban houses, and indeed many are adorned with houseplants, cut flowers, and, increasingly, items of cane furniture.

Clearly, such structural accretions are statements about the residents' identity and status as owner-occupiers, rather than being functional extensions to the property. Few porches I peeped into, for example, had coats or muddy boots in them. The porch is a relatively inexpensive but definite emblematic alteration, and is a possibility available only to those who have broken free of regulation by local authority control. The porch is also a border territory, on the boundary between the public space of the estate and the private realm of the home. In this sense, it is a neutral zone in which visitors are formally received and then either admitted or turned away from the private sphere.

Yet porch erectors themselves are not necessarily aware of their cultural signings. Among those I questioned, most initially emphasized a supposed utilitarian function of the porch: "It helps block off drafts and keeps the house warmer"; "We thought it would be somewhere to keep the little 'uns' things, their toys and that"; "It stops

5.3. Two distinguishing totem architectural expressions: the enclosed glazed porch and the front boundary fence, 1995. Photograph by John A. Dolan.

you getting as cold [as formerly?] when you answer the door, doesn't it?" However, the ideological symbolism that I am claiming for the porch is perhaps intimated in the response from the houseowner who was actually in the process of porch construction: "We thought that now it was ours, we'd have a go at the job proper, make it more of our own place, like."

In most cases, the construction of a front porch is closely followed by erection of a front wall or fence. Though there were formerly few boundary markers on the estate at housefronts, the overwhelming majority of privatizers' properties are cordoned from neighbors and pavement by fence or wall. In a few cases, this boundary marker is privet hedging, but in more instances it takes the form of white-painted ranch fencing, presumably because it is cheap and quick to erect. Of course, the building of a fence denotes material expression of twinned desires: to mark off one's own property and to defend it against the incursions of competing values or interests.

Within the discourse of analyses of cultural politics, the erection of physical boundaries is articulation of privatized concerns, the construction of self from not-self, and the fear of difference. Jonathan Rutherford, for example, in his examination of the ideological relationship between culture and individual sensibilities notes that "The Right [and Thatcherism] always have promised strong political defenses and well-policed frontiers against the transgressive threat and displacements of difference" (1990, 12).

Even so, the construction of a ranch fence would seem to be an intermediate stage of boundary marking. An increasing number of houses on the estate boast low walls, usually of brick. At least one even carries the mark of the not-too-distant, upland landscape of the Peak District and has a drystone wall. Interestingly enough, a growing number of homes unite the privatized ideal with heritage idyll and incorporate vestigial, heraldic features (either as gates or low capping fences) such as wrought ironwork and statuary (see also illus. 5.2). Indeed, the man building his porch told me that he would place a (concrete) lion beside his own porch when completed, because: "I've always fancied owning me own lion, like on a coat of arms or something."

A very few privatizers even manage to demonstrate the niceness of demarcation between themselves and transformers by adhering stone cladding to the facades of their houses (illus. 5.4). A stone facade apes, albeit subconsciously, the prestigious social status still so often attached in the United Kingdom to idylls of rural life and living.

Given that many former tenants as houseowners remain tied to their original homes of purchase, such falsifications may be symbolic attempts to shift the *site* of the home to a neighborhood characterized by a different type of construction material from that found on the estate. Baltzell's work (1962) on the defining characteristics of status symbolism ranks site along with style as a critical variable in the denoting of respectability. However, the use of cladding materials may also be an unconscious expression of the ambivalence of purpose between the two groupings of homeowners, perhaps itself reflecting the tensions and contradictions of Thatcherite ideology.

However, the transformers and the privatizers are linked by their enduring commitment to living on the estate. Among my informants, all had been long-standing residents in the homes they had recently purchased, and none expressed any formed intention to leave the estate.

5.4. A stone facade apes the prestige attached to idylls of rural life and living, 1995. Photograph by John A. Dolan.

John A. Dolan

The Market Traders

There appears, finally, an emerging third grouping, constituted chiefly of children of the estate settlers, who espouse the market trader values that are most readily associated with the economic structures of Thatcherism. For these people, the immediate urge is to turn a home into a market commodity for future *trading and profit*, and this invariably necessitates that they invest early in the construction of a private garage within the house plot. At the time of the estate's original construction, of course, no thought was given to the needs of private motoring, because few of the (then) tenants owned a motor vehicle. The National Association of Estate Agents has consistently reported in recent years that a garage is the most cost-effective household improvement, and this market awareness appears strong among those who see the right to buy as their opportunity to move on.

The decision to build a garage, or garage extension to one's property, would seem to be an expression of market ideology, translating "home" into commercial "asset." However, the legislative regulation requiring purchasers of local authority houses to return their tenants' discount on the original purchase price if they sell within the first five years after purchase may mean that the decision to build a garage is delayed.

Market traders exhibited no loyalty to the estate, and indeed spoke of it in disparaging terms. However, such attitudes contrast sharply with the many examples of investment in the estate of all types, made by both individual householders and the local authority itself, which has a major Action Area Scheme in operation to improve residential conditions on the estate. Their interest in translating "home" into marketplace "commodity" also means that the emblematic features of Thatcherism (such as residual heraldic motifs) are absent from their home-improvement imperatives (illus. 5.5). Essentially, the market traders embrace commodity relations at the expense of the more subtle cultural relations of Thatcher's "property-owning democracy," in which the emphasis is on ownership and nation, rather than on selling.

Conclusion

Of course, such a small-scale, localized investigation as the one reported here makes any mapping of the ideological signs and symbols attached to exterior house style and decoration provisional. It is likely, too, that there is ample room for refinement for the interpretations offered here, not least in respect to the gendered experiences and motivations of homeownership (Madigan, Munro, and Smith 1990). For example, it may well be that, for women, decisions about exterior decorations and structural extensions have to do with affective and family priorities, whereas such decisions

5.5. To translate "home" into marketplace "commodity" means that emblematic features are absent, 1995. Photograph by John A. Dolan.

for men may relate more to their sense of themselves as social agents, and particularly as participants in relations of exchange, consumption, and competition.

Stewart and Burridge (1989), for example, discuss house purchase decisions as a function of an individual's buying power within social markets. Fairly obviously, the size, style, and location of one's home is—at least in part—a function of the householder's economic status. On top of that, access to social assets such as schools, health care services, and recreational amenities varies in quality and supply between neighborhoods and communities. In such a stratified context, decisions regarding house purchase, and about what to do with the house thereafter, are as likely to be determined by an individual's sense of social identity and ideological aspirations as by personal whimsy or pragmatic needs.

It would seem that there are grounds, then, for believing that the political and economic imperatives of Thatcherism have had an impact on the private actions of former tenants of the local authority, and that this impact is capable of observation and

John A. Dolan

ideological codification. Whether this proves to be a subject for enduring inquiry, or one of merely passing interest, depends upon the outcome of the genuine tensions between the settler instincts of transformers and privatizers, with their commitment to permanency and community, and the commercial instincts of the market traders, who translate all social experience into commodity transactions for personal gains.

In either case, the visual evidence from this study of homeowners' stylistic and decorative choices of external features strongly suggests that the privatized and imagined "transcendent and eternalized . . . imperial national identity" (Wright 1985, 27) at the very center of Thatcherite public rhetoric and policy has found a place in the definitions of social self available to new owner-occupiers on former municipally owned estates.

6

Bringing Modernity Home
Open Plan in the British Domestic Interior

Judy Attfield

O PEN PLAN is one of the most fundamental changes in the British domestic interior since World War II. By its radical reversal of focus from "closed" to "open,"
it embodied modernization in the form of the house plan, thus incorporating, if only
in theory, the notions of adaptability, mobility, and change. It paralleled, in microcosm, the utopian expectations of urban planning in the postwar period (Schaffer
1972; Ward 1993; Wright 1991).

Ideally, modernity in terms of housing was envisaged by designers as a universal
type of mass housing suitable for and accessible to all citizens. It gave priority to ease
of use and maintenance, rejecting traditional styles and unnecessary ornament in
favor of a minimal aesthetic. Domestic open plan placed an emphasis on the functions and layout of the interior, eliminating walls to create a multipurpose "democratic" living space.

The reconstruction program[1] for the rebuilding of Britain after the war was seen
as an opportunity to put ideals into practice. New towns were built, and residents
were imported from urban working-class areas to inhabit the new houses. The case
study of Harlow New Town illustrates the way in which domestic interiors embodied different versions of modernity—those of the residents and those of the designers. This chapter examines how tenants adapted to their new surroundings through
their own styles of interior decoration and furnishing.

---

1. "Reconstruction" is a general term used in connection with both world wars and referring to the government plans for postwar rebuilding of the physical structure of the nation
in the form of housing, schools, hospitals, etc., and the process of transforming a population
geared for war to peacetime civilian life. The ideals behind the concept of reconstruction saw
design and planning as a means of effecting social reform.

The study[2] is largely based on a series of interviews carried out in 1982 and 1985 in the postwar new town of Harlow in Essex, not only with local authority housing residents mainly drawn from working-class areas of London, but also with architects and council officers (Attfield 1995). It provides an ethnographic focus to the history of open-plan design as a cultural phenomenon.[3]

The modern open-plan living room arrangement, which replaced the conventional plan of separation between the little used "front room" or parlor and the all-purpose "living room," became a feature of public housing.[4] It is significant that in this case study of local authority housing the accommodation was rented rather than owned.

The ingenuity employed by occupants to superimpose their own interpretations of modern design highlights the importance of appropriation. Their "common sense" style of modernity, adapted from the traditions of their cultural background, was in distinct contravention to the designers' ideal version. It was the distinctiveness of the residents' style that marked the transformation of public housing into individual homes,[5] a process Daniel Miller (1990) has so tellingly called "appropriating the State on the Council Estate."

The engagement with modernity and social reforms that were embodied in postwar social housing in Britain met with resistance, which has in retrospect been interpreted by design theorists and architects as "the failure of modernism" (Boudon 1972). This chapter, however, argues that the history of open plan in the home, when studied as material culture rather than the failure of design theory, indicates how a popular adaptation of modern design was used to assimilate social change and modernization.

2. This chapter developed out of an ongoing study of the social history of domestic interiors (Attfield 1995). I would like to express my thanks to the many people who helped me in various ways with this project, but in particular to the interviewees who shared their experiences so generously with me.

3. One of the distinguishing features of the relatively new discipline of design history, from which this study emerges, is its conscious break from conventions within art history. The adoption of ethnographic practice in researching the social significance of the history of design removes it from a discussion of theoretical ideals and recontextualizes it as a quotidian and integral part of the material culture of everyday life (Attfield 1996; Putnam and Newton 1990; Woodham 1995).

4. Open plan in Britain was not generally adopted in the private speculative housing sector until central heating became common during the 1960s.

5. The term "home" is used here according to Tim Putnam's definition: "The home is at once an idea, a social institution, and material reality" (Putnam and Newton 1990).

Open Plan as Modernism

The concept of "open plan" used in the interior living space of the house can be defined within the context of the history of British housing design as echoing some of the characteristics of modern town and country planning based on rational design theory (Abercrombie 1945). The main purpose of a town plan in the postwar reconstruction period was expressed in social terms. According to Frederick Gibberd, one of the new generation of architects and town planners emerging after the war, it was "to give the greatest possible freedom to the individual . . . by controlling development in such a way that it will take place in the interests of the community as a whole" (1953, 21–22).

Writing in 1942, the architect Ralph Tubbs encapsulated the ideals of the reconstruction and its hope for the future: "The folly of the last century must go, the chaos, the slums and the dirt; so also, the crimes of our own century, the mock-Tudor suburbs, the ribbon development and the imitation Classic. . . . New ways of building will free us from the limitations of the load-bearing wall. Let the plan reflect new freedom of spirit. . . . Analysis of requirements is the basis of all planning—the same principles apply to the house or the city" (1942, 33, 38).

The construction of "open-plan" buildings depended on the reconsideration of conventional methods of construction, greater use of glass, and the elimination of walls in order to maximize internal space and open it to the outside to create a more direct relationship to nature. Open plan marked the culmination of technical developments that enabled the spanning of large areas, dispensing with the need for masonry and hand construction.

The load-bearing properties of steel and concrete offered architects exciting new possibilities of treating architecture as the enclosure and ordering of space according to logic, rather than conforming to traditional forms and conventional patterns of room arrangements (Le Corbusier and de Pierrefeu 1958). Ideally, the form was supposed to result from rational planning based on social considerations rather than from aesthetic conventions.

The well-being of a building's occupants was one of the fundamental demands placed upon modern architectural design. This entailed planning the relationship of internal zones, both to each other and to the outside, so as to obtain the optimum conditions with regard to quantity and quality of fresh air, sunlight, and proximity to nature. Labor saving and efficiency were principles applied to the design and equipping of the house, using "scientific planning" techniques derived from factory organization, based on time and motion studies (Denby 1942, 1944; Giedion 1969).

More important than the technology that generated the development of open plan were the utopian ideals. In house design, social convention had formerly determined a hierarchy of rooms that divided the servants' quarters from the employers' and designated certain rooms according to gender (Davidoff and Hall 1987; Davidoff et al. 1983). The segregation of genders and classes gave way to a more ambiguous open plan with its attendant implications of modernity: social equality and adaptability to change. Above all, it took into account the economic necessity of the building of "suitably sized" houses by local authorities for rental to low-income tenants (Lewis 1952, 226–30).

In emphasizing the need to make every inch of the well-designed house functionally meaningful, the Dudley Report *Design of Dwellings* (1944), prepared in anticipation of the reconstruction, explained its refusal to use the term "parlor" expressly because it carried "old-fashioned and obsolete" connotations (*Design of Dwellings* 1944, 14). This illustrates the climate of change that sought to question and eliminate tacit customary practice in favor of an innovatory strategy for tackling problems of space.

Experience has since taught designers that it is impossible to create neutral spaces devoid of cultural connotations. Attempts to do so by the modernist designers of the time can be explained by their optimistic belief that it was possible to create a dwelling type to suit a new way of life. However, both open plan and the modernity it represented meant different things to different people.

Originally for the designers, "open" was seen as synonymous with free (as in Le Corbusier's *plan libre*). To the occupiers of the new houses who ascribed more value to privacy than almost anything else, "open" meant something else; it was about being able to control access to their own space. They spoke of the pride they experienced from "having my own front." And while the front door was about being able to shut the outside out, the back door was about opening: "I could open my back door and go into a garden and that was a thing I had never had before."

The social and economic program responsible for the building of postwar public housing gave residents access not only to the open countryside but also to opportunities that many had not had before. As another tenant said, "The fact that there was a garden . . . made one appreciate that you'd come not only into a new town but into a new way of life."

The argument often leveled against public housing is that of uniformity, a criticism that a cursory study of just some of the designs produced would soon prove inaccurate. It is in fact in the private sector that we find the uniformity. By the 1960s open plan became general in the popular house that had reached such a degree of impersonal blandness that it earned the label of "universal product" (Cowburn 1966).

Its success was attributed to the builders' and property developers' skill in creating the ultimate popular commodity—a product that could easily be resold because of its universal appeal. The easy adaptability of open plan as a frame for ephemeral interior decor also lent itself to the quick changes required during a period of great buoyancy in the property market when it was usual for houseowners to move every few years.

The other criticism applied to public housing, and new towns in particular, is the sense of dislocation and lack of community to be found in a place that has not had enough time to establish roots. There was much evidence of residents' difficulties in adjusting to new accommodations and new towns. However, with historical perspective it is just as possible to cite examples of how people overcame these difficulties and managed to "settle" in the new towns and dwellings.

A case illustrating this point is that of a family who remained corporation tenants and had no aspirations to own their own house. They felt settled and did not want to move, although they were both retired. By that time they had nine grandchildren living in the town, some of them "just around the next turning. . . . It's just like it was in the East End."[6]

Current sensibility about the need to acknowledge cultural diversity was a missing ingredient in modernist design theory in the postwar years (Ward 1993). This, however, did not inhibit residents from making themselves "at home" in a variety of ways that subverted the homogeneous unity of modern design.

Killing Off the Parlor

The social reform movement of the nineteenth century sought to effect its ideals through well-designed working-class housing in the form of model cottages set in ideal villages. In a failed attempt to eliminate the social pretensions represented by the middle-class parlor,[7] reformers like Barry Parker and Raymond Unwin also favored the all-in-one living room for functional reasons (Matrix 1984, 29). Mid-twentieth-century design reformers[8] tackled the recurring problem in a different way. They attempted to eliminate the "room" altogether as an outdated architectural unit of enclosure that defined the house plan according to an unquestioned traditional social hierarchy.

6. The studies carried out by Young and Willmott (1957, 1960) confirm the importance of family ties in establishing a sense of place.

7. The typical nineteenth-century town terrace had a kitchen and/or living room at the back and a little-used parlor or "front room" kept for occasional public and formal use (Chapman 1955).

8. Le Corbusier, the Swiss architect, is credited with the concept of *"plan libre"* (free plan). It was first introduced in a prototype for a low-cost worker's dwelling using preconstructed standardized parts (Giedion 1969, 498; Le Corbusier and de Pierrefeu 1958).

With open plan, the tearing down of dividing walls united rooms to make "spaces." The function of spaces became a primary source of reference in the architectural design process determining the plan's ultimate form. Rooms became "areas" within spaces, mapped out according to circulation patterns related to different activities. Thus the relationship between areas became more significant in the design process than the consideration of the specific features of each room. The intention behind this type of modern design methodology resulting in the open plan was to create integrated, flexible, and efficient space (Burnett 1978, 266–67).

When the theory was applied in practice it did not work out quite so logically. In reviewing the state of postwar housing in Britain, Stanley Alderson (1962) remarked on the success of the parlorless plan in persuading tenants to "move to the front" and make everyday use of the space that would otherwise have been a "front room" reserved for special occasions only.

However, he also commented on the resistance to use the open-plan living-dining room in the way that it was intended, noting that most residents preferred to eat in the room where the meal was cooked: "In the last analysis the consumer has asserted his sovereignty. The ministry's [British Ministry of Housing and Construction] research and development group found that, even where an architect had deliberately left no room for eating in the kitchen, people managed to force a table and chairs into it in order to eat some of their meals there" (Alderson 1962, 26).

During the 1950s the variety and ingenuity of do-it-yourself (DIY) alterations carried out by Harlow residents to individualize their rented homes caused bitterness and resentment among the architects responsible for public housing (Attfield 1995, 222). Although at first tenants were not allowed by the new town corporations from which they rented the houses to make structural alterations, this did not stop them. Contravention became so usual that it was finally accepted by the local authorities as common practice and a formal system for applying for permission was instituted.

Alterations often entailed closing off the open plan by building walls between the dining and sitting areas and, where the house plan was of the "dining-kitchen" type, between the kitchen and the dining area. This was a popular modification in spite of the two extremely small rooms that resulted from the division of an already minimal space limited by the imposed economies of low-cost public housing.

In some cases the same household would demolish the dividing wall when family circumstances changed. Modernity in this context was expressed through the adaptability with which families constructed and reconstructed their surroundings to fit in with their changing lifestyles rather than passively accepting the aesthetic styles the design experts tried to impose upon them.

A major objection to the apartments of the first tower blocks was the lack of space to accommodate kitchen appliances. Prospective tenants were told to keep their washing machines on the balcony and the refrigerator in the hall or living room, because insufficient space had been allocated for them in the kitchen. This caused considerable indignation, not only because of the lack of accommodation based on the assumption that tenants would not own the latest type of kitchen equipment, but also because they were expected to place appliances in inappropriate areas.

Designers were not unaware of the problems resulting from lack of space in postwar housing conditions. The Festival of Britain exhibition of 1951 displayed a series of domestic room settings in the Homes and Gardens Pavilion to offer the public design suggestions for modernizing their homes in light of "the problems of (limited) space" (Cox 1951, 69–72).

Conscious that a functional approach was contrary to traditional furnishing habits, the writers of the exhibition guide acknowledged that: "Many people still feel the need for a room apart, where photographs and souvenirs can contribute to memories and where the fireplace can be treated as an altar to household gods [while] the rooms of today must often serve more than one purpose" (Cox 1951, 72). It proposed reserving a corner as a "token parlor substitute" in the open-plan living room, referred to as a new type of "larger living room."

House occupants, however, did not need any advice on how to display their nonfunctional possessions. What they did need in the modern house devoid of dust-catching ledges and old-fashioned mantelpieces was horizontal surfaces on which to place them. Some early new town corporation houses included built-in glass-fronted bookcases in the open-plan living room. These were soon adapted by tenants to display their best china.

One interviewee recalled her pleasure on moving into a modern council house to find that there was no mantelpiece. After having had to clean the parlor every week as a girl in her family home, the fireplace mantle signified interminable hours of boring work dusting the old-fashioned fussy Victorian bric-a-brac. Yet her house contained ornaments and souvenirs in profusion, which she displayed on the top of a modern wall-hung run of storage units, with no hint anywhere of Victorian antiques. Unlike the architects' version, this occupant's interpretation of modernity included the display of ornamental nonfunctional objects representing memories and personal associations as well as a number of contemporary items showing her interpretation of the modern aesthetic.

In 1959 the design experts, in the form of the Council of Industrial Design (CoID), were still trying to coax the public to adopt modern functional design values. One of the features that proved most intransigent to modernist reform was the primary focus given to the fireplace in the traditional interior. The CoID magazine, *Design,* addressed this in an issue devoted to "focus" in which the director of the council, Sir Gordon Russell, asked: "Do you sit and stare at blazing logs, flames leaping high, a symbol of another time and place? Do you pull up the chairs, tight-circled; or make believe with artificial flames that give electric warmth? These are not for honest men today, focus rather on a friend's face across the coffee table. . . . Break up the circle, rearrange the chairs" (1959, 33).

The only evidence that could be found of the ideal square seating layout, with arm-chairs in a parallel arrangement facing each other across a coffee table, was in a room setting designed by the council for an exhibition to demonstrate "good design" principles. Even after central heating became more common and there was no longer a practical reason for grouping the furniture around the fireplace, it still formed the main focus of the living room. The introduction of the television, however, brought in a competing feature that did not altogether manage to displace the fireplace in the British domestic interior.

Because of its relative low cost, the coffee table was one of the most popular pieces of furniture brought in to add a touch of modernity to a household that could not afford to buy new furniture. Although design experts like Russell presented the coffee table as an alternative to mark the center point of the seating area, it was most often used as a side table or placed in a corner as a small altar featuring an ornamental arrangement of objects.

Fashioning the Home

The aesthetic ideal of modernism is usually associated with the search for the eternal classic form that supersedes any sense of passing time. The antithesis is the fashion system most commonly associated with women's high-style clothing, characterized by endlessly producing new forms, ephemeral in nature, and is often represented as superficial and trivial because it colludes with commercial interests to keep the consumer constantly buying in order to be "in fashion." Yet the quick changes in the fashion system could be posited as more symptomatic of the temporality of modernity with its never-ending search for the better in the new.[9]

The distinguishing characteristic of modernity referred to here—the condition of temporality—remains invisible in the static aesthetic of the modern movement. Where temporality is best expressed is through the changing tides of popular fashion trends evidenced in superficial stylistic changes. In recent years domestic areas formerly considered utilitarian have also become susceptible to fashion. Kitchen cupboard fronts in the latest styles can be purchased for storage units without having

9. Recent historical and cultural studies of consumption posit the fashion system as the objectification of cultural identity in a period of constant change (Miller 1995; Wilson 1985).

to change the cabinet work behind. And where the chosen style is antique, paneled doors can be supplied to conceal modern electrical appliances.

During the period when the first crop of reconstruction housing was newly inhabited, tenants were not in a position to be able to create an integral "scheme" in which colors, patterns, and styles of furniture could be matched (Attfield 1995, 223). Even had they been able to afford the modern Scandinavian style favored by the professional designers, it remained for the most part inaccessible to them, as that kind of furniture was stocked by only a few metropolitan furnishers. Scarcity and lack of funds meant that most newlyweds who came to live in Harlow acquired much of their furniture from parents, relatives, or secondhand shops. As one interviewee said with hindsight, "I couldn't afford taste in those days. It was what you could get."

Architect interviewees' responses to tenants' styles of furnishing the new housing were also very revealing. They disapproved of old or reproduction furniture, clashing patterns, and nonfunctional items, particularly decorative textiles such as lace, net curtains, and tablecloths. Even the layout of the furniture was a preoccupation—so much so that the mere placing of a chair diagonally across the corner of a room was seen as completely at odds with the design of the house.

Yet it cannot be said that tenants rejected modernity as such, even when they clung to family heirlooms and traditional furnishing conventions. On the contrary, it was the adaptability with which tenants took over their domestic space, stubbornly arranging it in contravention to the designers' intentions, that shows how they appropriated modernity to their *own designs.*

Though reproduction and the rustic style of furniture were very popular among the older generation, some house occupiers adapted with ease and pleasure to modern-style decor. It would not have been the expensive and exclusive modern furniture and furnishings that the design experts would have chosen, but a style of popular contemporary that the experts disparagingly called "repro-contemporary."

One interviewee described the enthusiasm with which she and her husband tackled home decorating when they were first married in the early 1960s. "We were furniture mad. . . . All we could think about was the home." Among the items she recalled were bright color schemes featuring purple and orange, a tartan wallpaper in the bathroom, synthetic materials—Formica plastic-laminate finishes on furniture, nylon carpets, the futuristic styling of a spotlight lamp standard, and an orange swivel chair called "the Orbit." Their aim was to be "very modern" and to shock their friends and relatives with their "way out" decorating ideas. "You needed sunglasses to go into the living room," she said.

The members of the household described above clearly differentiated themselves from their parents' attitude toward the home, not only through their taste but by the priority they gave it in relation to other aspects of their life. The wife's father had considered it important enough to make the sacrifice of "uprooting" his family and moving into a new town "rabbit hutch" in order to give his son a "better start in life"; his son-in-law, however, considered his home so important that he changed his job in order to move into a higher standard of house.

While the parents kept their prewar furniture the whole of their married life, their daughter and her husband were always on the lookout for "anything weird," making numerous changes of decor, furniture, and furnishings to keep up with the fashion. Within the two generations there was a marked difference of attitudes toward family identity formation. In the older generation, identity came through the work occupation of the male branch of the family, and in the younger generation, through the home and its interior decor.

In the context of material culture studies, DIY can be studied as a subjective response to the perceived uniformity imposed by mass-produced housing with features like open plan (Miller 1987, 1990). In the cases cited it could also be observed that the "fashioning" of the home was a way of keeping in time with social changes for a generation that had to adapt to the "newness" of settling in a new town from a very early age.

Conclusion

Open plan formed the basis of modern public housing in Britain when the state undertook housing programs to provide a better standard of accommodation for working-class families. The ways in which open plan has undergone rejection, adjustment, and transformation before taking its place in the vocabulary of house design are suggestive of the difficulties of adapting to modernization in everyday life.

It can be seen that consumers were active participants in this process. The fact that people who occupied the houses did not use them as was intended by their designers may be, and has been, seen as a failure on the part of architects and planners to inculcate good design values. But this "failure of modernism" critique does not account for the way in which the interiors were actually used to create a popular type of modernity different from the stark avant-garde version envisaged by the designers.

What has to be recognized is the difference between the popular manifestations of modernity in the context of the "home" constructed by its residents and the designers' ideals in the context of public "housing" as an aesthetic expression of social reform through design.

7

The French Two-Home Project
Materialization of Family Identity

Sophie Chevalier

IN CONTRAST to the traditional and rural societies that cultural anthropologists usually take into account, this chapter focuses on modern urban society and, more specifically, on the inhabitants of a Parisian suburb. There seems to be a common understanding in the social sciences that after industrialization social life changed radically. Not only did the way people related to one another change, but the way people related to the material products of industrial production also changed (Baudrillard 1968, 1981). Mass-produced objects in industrial society, unlike manmade artifacts in traditional society, are not integrated into people's lives; they are proclaimed to be "alienated."

By taking the case of the two-home project of French urbanites I want to show similarities in the way people in traditional and industrial societies relate to their respective material environments. The French—throughout all social groups—have, or strive to have, two homes: one in the city that serves as their main residence and the second in the country that is used for holidays only. Both residences, but especially the second, can be considered as materializations of family identity. Using an anthropological vocabulary this could be called "the anchoring of the lineage in a materialized space," as Annette Weiner (1985) described property relations in traditional Maori society of New Zealand.

The French school in ethnology (Haudricourt 1987; Leroi-Gourhan 1965, 1973) mirrors in its material culture studies the focus on production in traditional societies. These scholars analyze how material culture is rooted in a specific group, region, and type of livelihood, and how it is linked to everyday life and celebrated in rituals. In the Museum of Popular Arts and Traditions (Musée des Arts et Traditions Populaires) in Paris, the material culture of traditional rural France is presented according to this approach (Tardieu 1976).

The ethnologists' focus on traditional production is based on the nineteenth-century schism between the traditional—and predominantly rural—mode of production, and the modern—and predominantly urban—industrial mode of production. Pertaining to these opposing modes of production are equally opposing types of social relations. Progressive urbanization and industrialization have destroyed traditional rural community life.

According to this point of view, our society is characterized by alienation, not only in our social relations, but also in our relations to the material environment, like the uniform buildings we have to live in or the mass-produced goods we have to consume.[1] The "uprooted," mainly working-class residents of the Parisian suburb Nanterre I studied are considered to live in an alienated situation (Chevalier 1993, 1994). This "alienation" refers both to their uniform and constrained housing and to their powerless socioeconomic position as mass consumers.

However, this division in modes of production is not paralleled in different modes of appropriation. Relations of alienation predominantly reside in the production process and in the built environment, but evidentially not in the experience of consumption and appropriation (McCracken 1988; Miller 1987; Putnam and Newton 1990). From this perspective there are no essential differences between the domestic projects of the residents of a Parisian suburb and the domestic projects recorded in traditional societies near or far (Douglas and Isherwood 1979; Kopytoff 1986).

Rural Roots

The phenomenon of the two-home projects of urbanites is related to the late industrialization of France in comparison to that of Britain. The end of World War I parallels the end of the French peasantry and marks the beginning of the depopulation of the French countryside, which would be accelerated after World War II (Weber 1976). However, this social transformation did not entail the fall of small landed property in favor of landlordism. France has a long tradition of landed peasantry, and the idea of owning land is familiar to most of the French people.

It is only recently that the French countryside has lost its productive dimension to become a recreational landscape. Unlike the nineteenth-century Swedish bourgeoisie, described by Jonas Frykman and Orvar Löfgren (1987), members of the French bourgeoisie did not become romantic lovers of nature. Therefore Strindberg's picturing of a bourgeois summer paradise in the countryside is typically Swedish and does not correspond to a bourgeois history of the French two-home project.

---

1. Simmel (1980) demonstrated very clearly the contradiction of modernity as related to mass consumption and money—on one hand, the opportunity for freedom and equality, and on the other hand, the possible alienation and exploitation.

For most French urbanites the countryside is a place of memory related to a recent rural past of smallholders and inherited property. Their link to the countryside is close in terms of family history, placing the family residence at the core of their identity. However, there is a class aspect involved in the relationship between town and countryside. Villagers often entrust the mayoralty to an upper-class urbanite who owns an estate or a family residence in the village. It is believed that their close contacts with the urban centers of power will be to the advantage of the village. This arrangement mirrors ancient, prerevolutionary sociopolitical relationships (Pinçon and Pinçon-Charlot 1989).

Since the 1950s most French urbanites, irrespective of social class, have owned or aspired to own a house in the country. They intend to keep or to buy a second residence, not necessarily to live there. In this two-home project their urban quarters serve as their main site of residence, but their house in the country symbolizes "the family" and is, so to speak, an anchorage for their lineage in rural space.

In the case of inherited family property, both husband and wife may have family residences in different regions. Having to sell one's family residence is considered to be a very painful affair, especially when the house has been in the family for generations: it is like losing a part of one's identity. Only in the case of serious financial problems is one liable to sell. The estate-owning aristocracy escapes this fate by opening their residences to the public.

In the purchase of an intended family residence the choice of the area, especially when husband and wife are from different regions, will more likely be based on preference and pragmatism. Proximity to the urban residence, so the family can more easily spend weekends or short holidays in the country, or proximity to a favorable holiday resort such as the seaside, may be more decisive than historical ties to a certain region. To buy an intended family residence is to create an anchorage for "the family," a meeting point for all the members of the lineage.[2]

The Suburban Apartments

The material presented here was collected in a two-year period, from 1988 through 1990, when I conducted ethnographic fieldwork in a residential district of council tower buildings called Les Fontenelles, situated in the Parisian suburb of Nanterre. Its residents are an ethnically mixed population of mainly blue-collar workers. Most

---

2. The reverse is also possible. Rural people may have an urban residence, for example, when they have spent a part of their working life in the city or by inheritance. Only the well-to-do can afford to buy an apartment in a city like Paris. The urban residence, however, will never be considered an anchorage of the lineage.

of my older informants belong to the first postwar generation who left the country-side to work in the big factories of the Paris area.

The tower buildings of Les Fontenelles look quite run-down and consist of cramped apartments with uniformly structured floor plans. The tenants are not allowed to break walls to create larger rooms. In other words, the residents must adapt to the flat and have to use their furniture and decorative objects to personalize the rooms. When moving in they appropriate the flat by renewing the carpet and the wallpaper and by bringing in their furniture and decorative objects. In this process of appropriation the flat is transformed into a *home.* By cleaning the lift and the entry hall they try to protect their "sacred" home interior from any pollution from outside contact.

I focused in my fieldwork on the lounge, the public-private domain of the household; for nonfamily members this is a domain to be entered only on invitation.[3] This space is not only a presentation of the self through objects, but also a representation of an idealized family home to the outside world as well as an objectification of family relationships (Csikszentmihalyi and Rochberg-Halton 1981). In other words, it is a space with an ideological aspect expressing the individual and familial identity of the tenant through a sense of being "at home."

In Western domestic architecture—even in the most rationally constructed flats —the lounge is intended to be the family room, symbolized by its communal use and family-related decoration. Bedrooms, especially the master bedroom, also contain family-related objects such as family photographs or inherited objects, but these elements often represent more intimate relations, such as a honeymoon souvenir (Halle 1993).

Every household displays in its decor elements that testify to everyday events, to individual or familial history, materializing social relations near or far, living or dead. It is important to realize that most family-related objects, souvenirs, and even heirlooms are created out of mass-produced objects. Gifts and purchases are converted into family property.

The lounge is a spatialization of time, a result of a construction process testifying to different stages of the household visible in the wear and tear and in successive furniture styles. In discourse, the objects are introduced in time and connected to events in the married life of the couple, the constructors of the "home."

The key analytical term of this research is "appropriation." This term can be understood to mean the construction of an inalienable environment through mass-produced objects. It refers to the ways in which consumers personalize objects of

3. Goffman (1959) used the expression "presentation of self" and "front stage" in relation to the lounge.

mass production, by integrating them into their way of life (Miller 1987). This chapter examines how ordinary consumers succeed in creating their own decor through a process of appropriation of mass-produced objects.

Decor in Discourse

In their discourses, my informants always began their comments on their basic furniture. This furniture is composed of two sets: a dining room set consisting of a table and chairs, often in combination with a sideboard, and a sitting room combination of a three-piece suite, coffee table, and television set. Young households stressed the second combination of basic furniture. A dining room set is often absent in these households; a modern sideboard is the last reminder of the obsolete combination. Young couples eat in the kitchen or sit on their sofas and have a tray with a plate on their laps.

The basic pieces of furniture characterize the lounge and are the basic embodiments of "home" and "family." The set bought at the start of the marriage symbolizes the new couple: the more formal dining set for the older generation, and the more relaxed three-piece suite for the younger generation.

These basic elements were fundamental in the discourse because they were used to express a model without revealing too early more personal links.[4] Then my informants spoke about their decorative objects, which often referred to events outside the family circle—to the professional world, for example.[5] Both television set and sideboard functioned as "domestic altars" on which people displayed their highly valued and meaningful objects.

The shared lounge is one large display area of family and regionally related objects, as in the case of the Rufins, who married in the early 1970s. They bought their basic furniture at the beginning of their marriage: a three-piece suite and coffee table, and a dining set and sideboard. The first furniture symbolizes the couple's creation of a new "family." Even the purchase of the television set was tied to a family event; it was bought when Mrs. Rufin was pregnant and had to stay home. After twelve years of marriage, however, she became dissatisfied with the white gloss-finish furniture,

---

4. Discourses construct a link between an object or a series of objects and a life event; the link could be true or make-believe. By their very nature, discourses are constructions of reality, and often in contradiction with practices—an observation worthy of serious consideration.

5. For some objects, use can be indicative of meaning, unlike decorative objects that are seldom used. Only the discourses, or sometimes the circulation of the decorative objects, can illuminate their meaning.

which was "difficult to clean." The couple purchased new sets of furniture: a three-piece suite in dark leather and a dining set, adding a few extra pieces, such as a chest and a writing desk.

Their decorative objects tell their own story. Some were bought by Mrs. Rufin in secondhand shops, like a statuette of a naked woman in Sèvres crystal. Most of their decorative objects, however, were souvenirs or gifts, linked to special occasions. Holiday souvenirs, like the Murano glass bowl from the couple's trip to Venice or the Algerian plate from their African holiday, are reminders of family happenings. The clock that decorates the wall was presented to Mrs. Rufin as a parting gift from her colleagues when she quit her job after the birth of her first child. Wedding gifts, like the decorative fish plates from Quimper (Brittany) and the magazine rack, are icons of matrimony.

The stuffed birds that decorate the walls (illus. 7.1) are gifts from hunters of La Creuse, a region in the middle of France. The couple comes from this region, and their families still live there. They also inherited a house in La Creuse, which they use as a holiday home. Mr. Rufin, a blue-collar worker in the civil service, was transferred to Paris. Both are also very keen on Aubusson tapestry, because the town of Aubusson, famous for its tapestry manufacture, is close to their native hometown.

The Rufins' interior decor is an accumulation, over a period of time, of pieces of furniture and objects. In themselves, these objects are nothing special, because they are mainly mass-produced goods. However, the created relationships among the elements are specific and significant in their expression of the identity of the residents. The created relationships—I will call them "affinities"—are based on specificities of the objects, which I have called "echoes."

To come back to the Rufin family, the obvious affinities among their decorative objects are their relationships to La Creuse, their home region. The affinities among these objects are not given a priori, but built by the actors, based on "echoes"—in this case the Rufins' probably romanticized ideas on the unspoiled nature of the region, represented by the stuffed birds and the traditional craft of tapestry.

Beyond the specificities of each lounge, a common affinity exists between the pieces of the basic furniture found in most lounges. The discourses confirm this observation: they are considered to be the necessary elements of a living room. Following certain affinities that reflect the household's identity one adds other furniture elements and decorative objects. The affinities between the basic furniture elements articulate a sociocultural model related to a bourgeois past and to a certain age group.

Some affinities are easy to detect, like those linked to function, form, color, or material; others, however, like the "reminiscent" affinities, are only apparent in

7.1. The stuffed birds that decorate this wall are gifts from hunters of La Creuse, the couple's home region, 1995. Photograph by Sophie Chevalier.

Sophie Chevalier

discourse.[6] Pieces of furniture or decorative objects can be reminiscent of specific events such as weddings or holidays, or more in general of a life history, or of individual persons, such as parents, children, or friends.

For example, the wall of Mrs. Faivret's lounge is decorated by a plate with the pope's portrait. Mrs. Faivret is Italian and Catholic. Both elements could be related to her decorative choice, but her comment illustrates her reminiscence on the plate: "My daughter gave me this plate; she did a trip to Rome with her students."

Inherited objects are the most powerful reminiscent items, and they often constrain the construction of the household's decor. Although an heirloom is handled with respect it may not suit the household's taste. This is illustrated in the case of a young woman who took care of an inherited clock that did not match the style of her decoration. Knowing, however, that her husband cherished the clock for being a memory of his father, she compromised by hanging it unobtrusively in a corner of "her" lounge.[7]

The contrary, however, is more often the case: people try to highlight an heirloom, to find objects and pieces of furniture that match or exist in reminiscent affinities with it. For example, the middle-aged Probst couple dreamed of building their interior decor around a few inherited objects. However, the present furniture is predominantly in the 1950s style, marking the date of their marriage, supplemented by furniture elements of more recent date. Mrs. Probst would love to buy matching pieces of furniture.

The Probsts' lounge is divided into a dining room and a sitting room. Only the dining room contains antique and delicate objects of considerable value. For example, the plate decorating the wall above the sideboard comes from a former Élysée service and is a real collector's item (illus. 7.2). The plate testifies to a presidential tradition: every newly elected French president orders a uniquely designed service to be made in Limoges (a town famous for its porcelain factory) and to adorn the state banquets at the Élysée Palace. The plate and the objects displayed on the sideboard were inherited by Mrs. Probst from her maternal kin.

By buying antique objects, some residents of Les Fontenelles invest a lot of money in the constitution of a "furniture capital": pieces of furniture they would like to leave to their children. Collecting objects from their kin is another possibility. However, without previous ancestral transmission, few residents of Les Fontenelles really succeed in creating a furniture capital.

6. However, the distinctions made are artificial, for the aesthetic and the reminiscent are often closely related.
7. Women are not only the main constructors of the decor, but also its curators. McCracken (1988) discusses the role of the older female "curatorial consumer" in guarding heirlooms, but as illustrated in this case, young women can also have this role. When family residences are concerned, even if inherited from the male side, women act as such.

7.2. The plate decorating the wall above the sideboard comes from a former Élysée service and is a real collector's item, 1995. Photograph by Sophie Chevalier.

The family identity, including the idea of lineage, is materialized in furniture items and decorative objects, and by its very material nature the family identity can be transmitted. The elaborated decor itself, however, cannot be transmitted for it expresses not only the material but also, and more so, the symbolic dimension imbued by the couple who created the interior. Heirlooms—mass-produced or antique—are objects transmitted without context, although individual pieces may very well have symbolic or emotional meaning to their heirs.

For example, when the couple has died and their apartment needs to be cleared out, their belongings undergo a process of desymbolization. In this process their created "home" will wither and be transformed into a flat with its contents.[8] Only the decor's material—and not its symbolic—dimension will survive. The affinities be-

8. The process of desymbolization starts as soon as those who gave meaning to the created interior are absent.

tween the elements linking them in a characteristic combination, created over many years, will be disrupted for good.

Aware of their inability to create a furniture capital, most residents of Les Fontenelles focused on their second house to anchor their descendants. Nevertheless, they also embodied their lineage in furniture items and decorative objects in their apartments in Les Fontenelles. In doing so they have converted their flats into homes, while realizing that a rented flat and its decor—despite all its financial and emotional investments—is a transient elaboration.

The Family Residence

Mrs. Lemant is an elderly woman who worked her whole life in the factories of Nanterre. Like most of my informants she is also the proprietor, in joint property with her brothers and sisters, of a big family residence in the Ardennes region situated in the north of France. The house is seriously neglected. War damage, owing to its positioning amid the battlegrounds of both world wars, was never repaired. Having no funds for repair, the siblings still decided to keep the house, along with all the furniture in it. However, because of its deplorable state and lack of comfort, no family member ever spends holidays in the house. Nevertheless, Mrs. Lemant frequently discusses "her" house and gives lively descriptions of its antique family furniture.

One could argue that the affinities created by Mrs. Lemant's ancestors are still there, though "fossilized." The fossilization process takes place when objects are neither used nor looked at, but still remain in position. However, even if a house is never or seldom used, its decor will not necessarily fall into fossilization if it is reactivated over and over again in discourse. A constant reactivated meaning, as in Mrs. Lemant's case, prevents not only fossilization but also desymbolization. Yearly family meetings in the family residence serve the same purpose.

In France, there is a history of the embodiment of the lineage in material culture, especially in a family residence.[9] Objects and houses "contain" the lineage in time. This function of "kin keeping" sometimes includes the extended family. The purchase of a family residence is not necessarily related to an identity dimension and does not need to be in the familial village. The aim is the symbolic anchorage of the lineage in a materialized space: a home the family owns solely or as jointly held property.

Family residences become as inalienable as some objects from traditional societies: they are taken out of the market exchange. Time plays a fundamental role in this construction; the process of "anchoring" is necessarily long. The houses and the objects

9. The family residence is not only important to the French residents of Les Fontenelles, but also to an Italian, Mrs. Loral. In a period of marital problems she neglected her Nanterre flat and left for Italy to take care of her family residence.

in them circulate slowly outside of the sphere of market-related commodities eventually to become inalienable. The longer the residence is in the family the more legitimate its claim. In traditional society, the longer the constructed genealogies the more legitimate the lineage.

As the contents and decor of the family residence are also inalienable, no family member moves furniture items from the family residence to his or her apartment. This is not only for practical reasons, because these old pieces of furniture are often too big for a flat, but also for symbolic reasons, because these pieces belong to the family residence. There is a strong link between the decor and the house itself, between the architecture and the style of the furniture.

This practice brings into dispute a familiar Western distinction between movables and immovables, for the furniture of the family residence becomes an immovable part of the building. At this point it will be illuminating to compare the French case with the case of traditional Maori society of New Zealand.

In her reanalysis of the Maori case once described by Marcel Mauss in his famous book *The Gift*, Annette Weiner (1985) designates some objects as "inalienable wealth," meaning movable objects that become immovable because they are tied to their setting of origin. Weiner distinguishes two types of inalienable wealth: possessions that are tied to their settings and possessions that, under certain circumstances, are allowed to circulate and to be given on loan (1985, 210–12).

The French family residence functions much as do the sacred Maori bones and stones that are believed to "anchor" a lineage to a particular locality, physically securing the descendants' ancestral rights (1985, 211). In the French case, one can use the housing or commodity market to create as many "bones" as one likes to anchor one's lineage. However, a family residence can be bought but never, or only under very special circumstances, be sold again.

The Maori objects allowed to circulate and to be loaned are comparable to some objects in the flats of Les Fontenelles. Although these furniture items and decorative objects are perceived to belong in an inherent way to their recent owners who imbued them with affective qualities, they can be inherited—loaned out to the next generation—and removed from their original setting. Both types of possessions act as vehicles for bringing the past into the present (Weiner 1985, 210).

Conclusion

The French two-home project illustrates the way in which so-called alienated urbanites create a meaningful universe, not only in their rented apartments, but also by investing in a family residence in the country, in response to their rural roots. The residents of Les Fontenelles transformed the space of their apartments into "home" by the appropriation of mass-produced goods. They created their own meaningful decor by relating it to everyday events and to individual and familial histories.

The meaning of objects is not only constructed by, or activated in, discourse but also by and in its use. In the process of meaning construction, decor elements are related to each other by affinities, linked to function, form, or reminiscence. These affinities are material articulations of sociocultural conditions, represented in styles and types of furniture and decor, and highly personal conditions. However, appropriation is not only objectification but also mediation: objects are by their material condition a reminiscent link to other individuals.

Heirlooms are often created out of mass-produced objects. Inherited objects, including the family residence in the country, tend to become inalienable. The inalienability creates constraints: one has to keep the inherited objects as one has to keep the family residence, even if the heirloom or the house does not suit one's taste or budget. However, these constraints also motivate urbanites to buy an intended family residence in the country to anchor their lineage.

In the comparison with the Maori case as described by Weiner, similarities appear in the materialization of family or lineage identity by "alienated" consumers or "uprooted" urbanites and people in "traditional" societies. In both societies there is a class of inalienable objects that are believed to anchor a family to a particular locality.

However, there are also differences to account for—difference of degree not only between the two societies but also between the two domestic projects, related to the possibility to choose, to move, or to discard the objects. Discarding is permitted and even encouraged by the transient reputation of mass-produced goods, contrary to seemingly cherished artifacts.

Nevertheless, Weiner's comment on traditional societies is also true for my French informants: "An individual's role in social life is fragmentary unless attached to something of permanence. The history of the past, equally fragmentary, is concentrated in an object that, in its material substance, defies destruction. Thus, keeping an object defined as inalienable adds to the value of one's past, making the past a powerful resource for the present and the future" (1985, 224).

8

Home
The Experience of Atmosphere

Paul J. J. Pennartz

ATMOSPHERE is an inherent aspect of habitation. Yet it appears to be irrational and indeterminate, and therefore difficult to study empirically. The phenomenological method and semantic analysis have proved to be valuable research approaches to everyday experiences. This study focuses on the experience of atmosphere in the home. Information was collected during in-depth interviews with people living in public housing projects in the Netherlands. A semantic analysis of the interviews resulted in the identification of several themes in the experience of atmosphere related to spatial characteristics of the dwellings involved.[1] Our results are of vital concern to architects and policymakers.

Atmosphere and Place

This study focuses on the interaction between architectural and (socio)psychological factors in the experience of atmosphere in the home. The central questions are: Are there consistencies in the way specific situations within the home area are experienced as having "atmosphere"? and How do spatial characteristics of the dwelling contribute to the experience of atmosphere? Atmosphere manifests itself as a double-sided process: the atmosphere of a room works on an individual, and conversely an individual projects his or her specific mood on the room.

In other words, atmosphere is the most comprehensive characteristic of a place. Places incarnate our experiences and aspirations and are foci of meaningful events

This chapter is an abridged version of "Atmosphere at Home: A Qualitative Approach," *Journal of Environmental Psychology* (1986) 6: 135–53.

1. Related research deals with differences in social climate and in conceptualizations of home between people of different social classes, or different stages in the life cycle, or living in different types of houses (cf. Sanchez-Robles 1980; Inman and Graff 1984). McCracken (1989) focuses on the meaning of consumer goods in the construction of a homey atmosphere.

in our lives (cf. Tuan 1971). A place, according to Norberg-Schulz (1971, 1980), is a "total phenomenon," which cannot be reduced to its individual components without losing its qualitative character. The human geographer Relph (1976) states that the essence of place lies in a largely unself-conscious intentionality that defines places as profound centers of human existence.

However, what is unself-conscious is difficult to investigate. A more workable definition put forward by Canter (1977) conceives place as an amalgam of related activities, conceptions, and material attributes. Conceptions of public and private places, and actual behavior in places, have been studied empirically (e.g., Nasar 1989b; Pennartz 1989, 1990), but how are conceptions and behavior related to the material attributes of place?

The urban sociologist Gans (1972) clarifies this relationship by distinguishing between the potential and the effective environments. The material and architectural attributes are the *potential environment*. The cultural or individual conception of the potential environment is the *effective environment*. In this view, the material environment is not effective in itself. Its potentiality has to be made effective on the conceptual level. In the present study, we attempt to distinguish those components of the home environment that are likely to function as *effectors* of the experience of atmosphere.

Phenomenological Method

What is often lost in social research is the everyday life-world. Phenomenology is a philosophical tradition that takes as its starting point the phenomena of the life-world of immediate experience, and seeks to clarify these in a rigorous way by careful observation and description (Relph 1976). The phenomenological approach is rather akin to the ethnographic tradition (MacPherson 1984; Spradley 1979).

In the present study, we decided to use in-depth interviewing and to have the respondent determine the precise meaning of the topic.[2] The number of households to be interviewed was not fixed in advance. We continued until no new information emerged. Glaser and Strauss (1967) termed this phase "the saturation of the sensitizing concepts." After about twenty interviews this point seemed to have been reached. In sum twenty-five households were interviewed including seventy-one individual respondents. All households lived in public housing projects and consisted of parents and children with at least one adolescent child. These households were se-

2. The concept of atmosphere was specified and operationalized by the Dutch word *gezelligheid*. This word has been translated into English as "pleasantness." Pleasantness refers to both a spatial and a nonspatial quality. Its translation depends on the object to which it refers: people are companionable, convivial, sociable; a family is chummy or matey; a room is pleasant.

lected at random from a larger sample of 250 households who participated in a quantitative survey and who lived in different types of dwellings within a large provincial town in the eastern part of the Netherlands (130,000 inhabitants).

Those interviewed were encouraged to express freely their experiences. Two pairs of introductory questions were used regarding pleasantness of the home atmosphere. The first pair was phrased "*When* is it most pleasant or unpleasant at home?" and "Can you tell me why?" The second pair of questions was expressed simply as: "*Where* in the house is it most pleasant or unpleasant?" and "Why in this place?"

Replying to the question, "When is it most pleasant at home?" respondents did not hesitate to refer to a special time of the day or the week. But when the interviewer went on to ask "Why?" most began to stumble, or stopped to think and responded with a statement such as, "Well, it's just quite pleasant then!" The interviewer had to help the respondent to be more specific by posing: "Try to recall a pleasant situation that recently happened. . . . What was happening then? What were your feelings about that?"

The question, "Where in the house is it most pleasant?" directed the attention of the respondent toward spatial characteristics of the dwelling. In general, this question elicited a straightforward answer, but again it appeared to be more difficult to give specific answers to the question, "Why in this place?" Alternative questions were: "What other rooms are rather pleasant or unpleasant and why?" and "If an architect were to design a pleasant house for you, what would be especially important to you?" When the views of respondents within the same household differed, the interviewer tried to offer each an opportunity to explain his or her point of view.

The analysis aimed to discover themes in the descriptions of a pleasant or unpleasant atmosphere. The transcripts were scrutinized for fragments that could be given provisional labels (Glaser and Strauss 1967; Korosec-Serfaty 1984). Passages containing clear descriptions of experiences of a pleasant atmosphere were grouped into chains. A chain of passages usually begins with a frequently mentioned and obvious aspect, after which each passage unfolds a new bit of information.

This analysis is in line with a semantic approach, which assumes that all individual variations in the expression of experience contribute to the comprehension of a phenomenon (Korosec-Serfaty 1984). Contrasts in the experiences of pleasantness between members of the same household assisted not only in refining but also in distinguishing themes.

In regard to the relationship between potential and effective environments, we decided to arrange first the selected passages about sociopsychological elements into chains developing certain themes. Then, the passages and labels referring to architectural elements of home situations were arranged according to three spatial characteristics that recurred frequently in the interviews: the arrangement of and connections between rooms, the size of rooms, and the form and physical enclosure of rooms. Finally, we focused on the interaction between architectural and so-ciopsychological factors in the experience of atmosphere.

Sociopsychological Factors

The first and most dominant theme in the experience of pleasantness is labeled "communicating with one another." Asked when it is most pleasant at home, a mother replied, "Well, I think . . . when children come home from school. . . . We always chat for a while. . . . Then it feels most like it." In households with older children, the time of pleasantness is different, but the activity underlying the experience of the situation is the same. A father explained, "What I mean is, you are at work all day. . . . I mean away from each other and when you come home in the evening with your problems . . . and one has done this, and the other that . . . then it's pleasant for me. . . ."

Time becomes meaningful because of the activity going on. Evening is especially a pleasant time, but it is not the evening as such. Often a specific evening was mentioned, Friday night, and in some cases Saturday night. As expressed by a daughter: "I think, it is pleasant at night and on the weekend. . . . Then we are all together . . . Friday night." A mother added, "And usually we play games with the children. . . . We like playing games, you know." Playing games may seem to be a somewhat trivial activity, but the players are engaged with each other.

With reference to pleasantness of the atmosphere, watching television is an often rejected form of leisure. Being engaged with one another seems to disappear, as expressed in the words of a father: "A TV at home . . . yes, when you are alone or just the two of you, then it is not too bad. . . . But it is always a contradiction, I think. . . . If there's a film to watch . . . everybody has to shut up."

It would seem that watching TV and talking together are necessarily mutually exclusive activities. However, not all programs have a detrimental effect on atmosphere. Preference for a certain program, at least for some people, seems to depend less on the program content than on the social configuration of which watching is only part. Watching television seems to be pleasant if there is opportunity for communication. In all these fragments the experience of pleasantness seems to vary with the actual communication taking place. Therefore, "communicating with one another" as a theme is considered to contribute to the experience of a pleasant atmosphere, but is not the only aspect.

The second theme we called "being accessible to one another." There are some activities in which individuals do not actively participate together, but evidently these contribute somehow to the experience of a pleasant atmosphere. A mother stated, "With nice music on the radio . . . I don't need to do anything else and I pick up a good book or something . . . but then I think it would be a sin to lose myself in that book . . . while it's so pleasant all around me . . . I can't bring myself to do that. . . . When we are together just quietly, that's also very pleasant, Sunday evening, Saturday night also. . . ."

It may not necessarily be the spatial characteristic (being together in a strict sense) that determines whether an experience is pleasant or not. There is another common characteristic when people are busy in some way. Frequently, it was stated: "It is quite nice when the children are here, all pottering about." Being together does not necessarily mean being in the same room. When everybody is at home, there is at least the opportunity to be together. As a father remarked: "I think . . . people ask sometimes . . . friends: Are you coming to play cards? I don't think it's pleasant to go out on Saturday night. . . . That is the idea, Saturday night we should be at home all of us. . . . That does not mean, that they, especially our oldest son, should be downstairs here. . . . I don't think it's nice, when he comes down and we are not there. . . . The idea is we ought to be together."

Evidently, not only actual behavior, but also possible behavior, is relevant to the experience and meaning of a pleasant atmosphere. However, more important, being together in a spatial sense may also mean wanting to be near each other. Pleasantness and atmosphere do not occur, they have to be created; that is, they result from action or intentional behavior. The quality of atmosphere depends essentially on the quality of the interpersonal relations, more specifically on the degree to which people try to approach each other.

Poor relationships are also expressed in observable, spatial behavior, just because the behavior is intentional. A woman remembered:

I was not at home much of the time, I was not close to my parents . . . because the marriage wasn't good and I tended to avoid being at home . . . because of those periods. . . . Half a year, oh Lord, that was nothing, they said nothing to one another . . . well, at dinner something 'May I have the potatoes?' . . . and for the rest of the time the conversation developed through the kids, my brother and me. . . . No, with us, the room was really not pleasant. . . . It is the atmosphere, purely the atmosphere. . . . You may sit in a very bare room and still there may be atmosphere.

Negative orientation of people toward each other evidently has a detrimental effect on atmosphere. The experience of a pleasant atmosphere varies clearly with the degree to which people are accessible to each other.

The third theme, "relaxing after having finished work," may even contradict the second theme, considering the next fragment. To the question, "When is it most pleasant at home?" quite surprisingly, the following answer was given by a mother: "I think it is most pleasant when I am completely on my own, yes. . . . Then the children are in bed and my husband is out, which he is most nights. . . . I enjoy that . . . nice and quiet on that couch, cup of coffee, watching TV . . . then I can really relax. . . . No cries, the children aren't shouting about the place." "When I am completely on my own" contradicts the proposition that togetherness and pleasantness go together. However, "being on my own" was stated in a specific context: "I enjoy that . . . nice and quiet . . . then I can really relax. . . ." Relaxing was given a high priority by this respondent, and as a theme it seems to be quite distinct from the themes already discussed.

Relaxing and being tired also occurred often in other fragments. A mother told us: "Mostly, on Thursday night the atmosphere begins to disintegrate. . . . It becomes somewhat unpleasant, because they are all a bit tired and Friday night with the weekend in sight. . . . When they come home they begin to droop . . . but by about seven on Friday night when they have had their dinner, their spirit begins to return." Relaxing is also related to a feeling of having finished work.

Work and pleasantness appear to be opposite phenomena. When asked, "When is it most pleasant?" a woman replied: "Well, when I have the housework done . . . everything is nice and clean. Like this morning, I dusted all chairs, vacuum cleaned . . . took everything out of the room. Then I did the kitchen and I put all the small things over there. . . . When I had finished, I thought, now it is pleasant again." Having finished work is often the reason given, especially by mothers, for Sunday morning being the most pleasant time of the week at home, because everybody is not running about but is sitting down relaxing.

Freedom from obligations and "being able to do what one likes" seems to form an independent fourth theme. For some people, Sunday is the day when they are not bound by time or by a rigid schedule. A mother explained: "That is, of course, an advantage of Sunday. . . . On Sunday I always try to disregard time as much as possible. During the week you have to watch time, but not on Sunday. . . . That is really Sunday for me. . . . Sometimes I say to them [the family] I am not watching the time on Sunday. . . . It is not that I don't cook . . . but maybe meals are half an hour later than usual. That is the advantage of Sunday, at least for me."

For others, however, Sunday is a day of obligations and thus cannot be compared with other days of the week in regard to being pleasant. Evidently, it is not the day or the time of the day as such that determines whether an experience is pleasant or not, but what is happening during the period. A mother told us: "On Sunday, we get up later. . . . We are Catholic and we go to church, the children also. . . . Before everyone is ready for coffee . . . it is often twelve o'clock. My daughter sings in the youth choir, that begins at twelve . . . and I still have parents to visit. . . . I visit them quite often."

For some people Sunday is less pleasant because they have certain obligations. Friday night was most often put forward as the most pleasant time of the week, perhaps because of the absence of obligations. As a father said: "Intuitively, it's Friday night which is relatively pleasant. . . . I always have a feeling that Friday night goes on for a very long time . . . yes, that is because of the idea that so many things can be done." In the words of a son: "Well, when I come home from school . . . a nice weekend before me . . . sleeping in, I really enjoy that. . . . I have no homework to do. You come home and you think I don't have to do anything . . . but I can do homework in the weekend if I want to. . . ."

As shown, obligatory activities are not confined to paid work or schoolwork. Going to church is an obligation for some, and for others specific recreational activities have a meaning of obligation. A man explained: "I find . . . the most pleasant night of the week is Friday. . . . ["Why?"] I don't know, but I think . . . yes, perhaps it's my life style. On Saturday I have to form the football team . . . that's what occupies my thoughts. But Friday night for me is the most pleasant night of the week. . . . On Saturday my thoughts are elsewhere in fact."

Having nothing to do, when wanting to do something, is the fifth theme in the experience of pleasantness and unpleasantness. This theme in more positive terms was labeled "being occupied, absence of boredom." It was, however, the most difficult to discern. In fact, it was mentioned explicitly only once, but it was implicit in many other reactions.

In the next passage, which is an answer to the question, "When is it *least* pleasant at home?" it comes to the fore. A mother and housewife reacted by saying, "Some days, I'm depressed. . . . No, I can't say when especially. . . ." Her husband intervened, "Well, in the course of a day . . . when everybody is out . . . probably only in the morning." She confirmed initially, but changed her mind, "No, I think in the afternoon . . . because in the morning I'm busy with the housework. . . . But in the afternoon . . . yes, for a few hours . . . from about one to four o'clock. . . . At three o'clock I start cooking again. . . . Then the boys come home, but they go upstairs to do their homework. . . . I rarely see them. . . . Yes, just me . . . it's a couple of hours in the afternoon."

It is not the morning when she is alone and busy that is experienced as being least pleasant, but the afternoon when she feels aimless. This is similar to the case of children of religious families who often hate Sundays, because "you have nothing to do" between going to church, drinking coffee, and doing homework for Monday. The idle hours are considered to be unpleasant.

In sum, five themes have been elicited in the analysis of answers to the question, "When is it most pleasant at home?": (1) communicating with one another; (2) being accessible to one another; (3) relaxing after having finished work; (4) being free to do what one wants; and (5) being occupied, absence of boredom. The next question we will turn to is whether and how these themes we have identified as sociopsychological factors clarify the relationship between architectural environment and experience of atmosphere.

Paul J. J. Pennartz

Architectural Factors

The spatial characteristics of the dwelling also affect the experience of atmosphere. Three architectural themes emerged in the responses: (1) the arrangement of and connections between rooms; (2) the size of rooms; and (3) the form and physical enclosure of rooms. The way in which these themes contribute to atmosphere can be clarified and, in a certain sense, explained by the sociopsychological factors mentioned above. The manmade "potential" qualities of architectural characteristics are transformed into an "effective environment," according to Gans, on condition of being empowered on the individual's conceptual level.

The first characteristic of the home environment that, in the interviews, was related to pleasantness is "the spatial relationship between kitchen and living room." However, opinions differed widely, and different sociopsychological themes appeared to be prevalent. A mother expressed her preference for an open kitchen: "An open kitchen, that's also nice, because . . . when I am in the kitchen . . . and the whole family is here, you are so shut away . . . it's not so pleasant." Being shut away or feeling shut away is not a static feature of a situation. It changes continuously with the actions of people and the use of architectural elements. Another woman added: "Now, you close the door and I am in the kitchen, . . . and when you have an open kitchen and someone calls you . . . you don't need to open a door." Such a seemingly trivial action as having to open a door evidently influences the experience of space.

Yet the visual relationship between kitchen and living room is the reason others do not favor an open kitchen. A man stated: "I always advocated open kitchens. . . . We used to have a living room–kitchen at home, so . . ." His wife intervened by saying: "Yes, but it should also be practical. . . . You know, we have two boys who are fond of playing football . . . so, you understand, very often they come in with muddy boots or shoes, so that's quite a mess. . . . Therefore it should be practical and it doesn't need to be very beautiful, because then you are always worrying about it."

Walls may function as barriers to communication and therefore give one a feeling of being shut out. This corresponds to the first sociopsychological theme in the experience of pleasantness, "communicating with each other." Yet walls within a dwelling may also function to separate the usual household activities and are quite functional for those who object to certain spheres being mixed. One woman objected to eating in the kitchen: "When there's only the three of us . . . that's all right . . . but I think it is very unpleasant to sit down and look at that kitchen dresser. . . . That would be all right if we had a very large kitchen, you would not have to sit quite so near the sink . . . because nothing is so awful as to look at dirty dishes . . . to stare at. . . . No, I think it's too messy."

Messiness or disorderliness is a curious phenomenon, because sometimes it is attributed a positive meaning as the opposite of being too neat and fussy, and sometimes a negative meaning such as a lack of care. Which meaning prevails depends on the situation and the individual involved. Asked why pans scattered all around, dirty plates, and dishes piled up "for everybody to look at" gave her an unpleasant feeling, a woman replied: "Because I get nervous while eating, I can't stand it. . . . I like to relax while I am eating, I don't taste the food when everything is in a mess. . . . ["Why?"] Because I feel haunted by the work waiting for me . . . or for the others . . . because they are in a hurry . . . they have so little free time."

"Because I feel haunted by the work" corresponds to the third sociopsychological theme in the experience of pleasantness, "relaxing after having finished work." The theme could not become more manifest than when it refers to the unpleasantness of disorder, which for this woman means work to be done. Openness and continuity of space are spatial features of a floor plan that are favored by many designers. However, appreciation of these features by the inhabitants seems to depend on the relevance of certain sociopsychological factors in everyday life.

The second characteristic of the home environment that, in the interviews, was related to pleasantness is "the size of rooms." The effect of the size of a room on atmosphere seems to vary considerably. Some refer to a very small room as being extremely pleasant; others complain that such a room is good for nothing. Thus, it is necessary to find the themes that underlie these divergent experiences.

When asked, "What is important for a pleasant home?" a woman referred explicitly to a limited size: "A nice house . . . the living room does not have to be so large, and an open kitchen as in many houses these days." But a man complained about the limited size of the kitchen: "You cannot make this kitchen pleasant. See, if I could put a small table and two small chairs there . . . then it might begin to be pleasant. . . . ["Could you explain this a little more?"] Look, if it were larger, you could make it more pleasant with a table and stools. . . . If it were large enough, the children could eat here at noon. That would make it more pleasant, . . . or you could sit down in the kitchen to drink coffee or tea for a while."

It is not space in itself that creates atmosphere, but some kind of social action that takes place in the space—for example, having dinner together or drinking coffee. The size of a room is a potential architectural characteristic as it affects collective performance of activities and mutual communication. Communicating with each other was the first and most important theme in the experience of pleasantness.

The kitchen in most dwellings seemed to have been designed on the assumption that activities there are carried out by one person alone. This is often not the case, because many activities are shared by several members of the family. However, doing things together is not made impossible by the available space, but is rather impeded by it. This is illustrated by the comments of a woman asked if the kitchen was pleasant: "No, no . . . because it's barely possible for two people to wash up. . . . It is much too small. . . . You can't even put a table in it. . . . When you are washing up together

... the boys always help in the evening ... then they have to be at one of the drawers. .... While I am cleaning the gas cooker, you have to get out of the way, otherwise they can't get to the drawer." Being impeded influences the experience and meaning of space.

The relationship between size of rooms, communication, and experience of pleasantness was also noted elsewhere in the house, for example, in the entry hall. A woman stated: "I think that crowding and pushing in front of that coat rack ... when people are leaving or arriving at the same time ... well, then you have to stand in a queue ... and if you have such a small entry where you have to stand the one behind the other ... that's not so pleasant, is it?" Crowding, queuing, and pushing do not contribute to the experience of a pleasant atmosphere.

The impediments of the limited size of a room is also illustrated by the following reaction of a woman discussing the pleasantness of her living room: "When it is somewhat larger, it's more pleasant. .... Then you really can put nice flower boxes here and there. .... Now it's so small that you can't do anything interesting. .... We would like to have an aquarium. .... Where could we put it? We have no space for it. ... An aquarium is quite nice, isn't it?" It is important that objects belonging to the atmosphere can be placed in the living room. Knickknacks, flower boxes, and an aquarium are hobby related. Their presence and potential characteristics affect the experience of pleasantness as expressed in the third sociopsychological theme, "relaxing after having finished work."

A room does not necessarily have to be large to be pleasant, but it needs to provide opportunities for people to do the things they want to do. Asked "Which are the most pleasant rooms in the house?" a boy reacted: "My room. ["Why?"] Well, it is not too large and because of that, most of the time there is no empty space, and I work there most of the time. .... And everything is there ... records and books. ...."

As the combination of work and pleasantness was of particular interest, the interviewer continued by asking, "You work there most of the time. Is that why it's pleasant in your room?" The boy replied, "That gives me a feeling that there is no empty space, because there is a lot to do there." So it is not the third theme, "relaxing after having finished work," but the fourth sociopsychological theme, "being occupied, absence of boredom," that is most relevant here. A space that is not used becomes meaningless and is not experienced as being pleasant. For that reason a room is deemed to be "too large" when it is not completely used either actually or intentionally. The size of rooms and the minimal dimensions required are important issues in public housing policy. The interpretations of room dimensions and space, however, differ significantly.

"The shape and spatial enclosure of rooms" make up the third potential architectural characteristic affecting the experience of pleasantness. The use of several rooms in the house appears to vary with their sizes and shapes. A hallway that is long and narrow is an area only to be crossed, redecorated, and provided with new floor covering from time to time. Asked if a hallway was pleasant, a woman answered: "Well, I can't say that. . . . I have seen nicer. . . . No, I can't say that it is practical. . . . A pleasant hall . . . I think should be square. ["Why?"] I think that's nice . . . you can put a nice coatrack in it and furnish it more pleasantly. ["Why square?"] You have more corners to do something with . . . that's what I think."

The relationship between the ability "to do something with" and a pleasant atmosphere does not hold only for the passageway or hall area. In regard to other rooms, people also referred to the meaning of the shape of a room. Usually their comments had to do with deviations from rectilinear forms. The question "If an architect were to design a pleasant house for you, what would be your requirements?" was answered by a woman as follows: "I am fond of niches where you can put odd things in. . . . I like walls that aren't always straight up and down, so that you can build in cupboards and shelves and have built-in lights and things like that. . . . It gives such a lot of atmosphere at home. . . . In this house it's all straight and you keep hanging things up and putting things down, you can't have them anywhere else. . . . In a niche you can create something, do something, . . . and that's what can't be done here."

The desire to have niches and corners seems to be irrational, but, in fact, is only irrational insofar as their latent function or meaning is not made obvious. The function in this case is providing the opportunity to do or to create something meaningful and is related to the fifth sociopsychological theme, "being occupied, absence of boredom."

The walls of a room are also spatial elements "to do something with." When a girl was asked, "If an architect were to design a pleasant house for your family, what would be most important with regard to your room?" she was very specific: "Not very large windows . . . everything now is open and . . . more wall space. You can do much more with more wall space. . . . Now, I only have wall space on two sides of my room. . . . On the other side is a wardrobe, there you can't do anything, so the bed can only go there or there. . . . ["What would you like to do?"] Hang things up . . . more wall space and smaller windows, that's much nicer."

"You can do much more. . . ." Again it is not the spatial enclosure that determines the atmosphere, but the opportunity it provides. Rectilinearity and rectangularity are also disrupted in rooms with a sloping roof. A sloping ceiling fills a room up and eliminates empty spaces, which are experienced as spaces "where nothing is done or to be done." It is an architectural characteristic that contrasts with the fifth theme in the experience of pleasantness in the home environment, "being occupied, absence of boredom."

Conclusion

In this study, transcripts of interviews were scrutinized to determine whether there are consistencies in the way situations within the home area are experienced as having atmosphere, and whether and in which way architectural characteristics of the dwelling influence these experiences. Atmosphere was specified and operationalized by the concept of pleasantness.

The sociopsychological factors in the experience of atmosphere were identified in the themes extracted from the responses to the question, "When is it most pleasant at home?" We distinguished five themes: communicating with each other; being accessible to one another; being relaxed after having finished work; being able to do what one wants to; and being occupied, absence of boredom.

The question "Where in the house is it most pleasant?" resulted in three architectural characteristics contributing to the experience of atmosphere: the arrangement of and connections between the rooms, the size of the rooms, and the shape of the rooms. The way in which these three architectural factors contribute to the experience of pleasantness can be clarified and in a way explained by the sociopsychological factors mentioned above. The potential qualities of the architectural characteristics proved to be effective only if empowered by the conceptions of a pleasant atmosphere. These findings fit in with Gans's potential-effective environment scheme, as outlined in the beginning of this chapter.

Within the limits of the study, it may be concluded that the experience of atmosphere in the home area is neither irrational nor indeterminate. Policymakers and architects will benefit not only from understanding the qualities of a good potential environment, but also from understanding effective ways of achieving their best intentions.

9

Negotiating Space in the Family Home

Moira Munro and Ruth Madigan

THE CONCEPT of "home" embraces both a physical and a social space; the house itself is home, as are the social relations contained within it. The concept of "home" also carries a heavy ideological burden (Watson 1986); it can be seen as part of an ideological trinity: "family," "home," and "community." Ideas of what constitutes a "proper" family have shaped the ways in which individuals relate to one another in the intimacy of their domestic life, and the same ideas have influenced the physical design of the housing within which these social relationships are lived. The home thus provides an important *locale* within which individuals negotiate their daily lives (Giddens 1984).

Architectural historians have drawn our attention to the ways in which the design of nineteenth-century housing reflected the ideal of the bourgeois family, with its strictly demarcated boundaries between public and private, masculine and feminine, and rigidly differentiated internal spaces (Matrix 1984; Muthesius 1982). The ideal of the bourgeois family lived on into the twentieth century as a model of domestic respectability (Roberts 1991; Thompson 1982) and as a set of design conventions that continued to influence the style and layout of quite modest suburban housing (Burnett 1986; Madigan and Munro 1991).

Yet even the most conservative exponents (Mount 1982; Murray 1994) acknowledge that the expectations of family have undergone a transformation in the last thirty or forty years, witnessed not only in Britain, but also in most of the Western and Westernized world. In modern familial ideology, the family is presented as a much more democratic unit based on notions of a companionate marriage, joint decision making, and greater labor market participation for women, rather than the hierarchical and overtly patriarchal structure of the earlier model. Smaller families mean that child rearing occupies a shorter length of time, but children enjoy a higher status. The modern nuclear family unit is also presented as being more socially isolated and self-reliant, with a strong emphasis on shared activities (Pahl 1984; Saunders 1990). Indeed the family and the home in this version are presented as the main sources of self-identity for both men and women.

This idealized model is not, of course, a description of how people necessarily live their lives, and even within the ideal there are contradictory strains. Familial ideology emphasizes the importance of "doing things together"; shared interests and shared activities acquire a new importance as part of a consumer and leisure culture (Featherstone 1991). Yet at the same time there is a stronger emphasis on individual expression and self-identity. Women in particular struggle to reconcile these two demands, to find the space to exist as independent adults while at the same time taking on the major responsibility for sustaining the family as a collectivity (Hunt 1989).

The modern family ideal may espouse the idea of equality and shared decision making, but the evidence confirms that there is still a very marked gender division within the family home. Feminist writers have pointed out that the family home, far from being a "haven in a heartless world," can also be a prison and the locus of oppression, ranging from the frustration of women who find themselves tied to a narrow domestic role to those who are victims of sustained violence. An increase in divorce rates, longer life expectancy, and changes in work patterns have all contributed to the diversity of household forms. Children, too, occupy an ambiguous status within the family. On the one hand they are protected: taken to school, not allowed to play outside, and kept economically dependent as never before. On the other hand they are sexualized and targeted as consumers from an early age.

Even allowing for a certain conservatism or caution in designs for mass housing, which have tended to reflect dominant conventions of family life, we would expect to find substantial changes in the design and use of houses over the past three or four decades. Fox (1985), writing about the North American experience, suggests that postwar social and economic changes have affected both family relations and the design of the houses in which families live. He contrasts the formality of the "parlor house," typical of the 1920s and 1930s, with the more open-plan layout of suburban housing from the 1950s onwards. Parallel changes can be seen in the evolution of British housing (Burnett 1986), though space standards are lower than those for suburban housing in North America.

The high cost of land in Britain and the political drive to sell houses to people on more modest incomes has made it necessary to build on smaller plots (Karn 1993). At the same time modern aesthetics have created a demand for a greater sense of light and space. Builders have been able to reconcile these apparently conflicting demands by creating a single living area that runs the full length of the site, with windows at both ends. An alternative solution has been to save on space by including in the living room the hallway and staircase to the upstairs bedrooms.

It has been suggested that this reorganization of space in conventional suburban mass housing reflects the democratic family ideal (Madigan and Munro 1991; Watson 1986). The family home is centered on the one room that is necessarily a shared and communal space. It not only symbolizes the family together, but as an important pathway to the front door, to the kitchen, and to the stairs (Karn 1993), it cannot be closed off from any members of the household for private use. Bedrooms offer opportunities for individual privacy, but they are often very small and are not always considered appropriate for visitors; in addition, they are often shared. This is particularly true for married and cohabiting partners.

Our study examines how people use the space in their homes and how it affects, and is affected by, their views of family unity and individual privacy. Most discussion of privacy in the home has focused on the relationship between the household and the outside world. Here we wish to disaggregate the household unit and consider issues of privacy between family members and the resolution of conflicts over the use of space within their home. We wish to understand how families negotiate their relationships within the limitations imposed by the physical space of a conventional suburban home and the social space defined by dominant ideas of family and home.

Method

Our research was based on a sample of households living in modest, postwar housing, a mix of rented and owner-occupied flats and houses in the Glasgow area (Munro and Madigan 1993). In selecting our sample we deliberately sought the midrange of housing; excluding both the upper-income, executive-style housing at one end, and poor quality housing from the least attractive areas at the other. In terms of internal space, most of the houses fell within two broad types: those with a single lounge or diner plus a small working kitchen with no sitting space; and those with a slightly smaller living room with no dining space, but a kitchen just large enough to accommodate a table and chairs. Only a small percentage had a dining room as well as a living room and kitchen. Just more than half the sample would be conventionally described as manual working class, and the rest mainly white-collar or lower-middle class, which is broadly what one would expect in a city like Glasgow.

Our evidence is based on 382 postal questionnaires and 20 extended interviews with female respondents from households with at least three members.[1] This was done in order to explore the issues raised when there is a potential conflict over the

1. We wish to acknowledge the work of Hilary Parkey, who conducted the detailed interviews and administered the postal questionnaire. We are also grateful for the support of the ESRC for the costs of the empirical work.

use of space, which we assumed would not arise so sharply in one- or even two-person households. The dominant voice in our more qualitative analysis is therefore that of the traditional family unit. Although it is well established that this unit is no longer the most common household type (Watson 1986), these houses are designed as "family" housing, so analyzing their appropriateness for family households is relevant. We have deliberately focused on women as our chief informants because it is still true that family, house, and home have a particular salience for women, both ideologically in prescribing women's work and women's responsibilities, and in practice in that women still spend more time in the home, on housework, and on child care (Darke 1994).

Communal Life

A strong commitment to a view of family life that revolves around communal activities and shared experience was clearly articulated in our postal survey. The great majority of respondents agreed with the statement: "It is important to family life that everyone sits down to a proper meal and spends some time together whenever possible." The rest selected: "When people have busy lives, and with modern technology, you can be more flexible about meals: Individuals can please themselves and eat when it suits them." Less than 3 percent agreed: "It is better for children to eat separately so they can have what they like and adults can have more relaxed meals."

In the extended interviews, mealtimes were identified as being of central importance in maintaining communication within the family unit: "I really do think that we're less and less communicating with one another. I think that mealtimes should be the time that you sit down together" (Mrs. C, age thirty-eight); "I think that sometimes when you sit down to a meal you talk, that's when you—em—rather than the children sitting down in front of the television or whatever—you sit down to a meal and talk or argue! We try to sit, and we do, unless my husband is away" (Mrs. S, age forty-two).

For parents of younger children mealtimes play an additional role of socialization, in relation to teaching children the norms and expectations of polite behavior: "It teaches children how to behave in company outside their own house. Although we don't do it now, I know that my children know how to behave anywhere, and how to use knives and forks" (Mrs. B, age fifty-seven).

Despite their emphasis on the ideal of the family coming together at mealtimes, this ideal was not always achieved in practice. The complex timetables of different family members militate against strict mealtimes: breakfasts are taken on the run, and young children eat dinner early, perhaps before any full-time workers return home; shift workers may seldom eat with other members of the family; and young adults (children in the age range of about seventeen to twenty-three) are likely to help themselves to food when returning from a night out, or when entertaining their own friends. Further, the space constraints are such that in some of these houses, sharing a "proper" meal at a table can be difficult, requiring rearrangement of furniture, or even impossible.

In our postal survey we found that only 47 percent of people took their main meals at a dining table and a further 14 percent at a kitchen table. However, 37 percent of people took the main meal of the day on their laps, in the living room, often watching television together. In such cases, the ideal of families gathering around the table to talk is evidently only aimed for or achievable on special occasions like birthdays and Christmas. This ideal is apparent from the changed distribution of responses to the location of special meals, when more than 80 percent would eat at a dining table and only 14 percent in the kitchen. When asked why they took their special meals in the kitchen, respondents said: "Because the children aren't all that good at eating. The youngest one, he's four, so he tends to drop his dinner on the carpet" (Mrs. L, age thirty-four); "We generally eat in the kitchen. . . . We set the table up there because they're not all in at the one time" (Mrs. T, age forty-seven). The separation between the ideal and the practice was frequently recognized and rather regretted by our respondents, though they were ultimately pragmatic and resigned to the practical realities.

Though television is often seen as a distraction, interfering with the communal aspect of family meals, it can also provide a collective focus. Families enjoyed the sense of being together, sharing a favorite program or videotape. Most households had more than one television set in the house, and although this arrangement reduced disagreements about which program to watch, the fact that the children, particularly teenagers and young adults, chose to disappear into their bedrooms, seemed to some respondents to undermine the collective life of the family: "Their rooms are their own wee houses, which I don't know is a good idea either. Because I think that's when you lose them, they just do their own thing in their bedroom. Whereas [without their own TV] if they wanted to see the telly they would have had to come down here. I regret them getting television" (Mrs. R, age forty-five).

Negotiating Space

The design of these family houses is founded on the assumption of a "companionate" marriage, where the two partners are implicitly expected to share their leisure time in the main living room and share their nights in the master(!) bedroom. This bedroom, though traditionally the largest in the house, is frequently more formal and pristine than those of the children. In advertisements at least, the double bed often has a regal appearance, with drapes and ruches, even a canopy over it (a shrine to marriage?). In our sample, the bedrooms were a little more prosaic, but they were still formal, and they were not furnished as multifunctional rooms or dayrooms, in the way that the children's rooms were. Once the double bed was in place, there was usually no room for a desk or a comfortable chair. Though the bedroom was used for watching television, listening to music, studying, reading quietly, or just getting away from the others, it was an awkward compromise.

There is inevitably some tension in the use of the main room in the house, particularly when there is only one such communal space. Strategies for coping with this tension were varied and depended on the structure of the household, particularly the ages of the children. One strategy is obviously to allocate individual members of the household their own private space, usually their bedrooms. Respondents expressed an almost universal preference for each child in the household having a bedroom of his or her own, although it was not always possible to achieve this ideal, particularly for families with more than two children. Children, and that includes young adults, shared bedrooms in 28 percent of the family households in our postal sample.

Families trying to allocate two bedrooms among three children often found it difficult to decide whether to give priority to the eldest or to segregate by gender. Different households reached different solutions: "I don't intend being here longer than five years. The oldest kid will be fifteen, she has a room of her own now, the two younger ones share. Fiona will be twelve, and twelve is really an age when they can't share with a boy" (Mrs. P, age thirty-four; children ten, seven, three); "Victoria doesn't [share a room] because she's the only girl. Ideally I would like separate rooms for the two boys, because Matt is only four and Gary is ten so there's six years of a difference which is quite a lot. Matt messes up the place and Gary is left to tidy it up. Matt won't go to sleep so he climbs in with Gary and they have a carry on. . . . They don't get on, but I'll have to separate them" (Mrs. L, age thirty-four; children ten, seven, four).

Parents and Children

By contrast with the parents' bedroom, children's bedrooms were typically furnished and equipped as a multifunctional space, with play area and toy storage or desk and television or sound system, or both, and sometimes a computer. This gave a certain amount of discretion to the parents in the household. Children could be banished to their own rooms, leaving adults the use of the living room. By the same token, children could escape to their own rooms to avoid adult surveillance. In general respondents were very respectful of children's privacy, knocking on doors before entering their rooms, for example.

Fear of crime and of traffic has meant that children are increasingly encouraged to play indoors, but bedrooms are often very small, not really big enough for more than one child. Some households solved this problem by converting the loft into a play area. Other respondents who did not have this option expressed a desire for something similar: "I would love a big basement where you could say to the kids 'Right, that's yours, that's your place to take your friends,' so they could still have bedrooms that aren't all cluttered" (Mrs. H, age thirty-four; children eleven, fourteen).

Patterns emerged in some households where the living room was effectively *time-zoned* in that children had the priority in the early part of the evening, but the adults had priority later on (once their fathers arrived home). At this later point, younger children would go to bed, while older children would be expected to go to their own rooms if they did not want to join in adult activities. In this way, the same physical space can be made more flexible by the social norms that structure the way it is used.

Conflicts over space were sometimes more acute in households containing adult children. Young adults are clearly expected to have more rights over the family home, to come and go as they please. Their visitors can no longer be banished to the bedrooms, but must be treated as adults, deserving of adult hospitality (the use of the living room and the offer of food or drinks). Often this did not cause any great problems; the children's friends had grown up with them and were welcomed as honorary members of the family. It was also evident that, to a significant degree, young adult socializing takes place outside the home, avoiding any potential clashes over the internal space.

However, two types of concern were evident among the parents of young adults. In some cases older children and their friends could prove a dominating and disruptive presence at times, tramping through the living room, raiding the kitchen, and making a mess, and parents looked forward to their leaving home. In other households, the independence of young adults and their withdrawal from collective family life was very much regretted as a loss and a foretaste of losing them altogether.

Entertaining

This concept of time zoning (rather than space zoning) was evident in ways in which social norms and expectations were deployed in other types of conflicts over the shared space (McDowell 1983b). We explored with the respondents the possible conflicts that could arise when visitors arrived. Responses to this question varied, depending on the ages of the children. Very young children have to stay with an adult as they need to be looked after. Though their belongings sometimes seemed to fill the whole house, they may only intrude marginally on adult conversation, without raising concerns of confidentiality or suitability of conversation.

Older children could simply be asked to go to their bedrooms if parents thought it was not appropriate or desirable that they remain with adult visitors. All but the youngest children were expected to take their own friends upstairs to play, ensuring privacy for them and minimizing the intrusion on adults.

We tried to explore the conflicts that arose when a visitor wanted to speak to only one of the parents, at a time when the other was present in the house. For many, such questions were very hard to answer as respondents found it difficult to envisage occasions when such potential conflicts would arise, partly because the companionate ideal was so strong as to prompt the response that any visitors would "of course" be for both adults. With further analysis, it emerged that there were more subtle ways in which time zoning was taking place in many households. Women were more likely than their partners to be at home full time or to have only part-time jobs. Women were therefore often able to spend time with friends without ever coming into conflict with the rest of the family. Their friends became familiar with complex schedules of work, family commitments, and other activities. They could therefore "drop in" for what is, on the surface, casual socializing, but is in fact carefully scheduled to be mutually convenient: "If I have my girlfriends it's normally an afternoon visit, because they have husbands and families as well, you know, to attend to at night" (Mrs. T, age forty-seven).

Men appear less likely to use the home for socializing with their friends. When asked what happens when her husband comes home with one of his friends, one respondent replied: "That's something that doesn't occur in this house. We have mutual friends—other couples. So of course, if we have visitors the children are normally out . . . so we have this place to ourselves, you know" (Mrs. T, age forty-seven; children twenty-one, twenty-two).

This gender-differentiated pattern of socializing typically preserves the evenings as a family time when casual socializing is rare, though of course there may be occasions when people are invited on a more formal basis for a meal or drinks. In this context, it can be seen that the hypothetical event of a friend of just one of the adults appearing unexpectedly would be a relatively unusual occurrence.

Women's Space

Women's traditional responsibility for domestic order means that they are not always able to enjoy the home as a relaxing "haven" in the way that other household members can. This is true in relation to their responsibility for children, as seen above, but also implicitly emerges in relation to their partners: "If my husband goes on a night out, which he does one night a month, . . . that night I make sure that I have a couple of bars of chocolate and I'm a great reader and I have my book and I have my television and I make sure that everything is done by teatime so that I can curl up with my book and chocolate and my television and that's my night out—my night at home rather. . . . I do enjoy having the house to myself for a night's peace and quiet because I think personally if you sit down in the afternoon . . . it's always at the back of your mind that you've got a dinner to prepare" (Mrs. T, age forty-seven).

Women are typically responsible for the emotional needs of the household as well as the more familiar practical demands of food, clothing, and so on (Hunt 1989; Roberts 1991). In the light of women's role in the home, it is important to recognize that women need *time* as well as *space* to enjoy privacy within the home. When asked where she went to be on her own, one respondent replied: "There isn't really many places in the house that you can go. I mean I've tried going into my room—it doesn't work because the wee one of three, she's in and out—one's doing dishes and that—you know, they'll start arguing and they're in telling me what they're doing and so that doesn't really work. I don't really manage to get any privacy unless they're all out playing and the wee one is asleep—it's ideal, it's lovely, it's great!" (Mrs. V, age thirty-five; children fourteen, eleven, three).

Alternatively, women often create social space, and eased conflict, by using their role as "housewife" or "carer" to distance themselves, or subordinate themselves, to others in the household. They accepted other people's choice of television program because they were only half watching, while cooking or doing the ironing. They could distance themselves from a conversation between their husband or partner and his friend by engaging with small domestic tasks, such as making up sandwiches for the next day, attending to the children, or preparing coffee and tidying in the kitchen. This "busy-ness" creates a space, without the very pointed separation that would be indicated by deliberately leaving the room.

The Presentation of Home and Family

There are particular tensions between the alternative ideals of home and family that contribute to the demands placed on women within the home. On the one hand, an important meaning of home is as the archetypal "back region" in which everyone can relax and be himself or herself (Giddens 1984). Associated with this meaning is the idea that the home should also be relaxing and welcoming for visitors. When asked what impression they would like visitors to have of their home, the respondents gave remarkably consistent answers: "That you can come in at any time, that it's nice and homely"; "That it's welcoming, that it's clean, comfortable"; "That it's clean, that's the most important one for me."

Although at first glance these expressions seem closely linked, further examination reveals conflict between two strong ideologies. Because a core part of the definition of a "welcoming" home is that it should be *presentable*—namely, that it should be clean and tidy and there should not be embarrassing amounts of domestic clutter facing any visitor—this translates into a pressure to maintain high internal standards of tidiness and cleanliness, even where the home is being enjoyed by the family at rest (Hunt 1989). Women expect to be judged to some degree on the way their homes are kept and are anxious that they should not be classed as "dirty" or not "respectable."

The conflict between leisure activities and the desire to maintain a clean and tidy environment is particularly significant where there is really only one room that is suitable for both these functions. Typically, women bear the brunt of this work (Gittens 1993); tidying and cleaning around other family members to maintain their high standards: "I'm working constantly to keep the place clean. It's really not very easy with the kids, especially if they've been sick or something. It's quite hard to keep the place clean. Although I don't really get many visitors during the day, I do try to keep the place clean if they do come" (Mrs. P, age twenty-nine; children ten, seven, three); "The place is always tidy. I very rarely sit down" (Mrs. A, age forty-three; children seventeen, fifteen, twelve).

Many women are constantly on duty, attending to other people's needs and looking after the house whenever other members of the family are at home. In this way, they subsume their own relaxation to fostering it in other members of the family. This is not something that they complain about to any extent. This is partly because they have internalized standards of cleanliness and tidiness to the extent that they actually feel uncomfortable; they really cannot sit down when the house is a mess (Darke 1994). It is also partly because of the time zoning discussed above: women typically have more flexibility during the day and might therefore be able to create space and time to relax when other members of the family are out.

Conclusion

In this study we have been concerned with understanding how families negotiate their relationships within the limitations imposed by the physical space of a conventional suburban home and the social space defined by dominant ideas of family and home. Our focus on postwar family housing in Glasgow has produced a sample in which couples and nuclear families are the dominant household types in the postal survey. Nuclear families are even more strongly represented in our interview sample because we deliberately excluded one- and two-person households. In such a sample it is perhaps not surprising that conventional ideals of home and family find strong expression in the ways in which women use their homes and talk about their lives. On the face of it there would appear to be a "match" between the assumption of a shared, democratic family life, which is implicit in the physical design of the houses, and the aspirations of those who have chosen to live in them. Our work suggests, however, that everyday practice is rather more contradictory than this apparent "match" might suggest.

It was evident from their replies that our respondents continually sought ways of circumventing and negotiating the restrictions imposed both by the physical design of the house and by the sometimes contradictory demands of gender and family ideologies: the conflict between the public, respectable face of the home and the desire to create a relaxed "back region"; the individualistic imperatives for space and privacy and the notions of "togetherness" and communal life; the ideal of democratic, compassionate relationships and the gender differences in responsibilities for housework and child care. All these contradictory demands create tensions that individuals seek to resolve through complex patterns of time zoning and space zoning, and a differentiation in the rights and responsibilities of various family members: between men and women, and between adults and children. It is evident that these negotiations are not always easy to achieve, but it seems undeniable that the physical design of contemporary mass housing creates a restrictive and somewhat inflexible locale, even for the nuclear family for which it was designed.

10

The Domestication of Laundering

Rudi Laermans and Carine Meulders

WHEN WE HEAR the word "housework," we think of domestic activities such as cooking, cleaning, and washing. Within the family these household tasks are still predominantly performed by women, even those who have a well-paid, full-time job (Martin 1984). Housework appears to be the shadow labor Ivan Illich spoke of, hidden inside the house and closely bound to the domestic sphere. On the one hand, the home is the spatial locus of housework; on the other hand, it is also its object and requires maintenance. The dominant association between housework and domestic space ignores the "outdoor" history of household practices.

Numerous products that are today purchased in the supermarket were, a century ago, still anchored in the family economy, produced by and consumed in the same household (Frazer 1981; Laermans 1993). By and large, the loss of productive functions went hand in hand with the rise of more intimate family relations and with the feminization and devaluation of the remaining housework (Cowan 1983). The so-called mechanization of the household, i.e., the growing substitution of human— or better—female labor by technical artifacts, had radical consequences for the status of housework and the layout of domestic space (Heller 1979; Lupton 1993).

In this chapter, we will examine the historical development of one specific household practice: the laundry (Meulders 1992; Meulders and Laermans 1993). We will direct our attention to shifts in the locus of the laundry work. In this respect a trend toward domestication and privatization stands out clearly. In comparison with many other household duties that were progressively withdrawn from the family, the history of laundry work is paradoxical.

In the nineteenth century laundry work was an object of commodification and professionalization contracted out to professional laundresses or commercial laundries. However, when the washing machine made its way into the home, laundry work was deprofessionalized. The introduction of automatic washers in the 1950s definitively domesticated the formerly out-of-doors practice of laundering.

Purity and Hygiene

In the sixteenth century courtly circles "discovered" the attractiveness and the distinguishing power of immaculate white linen. The transformation of the nobility from a class of knights into a class of courtiers played an important role in the formulation of new and stricter rules of conduct. As members of the aristocracy could no longer derive symbolic authority from glorious military operations, they began to confirm their social identity by stylizing their nonproductivity (Elias 1983).

An immaculate appearance obtained a fixed role in aristocratic public life. Wearing fresh and splendid white linen, washing one's hands, later on also using a fork and knife, and other practices nowadays considered "hygienic" were not yet directed by a striving for personal health, though. Whiteness and cleanliness became synonyms of courtesy, just as etiquette was the courtier's mark.

Since fear of water was widespread until the middle of the eighteenth century, washing the body was unusual and white linen easily became dirty. Actually, it was the linen that washed the body and the linen was washed in turn by the laundress. "Linen absorbed sweat and impurities; changing it was, in effect, to wash. The shirt had become a sponge; it cleaned" (Vigarello 1988, 60).

The emergence of cleanliness and whiteness as almost self-evident attributes of the noble identity lowered the tolerance for different kinds of dirt. Social constraints became individually internalized standards of conduct: dirt was no longer avoided exclusively for social reasons. On the contrary, with the internalization of courtly manners, dirt and filth began to arouse real feelings of disgust and intense bodily effects (Elias [1939] 1978). Thus, at the end of the sixteenth century shirts were daily changed at the French court (Vigarello 1988, 67).

A neat look served as a highly distinctive mark and a symbol of status, and it became the object of a struggle for distinction between the aristocracy and the ascendent middle classes. This mutual display of symbolic power resulted in a tightening of the cleanliness requirements in the next centuries. Thus, wearing white collars and spotless cuffs was followed by the use of sweet-smelling nightgowns, stainless sheets, clean handkerchiefs, and spotless tablecloths. Around the middle of the eighteenth century, the rediscovery of water as an ally in the battle against bodily impurities brought new cleanliness attributes into fashion. Bath towels and washcloths had to remove bodily dirt and purify the skin, but they still should never look dirty.

This evolution had an important side effect: the social gap between the well-to-do aristocracy and bourgeoisie who considered themselves "civilized" and the popular masses was visibly widening. Onto the real social distance between the upper and lower class, a symbolic distance was engrafted, which was partly legitimized by the sharpened opposition between dirty and clean. The initial courtly striving to keep shirts white and clean in order to keep up appearances thus evolved into a radical, social segregation (Muchembled 1978, 1988; Stalleybrass and White 1986). The social upper classes shared a world of images, in which the common people appeared as "filthy" and thus were to be avoided.

The tightening of the boundary between dirty and clean paralleled the emancipation of cleanliness as a distinctive quality. In accordance with the noble ideal of nonproductivity, the courtier was interested only in an elegant appearance in the eyes of the others. The combination of the noble taboo against work and the emancipation of cleanliness as a central moral value inevitably stimulated the professionalization of laundering.

To comply with the courtly manners, the nobility had its dirty linen washed by professional laundresses. Keeping up appearances required high laundry expenditures. However, investing in an apparently futile striving for immaculate whiteness by means of regular, though expensive, laundering fit in perfectly with the aristocratic lifestyle of "conspicuous consumption" (Veblen [1899] 1945). Some noblemen maintained a laundry in their households; others sent their washes to small workshops in the vicinity. The very rich could afford to send their fine linen to specialists with an international reputation.

Gradually, however, the aristocratic ideals of highly visible cleanliness and good manners anchored in public display lost their credibility in bourgeois circles. From 1860 onward, a new bourgeois discourse about cleanliness highlighting virtues like strength, austerity, simplicity, authenticity, self-control, and productivity became dominant. Noble practices such as taking warm baths were exchanged for less pleasant but toughening activities like the cold bath (Vigarello 1988, 112–31).

What was first a moral-political attack on the aristocratic weakness and enfeeblement obtained a scientific basis with the breakthrough of medical-hygienic concepts of cleanliness (Goubert 1989). With "scientific" arguments, so-called hygienists and medical doctors confirmed the new bourgeois self-image. By linking these values to the notion of health—the central signifier in the medical-hygienic discourse—they affirmed that frugality and naturalness were necessary in the care of one's body and appearance. Frequently washing the body was better than attending the Parisian salons nicely powdered and perfumed. Clean underwear, though invisible, was not only "more hygienic," but also "healthier," and thus "better" than ostentatiously white collars (Perrot 1984).

As the medical-hygienic discourse gained social impact, the notions of dirty and clean were dissociated from the primacy of sight. Physical health was influenced by processes that were not perceptible at all. From the 1880s onward, the discoveries of Pasteur, Lister, and Koch confirmed the fundamental importance of the nonperceptible reality in matters of health (Latour 1988). Pathogenic organisms were soundless and invisible, odorless, and nondescript; they were microbes and bacilli, protozoa and viruses, visible only under the microscope.

Striving for cleanliness became an unceasing struggle against an invisible but omnipresent enemy that could be perceived only by scientists. In order to know what was dirty or clean, one had to rely on their judgments and statements. The medical world claimed that the "enemy" preferred to hide in dust, dirt, rotting waste, and impure drinking water. According to Vigarello, "the microbe thus materialized the risk and identified it. . . . The consequences were inevitable: To wash was, as never before, to operate on the invisible" (1988, 203). Disinfection became an important objective in the laundry process, accomplished by boiling and steaming the dirty fabrics. Especially in institutions like hospitals, a great deal of attention was given to the practice of regular disinfection.

Nowadays cleanliness has lost its distinctive power, having become too common. A youthful or fashionable appearance will render more distinctive profits (Laermans 1990). The introduction of the automatic washing machine not only devaluated the status of domestic labor, but also undermined the status of cleanliness. A neat and tidy outfit came within everyone's reach.

The triumph of cleanliness was soon followed by a loosening of clothing standards. Today many will ask themselves whether yesterday's shirt or a somewhat wrinkled pair of trousers will do. Cleanliness escaped neither the process of informalization nor its accompanying uncertainty. Ecological concerns increased this uncertainty even further. While advertisements by the detergent industry keep focusing on the "whiter than white" argument, environmental groups protest against the polluting effects of detergents. The political debate on "social" whiteness and environmental pollution proves that being clean or dirty, or purity versus pollution, is a crucial and unstable issue, even at the end of the twentieth century.

Women and Water

A fascinating study by the French ethnologist Yvonne Verdier (1979), based on interviews with elderly women about the way they used to do their washings, reveals how traditional laundry practices survived well into the 1950s.[1] Traditional washing was dominated by the difference between "small washes" and "the great wash." Small washes reflected domestic needs: owning only a small amount of linen meant many

---

1. Several sources indicate that until the 1960s traditional washing rituals were performed, not only in rural France (Wasserman 1989) and southern Europe, but even more so in central Europe, including Germany (Silberzahn-Jandt 1991; Orland 1991), Switzerland (Ehrensperger 1988), and Austria (Grünn 1978). In the geographical periphery of modernity, older women apparently had enough symbolic power to command respect for tradition. Northern Europe, including the Netherlands, lacks, however, a tradition of publicly performed washing rituals: it was more of a domestic affair, though not exclusively.

small washes. The rhythm of the transitional seasons determined the rhythm of the great wash. It took place at the beginning of spring or fall, when the weather was most suited, and when the women had free hands for the washing labor.

Apart from material conditions, symbolic meanings were fixed to the rhythm of the great wash. Like other major spring and autumn events—the great baths and cleanings—the great wash followed the seasonal calendar. The return of spring and the onset of autumn marked a transitional period, a passage in nature that deeply influenced the entire rural economy. The metamorphosis in nature was linked to the restoration of the cultural order within material reality. Just as winter turned into spring and summer into fall, what was dirty had to become clean. This ritualized synchrony between the natural and the religious calendar lent the great wash a supratemporal meaning.

Both the informal small washes and the strongly ritualized great wash proceeded in two stages: a private *and* a public stage (Helming and Scheffran 1988; Orland 1991, 53–59; Verdier 1979, 110). Doing the laundry demanded individual and collective efforts, performed at diverging rhythms and in different places. The first stage of the laundry process took place indoors, but it had a public extension. First, the linen was sorted, soaked, and boiled at home by the lady of the house or her personnel. This individual labor was time consuming and arduous, since buckets of water had to be hauled and heated. Following the calm rhythm of the chemical processes, the start of the laundry process was slow, serious, time consuming, almost solemn, individual, and, last but not least, domestic.

Within rural communities, the public stage of the great wash was a more or less collective ritual. With their piles of soaked and boiled laundry, the women of the village gathered around the communal washing place. Here the female community "sisterized" and transformed "what had to be done" into a festive event. The women exchanged the latest news and sang local washing songs together as they washed the gigantic amount of dirty laundry that had been accumulated over the previous months.

Traditional laundry work was embedded in a system of exchange relations. Not only soapy water but also laundry requisites were passed on to poor women or were exchanged between neighbors. Going to the washing place for a small wash implied asking around if a neighbor wanted to have something washed. Women also exchanged recipes and advice with regard to the removal of stains, the softening of cloth, or the perfuming of linen.

As a collective ritual conducting and condensing female solidarity, the great wash was also an important instrument of local social control. Indeed, during the public stage of the washing ceremony, differences literally came to light: the amount and quality of the linen displayed a household's wealth or poverty, just as the presence or absence of stains could reveal conjugal secrets. Washing together created "sister-hood," but in this sisterly community every woman judged the domestic life of her neighbors by the linen. The great wash was thus a crucial episode in the local struggle for distinction as well as in local gossip. The shame and embarrassment of poorer women who made their way to the washing place will remain a historically well-guarded secret.

As already stated, the traditional washing ritual linked the categories "dirty" and "clean" to natural and religious oppositions such as death versus life, and sinful versus righteous. *Doing* the laundry produced a symbolic surplus value: just as sins disappeared through active penance, cleansing required heavy duty of washerwomen. In short, *making* the transition from dirty to clean and enabling the ritual passage of boundaries was at the core of traditional washing.

In nineteenth-century Paris laundry work was still performed in the vicinity of streaming water: near ponds, wells, or fountains, and on floating laundry platforms at the banks of the river Seine, a situation akin to that of Zurich, Geneva, and Strasbourg (Heller 1979; Ungerer 1986). After 1850, the Parisian laundry barges were gradually replaced by public washhouses to meet the growing need for laundry facilities. In the name of health and hygiene, the Parisian authorities encouraged the building of public washhouses by private entrepreneurs.

Public washhouses offered general facilities such as washbasins and cold water; sometimes even hot water was supplied, or extra facilities, such as a heated drying room or a room for ironing, starching, and folding, were provided. Soap, soda, and chlorine water could be obtained from the male supervisor, who had a dual function. First, he was the disciplinarian and the controller of the laundry facilities. Second, he gave professional advice to the women regarding washing products and procedures. His presence anticipated the creation of the domestic sciences and is to be interpreted as an attempt to get a hold on the domestic affairs of the still "resisting" household in promoting rationalization and professionalization (Perrot 1980, 20–21).

The traditional link between women and water also persisted in urban areas: women hauled water for the family and did the laundry. It was a heavy burden for women, but it also represented freedom. The public washhouse was for women much like the local tavern was for men. The importance of washhouses as sanctuaries of female sociability is shown, for example, by the failure of one of Napoleon III's prestigious projects. In admiration of the technical advances of the British, Napoleon III sent a delegation to London and Liverpool to study the local washhouses. In 1855 the prestigious wash- and bathhouse of the Temple Quarter was completed, constructed under the direction of two London engineers. The building symbolized the great importance of hygiene and offered the most advanced technical achievements in laundering.

British steam engines and drying and ironing machines ensured that the technical side of the operation ran smoothly. New methods, such as steam washing, which had been in use since 1853 in military laundries, warm-air drying, the use of hot water from a tap, and ironing rooms complemented the new equipment and were intended to make the work of washerwomen and housewives less arduous. A vapor extraction system was even installed in order to maintain a healthy atmosphere in which to work. (Goubert 1989, 74; Perrot 1980, 16)

However, six years after its glorious start this "temple of purity" operated at a loss. The separation into cubicles in which women had to do the laundry not only in isolation but also in silence was at the root of the female boycott (Perrot 1979, 130). The construction of the Temple wash- and bathhouse realized first and foremost the elite's dream of an efficient and modern space dedicated to hygiene. However, it was also an intentional attack on one of the most important pillars of urban popular culture experienced by the authorities as disquieting and threatening.[2]

Almost exclusively women of low social status, like professional laundresses, domestic servants, and lower-class housewives, frequented the washhouses. Most members of this female washing community were still strongly related to the traditional rural culture. Laundering proved an obvious way for many women among the urban newcomers to earn money. Thus traditional laundering practices penetrated into the urban realm of the washhouse, making it into a meeting place of women. They chattered and laughed, learned the latest news, shared their concerns, and found female solidarity, or, as Zola magnificently described in *L'Assommoir,* fought out their disputes (Perrot 1980).

Tradition and modernity intermingled at the urban washhouses. Remnants of the traditional washing ritual transformed the urban washhouse into a public space for women. The washhouse was also the locus of modernization of the laundry process.

Modernizing Laundry Work

In a treatise written in 1766 titled *The Easy and in the Household Certainly Very Advantageous Washing Machine,* Jacob Christiaan Schäffer from Regensburg tried to convince the world of the great utility of his invention. In subsequent years numerous other machines were launched without any commercial success. The chemical revolution in the laundry business was more successful. Indeed, in 1784 Berthollet managed to gear the bleaching qualities of chlorine to the laundry practice. Some years later, in 1790, Nicolas Leblanc succeeded in developing a process for the industrial production of soda crystals. Both new cleansing agents were very welcome, not

2. In Hamburg and Berlin, the London model of separate cubicles was imitated (Orland 1991, 133).

least because the demands of cleanliness kept rising and started to trickle down the social ladder.

In cities like Paris and London, the triumph of the medical-hygienic discourse and the increasing demands of cleanliness coincided with a rapid growth in population, lack of space, and problems of water distribution (Dyos and Wolf 1973). Although cleanliness became "the luxury of the poor," a growing number of workers' families lacked space and financial resources required for a clean and healthy way of life. Urban living conditions demanded appropriate collective laundry facilities in addition to commercial laundry services.

The laundry trade was considered a slowly modernizing sector, partly owing to the inadequacies in water and energy supply (Malcolmson 1986, xiii). The development of mechanized laundries started by and large after 1860. The first washing machines were drums rotated by hand and had to be filled with buckets of water. Employing a laundress or a domestic servant was still cheaper than purchasing a washing machine. It not only saved the mistress space, effort, and money but also enhanced her social status, for commanding servants was still associated with the aristocratic lifestyle (Hausen 1987, 290–303; Riffault 1980).

The prerequisite for mechanization of the laundry process in the nineteenth century was the presence and the rapid expansion of professional laundry works in the cities. Commercial laundry works functioned as laboratories for further refinement of laundry technology. The daily confrontation with the faults of technology, thorough knowledge of the laundry process, and particularly economic interests stimulated experimentation and optimization of inherent possibilities.[3]

The Taboo of Public Places

Medical-hygienic discourse not only transformed the concept of cleanliness but also changed social relations and their representation. The notion of public space took on a new, medicalized interpretation. Streets, squares, alleys, cafés, public washhouses, markets, and other public meeting places were, first and foremost, possible sources of infection—potential threats to the individual bodily order, which was inextricably bound up with the health of the social body.

From the 1840s onward, health professionals translated their theoretical insights into innumerable recommendations and proposals with respect to (notably urban) public places as well as to domestic spaces: the domains of private family life. Proposals to clean up the old "unhealthy" quarters were usually accompanied by pleas

---

3. Because the more frequent changing of linen involved rising costs, many collective households, such as hospitals, prisons, and convents, decided to build their own mechanized laundry works.

for building large collective networks such as sewer systems and waterworks. The demands of hygiene "involved a total reconstruction of the world above and below the cities. Water was, without any doubt, one of the most important factors in urban rebuilding" (de Swaan 1988; Vigarello 1988, 230–31).

Health professionals assigned a major role to the housewife in the medicalization of private life and domestic intimacy, portraying her as the guardian of domestic health (de Regt 1984; Donzelot 1979). With the help of scientific arguments they promoted the ideal and moral of bourgeois family life with separate responsibilities of husband and wife. The man had to make money while the woman managed the household and dealt with the vicissitudes of husband and children. In the first half of the twentieth century, a variety of developments caused a further dissemination of the bourgeois family model and the image of women corresponding to it. With rising prosperity, also among the working class, the material conditions for observing the prescribed norms of cleanliness were in reach of a growing number of households.

For the first time female professionals responded to this situation. Nurses, midwives, social workers, teachers, and home economists took over the "civilizing torch" from the predominantly male health professionals. Home economists, like Christine Frederick (1914, 1920) and Erna Meyer (1926), were advocates of the "rational household." From the 1920s onward, the movement of the rationalization of housekeeping pleaded an efficient and professional approach to domestic labor, implying the retraining of the housewife to become a competent manager of the household. In saving the housewife's time and energy, rational housekeeping was a prerequisite for "emotional homemaking." The time and energy saved were invested in cherishing husband and children, in creating an affectionate and protective family life.

The Nomad in the Home

In 1889 American Nikola Tesla made a vital contribution to the mechanization of the household by reducing the size of a previously huge electric motor to minimal proportions (Giedion 1969, 577–60). Numerous electrical household appliances flooded the market and contested for a place in the home (Forty 1986). This development opened the road to the modernization of everyday life and initiated the domestication of laundering. In 1910 the first electric washers for domestic use were introduced in the United States.

> These non-automatic machines reduced labor more than time; although the operator no longer had to crank the machine, . . . she had to start and stop it, add soap, and remove water, and put each item through the wringer. For those with the required plumbing (often hot as well as cold) and draining facilities, electric machines

lightened the washday burden: water running into one tub eliminated all the heavy lifting, and electrically powered agitation did away with hand cranking and washboard scrubbing. (Strasser 1982, 117)

The industrial production of domestic washing machines increased rapidly in the United States; between 1930 and 1950 the electric washer became widespread. In Western Europe, though, the breakthrough of the electric washer had to wait until after World War II (Delaunay 1994; Giedion 1969, 568–71). Middle-class housewives were pioneers of the modern laundry practice by using the electric washer. They responded to the ideal of the modern, rational housewife who managed her household efficiently by using time-saving appliances. Although hygiene, cleanliness, order, and propriety remained central values, they were no longer ends in themselves.

Housekeeping became a condition of homemaking, not only for middle-class housewives but also for working-class women. Domestic labor became a token of the housewife's affection for her family. Laundering was not just laundering, but an expression of love (Cowan 1974, 16). In short, the new orthodoxy "emotionalized" domestic labor.

The modernization of living and housekeeping also aimed at a rational division of the living space (Laermans and Meulders 1993). Each space in the home was assigned its specific function. Although the modern housewife appreciated the coming of the washing machine and attached great importance to clean clothes and spotless household linen, she did not assign the washer a place of its own.

Likewise, the journey of the laundry through modern living space does not accord with principles of architectural efficiency and household rationalization. The storing of dirty laundry, the washing, the drying, and the ironing and folding, as well as the storage of appliances related to laundering and even the storing of clean linen and clothes in chests and wardrobes, are relegated to empty corners of different rooms. The possible detour through the garden or via the balcony or the terrace to dry the laundry reinforces the laundry's liminal position (Douglas 1979).

The laundry process and its attributes seldom received the special space to which they were entitled by members of the rationalization movement and their companions, the architects. Sculleries in family houses were the only places originally designed for washing (Lawrence 1983). The cramped modern apartments, however, lacked a scullery. Architects seemed to reduce the laundry process to the installation of a washer, discreetly hidden in the built-in kitchen or in the bathroom, neglecting the processes of collecting, drying, and ironing. The wandering washing machine still remains the nomad in the home.

Only if "excess" space is available are people inclined to create a separate laundry room. Material conditions may restrict the range of possible locations of the washing machine. The vicinity of a tap and outlet makes kitchens, bathrooms, cellars, and garages likely locations. However, the popular location of washer and dryer in the attic requires special arrangements. With bad weather, the attic is also a favorite spot for drying.

Apart from material conveniences, cultural conventions have determined the suitability of locations for the nomadic washing machine. Nineteenth-century interior design set the trend to cluster and "hide" all cleansing activities in the "backstage" areas of the house: the kitchen, the bathroom, and the toilet (Goffman 1959). These were areas that nineteenth-century visitors seldom saw.

The recent trend to push the washing machine out of the kitchen and bathroom into further removed "backstage" spaces, like the cellar, the attic, or the garage, complies with the inclination to hide the personal linen (an intimate matter) from the eyes of visitors. Depending on the available domestic facilities, the wandering washing machine and its accessories are usually driven to spaces that form the very edge of the private backstage. Today's domestic laundering is done in the liminal zones between private and public space where clean water comes in and dirty wash water leaves the house.

Conclusion

Today's commercial image of domestic laundry work is often represented as a push of a button, an image far removed from the traditional public washing ritual performed by washerwomen. The laundry process was subjected to a radical metamorphosis in the period between roughly 1750 and 1950. In fact, laundry work is a rare example of a household chore that "moved into" the home after it was mechanized and industrialized. The introduction of the domestic washing machine transformed a collective and public washing ritual into a private one-person job.

Social and cultural changes, usually summarized by the notion of "modernization," affected traditional laundry practices in many respects. Laundry work was not only mechanized and ultimately automatized, but also intensified because of rising standards of cleanliness. In a constant struggle for clean clothes and white linen, the frequency of washings accelerated, legitimized in the late nineteenth century by the "rational" pursuit of hygiene.

Traditional laundry practices brought women, water, and linen together in public places. In rural communities the women occupied the local public washing place and transformed it into a ritualized female space during the event of the "great wash." In cities like Paris and London, laundry work was professionalized, bringing lower-class women—professional laundresses, servants, and poor housewives—together in public washhouses. The nineteenth-century washhouse was in that period one of the few public loci of female sociability.

Today's laundering is domesticated, but it has never really been integrated into the domestic space. Everything concerning laundering—from washers and dryers to irons and laundry baskets—is hidden in peripheral areas in the home and was never assigned a place of its own. Although cleanliness standards rose, laundry work was deprofessionalized, devaluated, and obscured. The transformation of dirty into clean, of wrinkled into ironed, became a liminal activity warranting the privacy of liminal domestic spaces.

11

Constructing Home
A Crossroads of Choices

Elizabeth Shove

THE LOCATION, shape, and form of our homes impinge directly on the smallest details of our daily lives. No wonder, then, that sociologists, social policy analysts, economists, historians, and anthropologists have attended to the design and use of house and home. Acquiring the colors and complexions of their parent disciplines, these analyses tend to revolve around a familiar menu of established themes. Discussions of housing have, for example, echoed wider interests in inequality, the benefits and perils of urban life, the socioeconomic history of building and design (Muthesius 1982), gender and domestic power relations, and the cultural construction of the images and ideals of domestic life.

Much of this research addresses houses in the aggregate. Given the social significance of neighborhood and community and the importance of location and property in reflecting and generating cultural and material difference (Basset and Short 1980), *housing* has been the focus of inquiry. Housing conditions, housing areas and zones of cities, changes in patterns of tenure: these are the terms and units of debate. Thus welded together, treated as a generalized commodity and examined in appropriately anonymous terms, houses and homes have an accepted place in the social science agenda. It is a place that emphasizes relationships between supply and demand, and the politics and practicalities of housing provision (Saunders 1990).

Looking at the other side of the equation, and viewing housing as a form of consumption, addresses have long been seen as significant and easily recognized markers of social status (Douglas and Isherwood 1979; Goffman 1959). As every real estate agent knows, patterns of social and geographical mobility are intimately related. Areas move "up" and "down" in social standing, just as individuals travel "up" and "down" the finely graded scales of the property market (Rex and Moore 1967). Framed in these terms, careful inquiries into the bricks and mortar of social distinction have served to illustrate the cultural properties of the housing market.

In all of this, the house itself has disappeared from view. Specific choices about design and construction have faded into the background as have the decision-making processes leading people to their current and previous addresses. Researchers consequently study the contents of an estate or neighborhood without regard for sequences of domestic and commercial decision making that generated the present mixture of residents and without reference to future moves that may lie ahead. In effect, residence is taken as a fixed characteristic: by implication families live where they do because that is, in some sense, where they belong.

For the most part, analyses of housing routinely stop at the front door. Historical and cultural researchers have sometimes gone so far as to cross the threshold, taking the home and its contents as legitimate subjects of inquiry in their own right (Cowan 1985; Forty 1986; Halle 1993; Putnam and Newton 1990; Rybczynski 1987; Silverstone and Hirsch 1992). Although of a finer grain than the anonymous analyses of housing, such studies abstract and map sociocultural developments, detaching these trends from the specific conditions and circumstances of choice and from the systems of domestic and organizational decision making out of which they emerge.

By contrast, this chapter will focus on the choices of those involved in the design and acquisition of houses, and in their furnishing and decoration. In doing so it cuts across conventional lines of analysis, mixing stories from a handful of different research projects and borrowing ideas from other traditions in an attempt to broaden the agenda of housing studies. By looking at the process of decision making, we can begin to examine that elusive territory separating and linking the microexperiences of individual householders with developments in the industries of house building and homemaking.

Decisions about house design, layout, and specification are made by construction companies and firms of house builders. Yet decisions about buying and selling these properties are made by individuals, couples, and families. The house is thus the point where corporate and domestic decision making intersect.[1] Commercial and personal choices are so embedded in the domestic environment that it would be difficult to find a better context in which to explore the interweaving of consumer interests and the manufacturing of preference.

The house is also a focus for the creation and structuring of markets, representing the point at which images and ideas are converted into commodities and cash. The four walls of the house and the three-piece suites, lamp shades, ornaments, and pictures they enclose consequently embody a range of diverse and often very complex relationships between consumption and production. As Coward observes, personal style is a strange paradox: "Individuals have it but we can all copy it" (1984, 65).

---

1. In telling the story of the design and building of a single home, Tracy Kidder's book *House* (1986) explores just this relationship.

Not everyone has a psychological investment in the design and furnishing of a home, but it is often the case that people's identities are wrapped up in their chairs and tables as well as in their immediate physical surroundings. In any event, addresses and styles of decor inevitably carry some social significance. These clues and signs are read and interpreted by strangers and friends alike. In this way houses and their contents cross another boundary, bridging the divide between public and private lives.

There are further reasons for choosing to concentrate on the organization and structuring of home-related decisions. Choices about the domestic environment frequently reflect the roles and responsibilities of husband and wife. Accordingly, patterns of decision making embody and re-create expectations of gender-specific behavior within the household. Such expectations are in turn exploited and modified in the wider world outside, forming and informing marketing strategies and shaping people's actions as consumers and users of the domestic environment.

Mixing Methods

A new agenda emerges when we attend to houses rather than housing and when we consider the detailed decision making involved in creating and selecting domestic environments. This reorientation of inquiry suggests that we should reflect on two especially important interfaces—first between provider and consumer, second between the house and its contents. What has been missing, to date, is any systematic attempt to compare the structuring of choice in these very different, yet intimately related, domestic and commercial environments. How do house builders and furniture designers conceptualize their markets, and, for their part, how do house buyers and homemakers organize and manage consumption?

The next step is to consider the dynamic interaction between the domestic and commercial players, and between the commodities they acquire and produce. In the absence of any coherent research simultaneously exploring the perceptions and priorities of producers and consumers of homes and their contents, this chapter draws instead on three quite separate studies. Stripped of their real history and purpose, and selectively raided for illustrative examples, these three studies help to develop and refine the questions outlined above.

The first study reveals something of the interests and perspectives of companies involved in designing and producing new houses. Undertaken as part of a contract research project for the Building Research Establishment's Energy Conservation Support Unit at Watford (Shove and Connaughton 1990), this interview-based investigation focused on ten house-building businesses and on builders' beliefs about their customers' needs and preferences.

The second piece of research, undertaken in York in 1986, involved in-depth interviews with a sample of sixty-seven married women (Shove 1986). The sample, which included women of different ages with and without children, was also structured in terms of housing and material circumstance. Focusing on domestic decision making, the York study generated a wealth of qualitative data about the ways in which respondents made decisions both about their houses and about furnishing and decor.

The third source is a more recent research project funded by the Economic and Social Research Council (Shove 1995). This comparative study of "the division and integration of building professional labor" in France and Britain involved close collaboration with IKEA, the Swedish furniture company.[2] Though its real focus was on the design and development of two new stores, this project provided an opportunity to explore the commercial context of furnishing and interior decoration and to consider the interests and priorities of an organization involved in designing, manufacturing, and selling furniture and other homemaking commodities.

It is important to be clear about the illustrative status of this eclectic collection of empirical material, for these three pieces of research have specific shortcomings. Critically, new housing makes up a very small proportion of the total housing stock. Most decisions about buying houses are therefore decisions about buying "second-hand" homes. Equally important, IKEA operates within and seeks to develop just one segment of the total market for interior design, decoration, and furnishing. Individual choices about home decor relate to a much wider range of products, styles, and tastes. But, as a device for opening debate and generating new lines of inquiry, this curious juxtaposition of research has real advantages.

House Builders

Consider, for a moment, the sorts of decisions embodied in a new house. How should the rooms be arranged? How should the building fit on the site? How many socket outlets should it have? How should the walls be insulated? The list is endless. Somehow, house builders have to find answers to all these questions. More than that, they have to respond in ways that allow them to make a profit from the production and swift sale of a marketable property. They have to know all about "curbside" appeal in different market sectors, and they have to translate this understanding into buildable, technically sound, and economically feasible designs.

2. IKEA started in 1958 as a Swedish mail-order furniture firm. By selling unassembled furniture, IKEA was able to cut transportation and assembly costs (Löfgren 1993b; Mårtenson 1981). Its market philosophy worked out quite well, for IKEA is now a multinational corporation with 130 stores in Europe, Australia, Asia, and North America.

Elizabeth Shove

It is a complex process. Builders are known to be pragmatic. Although their economic equations are dominated by major items like the price of land, considerable attention is also paid to the cost of each and every element of the final product. The specification of door handles may, for instance, be the subject of heated debate between marketing and technical departments. More significantly, the costs of a real stone fireplace must be justified in terms of the additional value such a feature might add and with reference to its anticipated effect on the speed of sale and the final selling price. In this strange world, gut feeling and commercial instinct combine with precise financial calculation and careful estimation.

House builders claim that the three most important criteria are, in their own words, "location, location, and location." The first "location" is the geographical positioning of the site itself. The second relates to the situation of an individual house within an estate of other properties. The third most detailed meaning of "location" concerns the positioning of the house within its plot. It is one thing to know that these are critical features, but another to work out just what this means when it comes to the design and layout of a specific site. As the builders explained, these practical choices are informed by an understanding of what the "market" wants.

Though placing enormous faith in their ability to read and respond to market demand, these respondents also acknowledged that the market (potential buyers) for a new house is a strange concept, including, as it does, only those people in a specific area seeking a new house within a certain price range. The market for a house in Saxmundham consists, for instance, of only those people who want to live there, who have seen (or who might see) the details in the estate agent's window, who like the property, and who can also afford it. This is an unknowable population of potential customers, quite unlike that which preoccupies those trying to sell carpets, stoves, or even furniture.

So how do builders translate this mythical "market" into technical reality? How can concepts like the "market" be used to justify the addition of a stone fireplace or the selection of a cheaper door handle? How do builders make decisions about the shape and character of the domestic environments that they are constructing? As noted, gut feelings are all-important. There are, nonetheless, significant differences in the way in which these instincts are organized and managed.

As the house builders' survey showed, it is difficult to locate gut feeling within a major company organized around a complex hierarchical structure, with regional divisions and perhaps with centralized design offices. In this context, pattern-book designs embody and fossilize corporate feelings about the market, representing the relative influence of marketing departments balanced by the hard economics of accountants and their technical colleagues. By comparison, it is much easier to pinpoint the instincts of a local builder producing just fifty houses a year. In such an environment the hunches of the managing director are likely to be all-important.

Either way, gut feelings and tradition provide an unquestioned—perhaps an unquestionable—foundation for decision making. Having settled for, let us say, fifteen socket outlets, fifteen becomes the norm. Standard drawings embody past practice and in time they come to represent *the* way of doing things. Larger builders invest heavily in the development of their pattern-book plans, and subsequent modifications are always expensive. Smaller builders are equally wary of the technical and economic risks of change.

It is difficult to know exactly why a house did or did not sell and, unable to quantify the precise value of innovation or to unscramble the ingredients of success, builders routinely rely on previous experience. In their words, they know what sells houses because their houses have sold. And because they have sold, they must have provided "what the market wanted." This incipient conservatism is tempered by the need to keep up with the competition. Lacking any real market to refer to, builders create an illusion of market demand by constant reference to the actions and decisions of their immediate rivals. When it comes to it, houses seem to be built for other house builders rather than for actual customers.

Decisions about design, layout, and house construction are made within a tangled commercial environment. There is considerable scope for choice and intervention: company size makes a huge difference in the process of decision making; organizational hierarchies determine patterns of relative influence; and formalized divisions between marketing and technical expertise are of real significance.

Furthermore, builders share a common reluctance to tamper with a proven product. While acknowledging the peculiarities of the housing market and the primacy of location, interviewees consistently argued that their decisions were driven by market demand. As they saw it, they had no choice but to provide what they thought the market wanted.

House Buyers

How do the four walls of a house appear from the point of view of the potential buyer? How do people decide where to live, and why do they choose one house rather than another? The York study shed some light on these questions. The sample of sixty-seven respondents included tenants as well as owner-occupiers, but just about everybody had some choice about exactly where to live. In this context, housing decisions were negotiated and resolved within the family unit rather than within a complex organizational structure peopled by accountants, and divided into discrete areas of marketing and technical expertise. So how did these families choose their homes?

The interview material underlines the importance of location to the house buyers, echoing the views of the house builders described above. Although location was a key factor, the process of house hunting was itself extremely complex. Much depended on how much time potential buyers were able to spend looking around, on why they wanted to move, and on the way in which they organized their search. Their place in the housing market was also important. The York housing stock is such that those looking for a small terraced house had far more choice than those seeking a detached property with a garden.

In practice, the scope and scale of choice also depended on a number of factors, including time, price range, the nature of the building stock, the state of the market (i.e., the number of houses on sale at any one moment in time), and, of course, location. These considerations limited but did not obliterate choice, and respondents still had much to say about the special qualities of the houses that they eventually selected.

In telling these stories, respondents described the cyclical sequence of events and decisions that led them to their present address. As they explained, the process was one of review, rejection, definition, and redefinition of criteria, finally culminating in the decision to buy or rent a particular property. This curious mixture of the accidental (what was for sale at the time, which agent they went to, which street they drove down, etc.) and the inevitable (what could be afforded, where the property was, how many rooms it had, etc.) was presented in different terms by different sectors of the sample.

For some, the chosen house was the first one that fulfilled a few key requirements. In such cases, time for looking around was typically cut short, limited by the demands of a new job or the deadline of a wedding. Having found a property at roughly the right price and in roughly the right location, they then had no reason not to buy it. Given the pressure of time, there was often no choice but to take this step. As one newlywed explained: "We'd put our name down for it and before we knew it had all happened. . . . It was more a or less a joint decision but we didn't do a lot of talking about it." But for most there were real choices involved.

In describing their decisions, the more affluent respondents[3] tended to employ an essentially emotional vocabulary. Phrases like: "We fell in love with it on first sight" and "I knew it was right as soon as I walked in" were common. Such language made sense to these buyers, for houses were expected to have character and personality, so much so that hunting for the right house was much like hunting for the right partner. As this response illustrates, instant personal affinity was the key to it all: "We both knew what we were looking for. We came to see this one and without saying anything

3. The sample was designed to include couples with and without children, at different stages in the life cycle, and living in different parts of the town. Detailed analysis of census data, like car ownership, amenities, and household densities, allowed me to place ward areas into one of three categories, each representing a different level of affluence. In this chapter I have omitted the middle category in order to emphasize differences between the two extremes.

to each other we both knew that this was what we really wanted." Having fallen for a house, there is no way back; you have to buy it. So although this group of respondents described the searching process—and insofar as there was a search they did have choices to make—the end result was seemingly inevitable: this was the house for them.

By comparison, the less affluent people in the sample tended to adopt a more pragmatic approach. In this context, location was especially important. Sometimes unable to afford to travel far and often unwilling to move even a few streets away from close relatives, these respondents restricted their search to a comparatively small area.

This account was typical: "We needed to live near here in case I got a puncture. We wanted to be able to walk to work." These people wanted a house that was "no trouble," often favoring new houses or, as they put it, "nice houses." Questions of character and personality simply did not arise; decisions instead revolved around the key criteria of cost and convenience. These two demands themselves generated a sense of inevitability. Respondents consequently ended up in the one house that best met their current requirements.

These very different languages of preference echo the sorts of patterns and distinctions between "popular" and "superior" taste as described by Bourdieu (1984): the formalizing and abstracting of the more affluent respondents contrasted strongly with the matter-of-fact transparency represented in the accounts of the less affluent section of the sample.

Despite these undoubted differences there are, nonetheless, important points of similarity. While the terms of inevitability varied widely, both sections of the sample felt they had no choice but to pick their present houses. Either they had fallen for it, or it was the best possible alternative at the time. Once that decision was made, prior, potentially contentious issues about house-hunting criteria were rendered invisible, simply vanishing from the retrospective view.

To summarize, the process of selection, review, and redefinition of criteria is one that leads buyers, within the limits of time, price, and other factors, to the purchase of the one and only house that meets their requirements. Builders claim to have equally limited choice about the design and specification of new homes. They say they have no option but to provide what the market wants. If we are to take these accounts at face value we have to conclude that houses are designed, bought, and sold without anyone ever making any really significant decisions.

It is, perhaps, misleading to take these stories so seriously. After all, interviewees have a common interest in justifying their actions and in presenting credible and plausible explanations. However, by looking in more detail at these descriptions, we can begin to see that the terms of inevitability vary from case to case, and that each reflects a subtly different blend of hardheaded pragmatism, gut feeling, and emotion.

Elizabeth Shove

The Furnishing Store

Sofas and lamp shades come in all shapes and sizes, and there is endless variety in terms of style, price, color, quality, and material. Moreover, these items are available from literally dozens of different sources and in multiple quantities. In each of these respects buying a chair is quite unlike buying a house.

When it comes to chairs, there are many markets to be catered to and cultivated, and, as those in the furnishing business know, it is possible to experiment with different styles and try out new ideas. Customer reactions are easy to test, and careful reading of daily sales records can reveal even small swings in consumer preferences.

As a purveyor of fixtures and fittings, IKEA is no different from any other furnishing store. Where it differs is in the way in which it goes about its business. The average length of stay in an IKEA store is one and a half hours. This figure suggests that the store occupies an ambiguous position, being part leisure center, part art gallery, part restaurant, and only partly a place in which to go furniture shopping. Linking commerce and culture (Whiteley 1993, 1994), IKEA appears to be selling a series of images and ideals, carefully disguised as chairs, tables, and lamp shades.

Shoppers, or as IKEA calls them, "visitors," are invited to try out different identities and speculatively experiment with new lifestyles as they work their way through the maze of ready-made room sets. These artificial rooms inevitably contain many of the same items, and it is interesting to note that although the displays model a wide variety of lifestyle options, the evidence of the sales tills is surprisingly homogenous. The one hundred best-selling items are more or less the same in all of the twenty-four countries in which IKEA operates.

Decisions about the selection and presentation of the 11,600 "active articles" in IKEA's international repertoire are shaped and formed by the company's internal management structure. Store managers set prices and choose which items to promote and market, but they do not directly influence the range itself. Such decisions are made centrally and are, of course, informed by data flowing back from the shop floors.

Somehow, these central choices have to express the "soul" of the company, sustaining a generalized image—a gut feeling that is as vital to the total enterprise as hardheaded market analysis of the thousands of items on sale. Recognizing the commercial significance of its "soul," IKEA exercises extremely close control over some aspects of its business, like the look of the store and the design specifications of its products, while leaving local managers considerable freedom in other respects.

These few observations underline the different environments of marketing and selling that characterize the house-building industry and the industries involved in furnishing and interior decoration. As an international company selling a range of separate articles, IKEA is able to learn about and manipulate its market in ways that are simply unavailable to those involved in creating one-time products like houses.

Although it makes its money from the sale of specific items, IKEA does so by inviting customers to imaginatively indulge in one or more of the many lifestyles gathered under the same blue roof. This approach helps to structure the decision-making process by helping people to find themselves among the variety of options offered.

Furnishing Choices

Returning to the experiences and responses of those interviewed in the course of the York research, we can now consider the selection of settees and three-piece suites. How were these decisions organized within the household? How do couples cope when faced with such an overwhelming abundance of choices about home furnishing and interior decoration? Where do they begin? Again, responses differed significantly between the "better-off" and "worse-off" sections of the sample.

The more affluent respondents tended to discuss these decisions in terms of personal preference and aesthetic value. In case of conflict there was no reason that the taste of one partner should prevail over the other, for both agreed that husband and wife each had a right to his or her own view. Presented in this way, the furnishing of the family home was a matter for negotiation and compromise between two equal parties.

Taking a different tack, the rest of the sample routinely subscribed to a vision of wife as homemaker. Believing that "women know best" when it comes to making a house a home, and that "men don't even notice their surroundings," these respondents operated with reference to an established pattern of rightful authority. Such an approach presumes that interior design can be done well or badly and that women have some special expertise in this matter.

Decisions about the selection and combination of specific items were strongly influenced by one or another of these two styles of decision making. The more affluent respondents emphasized the importance of aesthetic quality. Pictures and items of furniture were chosen because they were thought to have some intrinsic artistic merit: "I just liked it, so I bought it." End of story. Components acquired in this way stood on their own as inherently desirable objects, whether located in the hall or in the dining room.

Yet the piecing together of these elements was an art in itself. Still guided by personal taste and preference, respondents sought to combine objects and color schemes so as to create an overall feeling or atmosphere within their home. One aimed, for instance, to give a "springlike feel to the breakfast room," selecting plants and wallpaper and incorporating her grandmother's wicker chairs in a concerted effort to achieve the desired ambience.

Such abstract aspirations were rarely shared by those who were less well off. Their decisions were instead guided by a strong sense of decorative propriety and by an implicitly shared understanding of the "ideal" home. Different sorts of pictures went in different parts of the house.

Design decisions often revolved around a few key elements such as the furniture suite or the carpet. Guided by the notion that things should match, respondents expected to update the whole room if they acquired a new suite or if they changed the carpet. Newness was often valued as much as style, and in this environment there would be no question of hanging on to Granny's old chairs if there was a chance of replacing them with something better.

Again we can recognize something of the different cultures of taste described by Bourdieu (1984), and we can surely acknowledge the force of McCracken's observation that "goods 'go together' in large part because their symbolic properties bring them together" (1988, 121). In short, we can identify two quite different forms of decorative order, each associated with strong, but contrasting, senses of what does and does not go together. The results, in terms of style and image, are tangible enough.

The fact that these differences in approach also bring with them distinctive patterns of domestic decision making is less immediately obvious. Those subscribing to the more abstract model of interior decor were, for instance, unable to imagine a slightly more cheerful Munch or a rather less yellow van Gogh. Art objects had an integrity of their own. As a result there was no room for compromise. Either you liked the picture or you did not.

By contrast, other respondents felt able to separate qualities of size, color, style, and image when choosing artworks for their homes. In practice this allowed them to embark on a search for a picture with an overall color scheme that would "go" with the rest of the room and would fill a specific space on a specific wall. In this context, husband and wife might disagree about subject, color, and content in ways that would be quite inconceivable for other couples.

Respondents also subscribed to correspondingly different understandings of decorative order and coordination. Women who believed there was a right way to do things also believed that they (like other wives) "just knew" when curtains and carpets went together but that their husbands had "no idea." These wives simply assumed total control of a whole range of homemaking decisions. In other families, such choices were expected to be the subject of joint negotiation and much discussion, touching, as they do, on the raw nerves of individual and family identity.

As these examples suggest, the terminology of personal preference, like that of gendered expertise, had real consequences for the perception of choice and for the structuring of domestic decision making. These two modes of decision making, the individualistic and the conventional, appear to influence both the selection of specific items and their combination within the home. However, it is important to realize that respondents from both ends of this spectrum draw upon the images and visions created and developed by companies involved in making and selling furniture.

From the point of view of the manufacturer, it really does not matter how the three-piece suite is incorporated into the domestic setting. Although IKEA clearly caters to a particular market sector, its appeal is really very wide, so there is every chance that identical IKEA settees will fit comfortably within more than one system of decorative order. The same item may be acquired for freestanding aesthetic reasons just as it may be incorporated into a traditional, conventionally matching decorative scheme.

Four Walls, Three Pieces, and Two Patterns

The house builder and furniture store studies remind us that the priorities and practices of such organizations are far removed from the perceptions of choice and the varied decision-making regimes of their customers—so much so that it seems that the two worlds meet only briefly, at the moment of purchase. United by a common commercial framework, the decisions of builders and furniture retailers reflect the organizational contexts in which they are made. Marked by hierarchical managerial structures of one form or another and by functional distinctions between technical and marketing divisions, decision making is a formalized, if not bureaucratic, process.

These decision-making environments are quite unlike those that surround choice and selection in the domestic setting. Domestic decision making is not a homogenous process, and the framing and making of decisions clearly takes many different forms. However, the two ideal patterns outlined above, one revolving around individualized personal preference, the other around the conventions of gendered expertise, appear to structure the process of decision making across a number of separate domains.

The York research certainly suggests that the two sectors of the sample, those who were "better off" and those who were "worse off," adopted characteristically different approaches to the selection of *both* their homes and their homes' contents. Those in the "better-off" category defined these two types of choice in remarkably similar terms. Within obvious limits, house buying and furniture shopping were apparently determined by individual preference and personal taste.

By comparison, those in the "worse-off" category described these choices in rather more conventional terms. Houses were "nice," furniture "matched," and decisions were underpinned by constant reference to what was presumed to be a shared vision of the ideal home. Women were expected to have some special understanding of this ideal vision and were consequently thought to be "better" at the business of making a house a home.

Reference to tradition and past experience, like reference to conventional norms and taken-for-granted ideals, tends to limit opportunities for further debate and discussion. In less affluent households, vast reaches of decision making were lumped together and parceled up as the proper responsibility of either husband or wife. In this context many "choices" never appeared as such. Rather, they fell into the normal band of routine responsibility and were dealt with and resolved accordingly. In such a context the only issue that might require special justification would be a decision to deviate from the accepted pattern.

Much the same sort of non–decision making goes on in the house-building companies in which current practice is both based upon and justified with reference to past experience. Pulling the threads together, we can begin to identify similarities between certain types of providers (i.e., house builders) and certain types of customers (i.e., those in the "worse-off" category), both of whom make choices within what they see as a relatively restricted range of options.

By comparison, furniture providers, rather like the more affluent members of the York sample, confront what seems to them to be a much wider set of choices. On both counts, conventional analytic distinctions between buildings and their contents, and between consumers and producers, begin to blur.

Conclusion

Houses, homes, and styles of interior decoration represent the end result of extraordinarily elaborate networks of commercial and domestic decision making. In glossing over the practicalities of this process, researchers have tended to overlook the interlocking of personal and commercial choices. Equipped with no more than a handful of rather different studies, I have sought to explore this territory. In doing so I have begun to unpack conventional distinctions between the house and its contents and between providers and their customers.

In certain respects providing organizations like builders and furniture retailers have more in common with each other than they do with those who buy their products. On the one hand, familiar analytic distinctions between the house and its contents, and between the study of housing and material culture, tend to get in the way of efforts to understand the differing commercial dynamics and priorities of organizations involved in supplying the materials out of which we construct our homes. On the other hand, it is important not to lean too heavily on a simple distinction between consumer and producer.

Taken together, the three studies point to systematic differences in respondents' perceptions of the range and scope of choice, and in the way in which they approach the decision-making process. Some householders and some commercial organizations claim to operate in a relatively open, and therefore potentially contentious, world of opportunity. There are lots of decisions to be made, and many options to review. Others portray a more limited landscape of choice already structured through established decision-making procedures.

If nothing else, this comparative exercise suggests that there is much to be gained from closer analysis of crosscutting themes and from detailed inspection of interfaces between housing and material culture, and between the familiar analytic categories of consumption and production. From a vantage point at the crossroads of all these themes, we can begin to employ new ways of looking at the construction of house and home.

12

"Postmodern" Home Life

Tim Putnam

DWELLING is at the core of how people situate themselves in the world. The boundary of the home is still the most culturally significant spatial demarcation, and the way in which homemaking is elaborated through life stages provides key terms for ordering one's past, present, and future. One's sense of home is bound up in a sequence of relationships usually termed "familial": parents, brothers and sisters, partner and children, but includes also a penumbra of significant others: friends, neighbors, and associates. The home thus organizes not only relations of family, gender, and generation, but also relations of class; it is a principal product of human endeavor. The home is a prime unexcavated site for an archaeology of sociability.

Home is not only a locus of memory and sociability, but it is in a sense also one complex artifact of material "life supports" structuring home life. Sewers, cables, and utility mains are nowadays self-evidential elements in a "home life-support system," structuring our home life in a tacit manner. Home and furniture arrangements by their emphatic presence structure and support home life more explicitly. Philip Larkin's verses testify to this: "Home is so sad. It stays as it was left / Shaped to the comfort of the last to go." The signs of past use, of outgrown care, of unrealized aim acquire pathos, causing one to contemplate life courses and realize their irreversibility. There is also a specific sadness about the inability of things to live. While the intimate involvement of home arrangements in patterns of living imparts the impression that they have a life of their own, we have to remind ourselves that it is people, and not their life supports, who live and have the ability to recall, reflect, and renew.

My interest in the material culture of the home is therefore not in things as such, but in their roles as life supports. I am not suggesting that we can read psychological or sociological characteristics of persons, families, or groups from material evidence. In a commodity culture where homemaking makes extensive use of impersonally produced goods, such an exercise would be quixotic. But even so, how do we interpret recent changes in home arrangement? For example, when a new mode of living is mapped onto a house or a new house mapped onto an existing mode of living, rooms may be without use or subject to an overload of competing demands; in other words, the meaning of domestic space is redefined. Similarly, design innovation takes place and objects are successively revalued and decorative principles reinterpreted in relation to major changes in paradigms for living.

The ordering of goods in the home into a "life-support system" is in my view to be considered not only as an act of individual psychology, but also as one of culture building. Changes in the material order of the home—as in the appropriation of domestic space, the choice and arrangement of furnishings and decor, as well as in domestic routines and provisioning of the household—reflect and indeed define cultural changes. I would argue that in our century there have been two successive transformations of contemporary modes of living from the traditional, nineteenth-century models.

The first transformation is associated with the emergence of the modern home in the domestic architecture of the 1920s until the 1950s when domestic space was designed around a technical core of sewers, water and gas mains, power cables, and telephone lines.[1] The technical infiltration of the household was paralleled by infiltrating economic and political structures affecting individual household members in numerous other ways. In the 1960s a second transformation arose as the technical, economic, and political structures of modernity became part of the background of modern home life and became literally "postmodern" (Putnam 1993). As the material life supports of modernity are taken for granted, home becomes the supreme domain for personalization and, by consequence, of endless negotiations.

Home as Technical Terminal

The modern home paradigm, created by engineers on the one hand and social reformers on the other, was established in the period between the 1920s and the 1950s. Its design reflected an accommodation between technical innovation and the optimistic ideals of democracy, so omnipresent in Europe's reconstruction efforts after World War II.[2] In operation, the modern home would have a technical core hous-

---

1. When describing the introduction of home utilities in the American middle-class house, Schlereth (1992) selects an earlier period—between 1876 and 1915—acknowledging, however, the uneven pace in different regions. The same holds true for Europe, but the 1920s, the reconstruction period after World War I, were crucial for the public housing reforms that also affected the housing conditions of the lower classes.

2. See also chapter 6, "Bringing Modernity Home: Open Plan in the British Domestic Interior," by Judy Attfield.

ing hygiene-promoting and labor-saving appliances connected to water and energy services (Lawrence 1986; Paravicini 1990; Sèze 1994; Wright 1981).

The installation of necessary infrastructures to realize the project of the modern home required an unprecedented collaboration between the state and science-based industry. It transformed the home into a terminal of technical infrastructures, culminating in the installation of broadcast media whereby people can in principle, and often in actuality, see the backstage activities of others. Also, the opportunities in the lives of members of modern households came to rely on external structures of education, employment, and social provision. Likewise, professional success became more dependent on education than on family contacts. In consequence of these changes, not only have perceptions of the boundary between the home and the outside world been transformed, but the use of the home in fashioning social identity has also changed.

The technical and social logics that placed the modern home as a terminal on a vast network also implied a different decorative syntax from the nineteenth-century principles of hierarchy and symmetry. The modern decorative syntax stressed functional arrangements, simplicity, and utility. However, as the 1937 Mass Observation records showed, only a few avant-garde British householders wholeheartedly embraced an overtly modernist aesthetic devoid of hierarchy or symmetry, while divesting themselves of accumulated "clutter." Most would-be modernizing households in Britain merely simplified their object registers and coordinated their colors and patterns, while retaining some elements of hierarchy and symmetry in object placement. While most new British householders after 1950 still eschewed an overtly modernist style as too bare, the departure from the practices of previous generations was striking, if not recognizably modernist, in the eyes of design critics (Putnam 1995).

Modern planning initiated the dismantling of social and physical barriers erected when domestic servants played a central role in defining their employers' social position. In the design of the postwar modern home with its open-plan living and multifunctional spaces, internal divisions of domestic space and separation of activities were greatly weakened. However, spatial shifting of activities had already begun in the British popular home of the interwar period, when everyday leisure shifted from the living kitchen to the parlor, a room previously reserved for ceremonies of the extended family or for receptions of notables.

The arrangement of the postwar open-plan living room revolved around the paradigmatic three-piece suite—the furnishing ensemble of the twentieth century in Britain. Postwar modernity really involved a simplification of decor. The elaborate overmantel mirror and shelves for the display of extended family and community icons went into eclipse during the interwar period. Since 1960 living rooms have become more casual, while the kitchen and bathroom have been drawn toward the front stage and made suitable for presentation. In several countries, home life has turned progressively inward, away from the street and the public realm, toward the backstage of the private garden (Bernard 1992; Gullestad 1992; Halle 1993; Löfgren 1993a).

The design philosophy of the modern home reflected a view of the outside world as an impersonal, rational, and technical organization. However, although the rational and technical organization of corporations and public powers has been vital to the development of modern home life, its presence in the contemporary home decor is often masked. Instead, the two most popular subjects of representation in the modern home are still unpopulated, benign, "natural" landscapes and the immediate family as captured by photography (Halle 1993; Londos 1993).

It seems as if the monolithic external world is to be held at bay, while the personal and anecdotal can stand in their own right, free of the obligations to be respectable or to carry the destiny of class and nation. This symbolic transformation evidences not only the ignoring of the technical infrastructure underlying modern home life or the attenuation of family hierarchies, but also the depersonalization of the external public space, including nature. In general terms it raises the question of the extent to which contemporary modes of home life have become recognizably "postmodern."

"Postmodern" Living

In passing from ideal to reality, the modern home and the modern "project" of democracy and self-determination have become part of the background of our home life. It is sometimes hard to see the fundamental changes they have brought about in ways of living. The dismantling of social and physical barriers initiated by modern planning paralleled the obsolescence of domestic service. "Labor saving" became an unspoken presupposition in the marketing of domestic appliances. The modern household abstained from production and became solely dependent on the consumption of commercially produced goods. With the loss of the household's productive functions the scope of family activity shrank to nurturance of the young.

The modern "project" with its individualizing ideals concerning opportunities in life, self-determination, and consuming choices has profoundly affected the quality of relations between household members (Lunt and Livingstone 1992; Miller 1987; Silverstone and Hirsch 1992). In their turn, the economic and political structures of the modern world address discrete individuals at each life stage. Children, not only the most protected but also the most impressionable members of the household, are addressed independently through education and cultural media long before they leave the parental home.

It is now increasingly normal for young people of both sexes to reside independently from their parents for a time before establishing a shared conjugal home. This period serves to consolidate the importance of individual agency in relation to ideals of living. Above all, it has very important effects on the process by which conjugal intimacy is formed and norms of domestic life transmitted. Norms of conjugal life must now in principle be chosen by the partners, even though "traditional" motifs in the domestic division of labor reemerge in resulting negotiations (Duruz 1992; Franklin 1990; Kaufmann 1992).[3]

To speak of negotiation may create a misleading impression as, in homemaking, differing rationales may be accommodated in a shared result. As one of the principles of contemporary legitimation is choice, couples ground their existence by insisting on the rightness of their joint home-founding choices, especially the choice of partner. As Kaufmann's (1992) study of laundry routines in French homes shows, partners often "swallow" potential conflicts arising from the clash of received expectations in the actuality of joint decision making.

The arrangement of homes in which both partners move comfortably in the larger world is now often a mutual process. Significant conflict about decorative order arises only when partners bring unrecognized ties to tradition into the process of negotiation. For example, men may insist on giving family memorabilia or an image with personal resonance a central place in a decorative scheme, while women often insist on their decisive role in decoration (Putnam 1995; Shove 1994). The emerging pattern, however, is one in which the symbolic work performed by couples subsumes differences in a joint life project.

In such homemaking projects, social differentiation gains new cultural parameters. A survey of home alteration studies carried out in Britain between 1986 and 1992 revealed two complementary patterns across myriad lifestyle differences. One type of home alteration project was undertaken by households that continually invest in personal developmental activities, redefining spaces to fit these new ambitions. This type of project, typically involving the adaptation of a spacious old property, was undertaken in midcareer when incomes rise and childbirth, although not child rearing, has peaked. Adjustments to the house over several years created a platform for personal growth and may be seen as a metaphor for the household's working of possibilities in the external world (Putnam 1993).

The other pattern was seen in households that practice a more collective consumption as leisure, which compensates for time spent at work. Here there was more

---

3. Where strong gender differentiation exists and employment opportunities for women are restricted, as in contemporary Japan, these individualizing effects are less notable. The diminished public role of families that accompanies modernity leads to the ascendance of nurturance in the home over the preoccupation with identity construction as in many European and North American homes (Kurita 1993).

acceptance of received definitions of roles and rooms. Couples undertook substantial new collective projects at an early stage in marriage, before childbirth, when both partners were employed. The character of the work each contributed to such projects tended to complement that of the other, helping to redefine but also maintain gender roles. Typical projects involved a modernization or extension, with a result that is achieved in order to be enjoyed (consumed) and displayed. This mode of home alteration may also be viewed as a metaphor for the household's approach to the global system.

Such distinctive modes of domestic consumption imply the reproduction of different aspirations and aptitudes; they indicate, better than differences of taste do, how class position may be transmitted from generation to generation in the modern world. While personalization could be expected to exacerbate competing uses of space and conjugal discord about decorative order, interview programs instead report increasing openness and flexibility in the negotiation of home arrangements between partners. The anomaly is only apparent as personalization appears to stem from the same forces that lead to a more open and deliberate approach to homemaking relationships.

Symbolic communication between conjugal partners increases in importance and complexity, as couples define a relationship between individual projects, and received norms and expectations. In this perspective, the growth in DIY activity and the proliferation of stylistic variety in home decoration can be seen to involve more than commercial promotions or a mysterious turning away from the public realm, or "cocooning." "Carpentry culture" serves to redefine complementary gender roles in a process of symbolic exchange. Here, as in the renegotiation of domestic routines, one may distinguish differing articulations of tradition and modernity and degrees of jointness. As several studies have shown, these articulations depend on how kinship, education, employment, and social reference groups are related in life trajectories (Gullestad 1992; Miller 1990; Pratt 1981; Programme 1986; Segalen et al. 1990).

New Uses, New Meanings

In the face of a desire for personalization, common elements of material culture acquire new meanings. The standard equipment of the modern kitchen may lose its definite "modern" character and take on the desired personality: "I definitely decided not to have pine in my kitchen because I didn't want to be associated with that kind of woman," said a working wife who chose to personalize her hard-surfaced kitchen units with terra-cotta and plants. Beyond the common commodity culture, it is an individualized perception of the social world that activates a strongly personalizing aesthetic.

The scope for personalization is increased as previously backstage areas of the home are opened to social visits. Several studies, including the large survey that Yvonne Bernard (1992) directed for Institut National de la Statistique et des Études Économiques (INSEE) in France, indicate increasing demands on the kitchen as a focal point of domestic life. The enlarged kitchen as a locus for eating and other family activities is valued by women in particular as the "heart of the home." However, what distinguishes this focal point from the living room is its recognition of domestic labor. Whatever the actual division of labor, there is an important connection between this visibility of domestic work and the choice of role in the founding of the couple. So the enlarged kitchen or the kitchen-diner combination has become a potential stage for the renegotiation of roles.

Increased social loads on the kitchen space may be seen as an aspect of what Löfgren (1993a) calls "informalization." In several countries, separate formal dining space derived from a servant-based bourgeois model is being abandoned or marginalized in use in favor of the "living kitchen" or hall found in early farmhouses and maintained in most working-class homes. Such informalization, however, is most marked where the individualizing address of the outside world is strongest: the privileged social strata that confidently navigate its structures.

Even though it is now fashionable to eat in the kitchen while watching television, it does not lead to the complete dissolution of traditional spatial models of family life. Bernard's study, for example, showed a staggering 85 percent of French respondents who occupied the same place at the table each day. Where informalization involves the greater access of nonhousehold members to areas previously not used for reception, it may also involve the "dressing up" of these previously backstage areas.

If the postmodern kitchen receives an increased social demand, the principal living and dining spaces are increasingly stripped of their certain roles. The new semi-detached suburban homes of interwar Britain, constructed for a middle class without servants, necessarily contained a dining room, but this was more likely to be used as a home office and workroom, as the everyday detritus recorded by Mass Observation in 1937 showed. With the reduced importance of local social hierarchy and extended family networks, dedicated space for reception and ceremony has been subordinated to other needs: family relaxation, whether shared or individualized, and various forms of individual domestic work, such as study, office work, sewing, or hobbies (Bonnes et al. 1987). The "sitting-up" postures of the dining room or area, or the "sitting-down" postures of the principal living room or area, continue to serve as a functional basis for organizing activities.

In Christine Morley's (1996) recent study, the three-piece suite of sofa and two chairs was found to still exert a powerful structuring of behaviors and reduce domestic discord in the evening. However, as children grow and parents elaborate other interests, the competition of individualized activities may lead on the one hand to a hiving off from shared space to private space, and on the other to the creation of a second living room as shown, for example, in studies by Hart (1992) and Swales (1990).

The arrival in the home of broadcast media, personal computers, and electronic cultural products with their differentiated and individualizing addresses greatly exacerbates the difficulty of shared use of space (Silverstone and Hirsch 1992). In some homes, rituals of active collective life, such as the shared principal meal or the piano, still occupy an important place; in others, a collective and hierarchically ordered practice of television viewing exists. Television, musical apparatus, and computers pose an increasing challenge to shared activities in "postmodern" family life.

In terms of material culture, most homes now conform to the modern home paradigm. Homemaking as the dominant activity of a household has brought into being a system of supports for a mode of living, in relation to which householders order their lives and place themselves in the world. Although "postmodern" dwellers inhabit the structures of modernity, they hardly do it in a uniform way. To the extent that formal higher education rather than family connection is a route to socioeconomic position, to the extent that labor market opportunities exist for both genders, and to the extent that the number of generations sharing a household at different life stages has diminished, households more closely approximate the modern ideal of democracy and individual choice.

Conclusion

In this chapter we have considered fundamental transformations in the way in which domestic space has been made and used since the interwar period. These transformations have been presented as a succession of phases. During the establishment of the modern home paradigm, between the 1920s and 1950s, the emphasis was on the reconfiguration of space associated with the installation of a technical core linked to external energy and communications infrastructures. In the subsequent "postmodern" phase, the emphasis has been on changes in modes of living associated with habituation to the many ways in which these infrastructures address householders and shape the whole range of opportunities open to them.

This phasing is artificial to a degree. While it is important to acknowledge that the fundamental innovations associated with the design of the modern home were led by interventions of science-based industry, changes in the making of the domestic environment and its equipment and use have proceeded in parallel throughout. Habituation to living in the modern home has also been habituation to moving as individuals in the extensive and elaborate spaces of education and employment, consumption, and politics characteristic of the modern world. Thus the influence of external institutions on the domestic sphere in this century has been more extensive than is often recognized. The ability to navigate in these institutions has been a solvent of tradition, feeding the autonomy of generations in kinship structures and of individuals in conjugal partnerships. It also emerges as a primary differentiating factor across a broad range of studies of home arrangement.

The breaks with traditional spatial structures of social hierarchy and symmetrical arrangement stand out clearly. The more democratic spatial structuring of the modern home was paralleled by more equal relations between family members, stressing individual choice. Although the resulting negotiations of tasks and roles seemed to defy traditional destinies of class and gender, these reemerge in inflected forms. Informalization related to more equal social relations also affected rooms, like the more casual style of decor and relaxed conduct in the modern living room. More recently the main focus of informal family life shifted to the "postmodern" living kitchen. Likewise the conjugal personalization first elaborated in the living room is extended to the kitchen and even to the bathroom, two former backstage areas in the home. The very exposure of domestic work in the living kitchen has turned it into the prime postmodern locus of negotiation in the household. In these ways home continues to be an evolving system of material life supports.

Works Cited

Index

Works Cited

Abercrombie, Patrick. 1945. *Town and Country Planning.* 2d. ed. Oxford: Oxford Univ. Press.

Alderson, Stanley. 1962. *Britain in the Sixties: Housing.* Harmondsworth: Penguin.

Allan, Graham, and Graham Crow, eds. 1989. *Home and Family: Creating the Domestic Sphere.* London: Macmillan.

Alpers, Svetlana. 1983. *The Art of Describing: Dutch Art in the Seventeenth Century.* Chicago: Univ. of Chicago Press.

Altman, Irwin, and Mary Gauvain. 1981. "A Cross-Cultural and Dialectical Analysis of Homes." In *Spatial Representation and Behavior across the Life Span,* edited by Lynn S. Liben, Arthur H. Patterson, and Norg Newcombe, 283–320. New York: Academic.

Amaturo, Erica, et al. 1987. "Furnishing and Status Attributes: A Sociological Study of the Living Room." *Environment and Behavior* 19, no. 2: 228–49.

Ames, Kenneth L. 1984. "Meaning in Artifacts: Hall Furnishings in Victorian America." In *Material Culture Studies in America,* edited by Thomas J. Schlereth, 206–21. Nashville: American Association for State and Local History.

Ardener, Shirley, ed. 1981. *Women and Space: Ground Rules and Social Maps.* New York: St. Martin's Press.

Attfield, Judy. 1995. "Inside Pram Town: A Case Study of Harlow House Interiors, 1951–61." In *A View from the Interior: Women and Design,* edited by Judy Attfield and Pat Kirkham, 215–38. 2d. ed. London: Women's Press.

———. 1996. "'Give 'em Something Dark and Heavy': The Role of Design in the Material Culture of Popular British Furniture, 1939–1965." *Journal of Design History* 9, no. 3: 185–201.

Attfield, Judy, and Pat Kirkham, eds. 1989. *A View from the Interior: Feminism, Women, and Design.* London: Women's Press.

Bachelard, Gaston. 1957. *La poétique de l'espace.* Paris: Presse Universitaire de France.

Baker, Victoria J. 1983. *Wooden Shoes and Baseball Bats: A Study of Sociocultural Integration of Americans in The Hague.* Leiden: Institute of Cultural and Social Studies of the Leiden Univ.

Works Cited

Baltzell, E. Digby. 1962. *Philadelphia Gentlemen.* New York: Free Press.

Barley, Nigel. 1989. *Native Land.* Harmondsworth: Penguin.

Bassett, Keith, and John Short. 1980. *Housing and Residential Structure.* London: Routledge.

Baudrillard, Jean. 1968. *Le système des objets. La consommation des signes.* Paris: Denoël.

———. 1981. *For a Critique of the Political Economy of the Sign.* St. Louis: Telos.

Beckham, Sue B. 1988. "The American Front Porch: Women's Liminal Space." In *Making the American Home: Middle-Class Women and Domestic Material Culture, 1840–1940,* edited by Marilyn F. Motz and Pat Browne, 69–89. Bowling Green, Ohio: Bowling Green State Univ. Popular Press.

Bernard, Yvonne. 1992. *La France au logis.* Liège: Mardaga.

Bonnes, Mirilia, Maria Vittoria Giuliani, Flora Amoni, and Yvonne Bernard. 1987. "Cross-Cultural Rules for the Optimisation of the Living Room." *Environment and Behavior* 19, no. 2: 204–27.

Boudon, Philippe. 1972. *Lived-in Architecture: Le Corbusier's Pessac Revisited.* London: Lund Humphries.

Bourdieu, Pierre. 1984. *Distinction: A Social Critique of the Judgement of Taste.* London: Routledge & Kegan Paul.

Boym, Svetlana. 1994. "The Archeology of Banality: The Soviet Home." *Public Culture* no. 6: 263–92.

Broos, Ben. 1990. *Great Dutch Painters from America.* Zwolle: Waanders.

Burnett, John. 1978. *A Social History of Housing, 1815–1970.* Newton Abbot: David and Charles.

———. 1986. *A Social History of Housing, 1815–1985.* London: Methuen.

Canter, David. 1977. *The Psychology of Place.* London: Architectural Press.

Capek, Karel. 1934. *Over Holland.* Amsterdam: Van Holkema & Warendorf N.V.

Carlisle, Susan G. 1982. "French Homes and French Character." *Landscape* 26, no. 3: 13–23.

Carter, Alice C. 1974. "Marriage Counseling in the Early Seventeenth Century: England and the Netherlands Compared." In *Ten Studies in Anglo-Dutch Relations,* edited by Jan van Dorsten, 94–127. London: Oxford Univ. Press.

Cats, Jacob. [1625] 1655. "Houwelick." In *Alle de wercken* (The complete works). Amsterdam.

Chapman, Dennis. 1955. *The Home and Social Status.* London: Routledge & Kegan Paul.

Chevalier, Sophie. 1993. "Nous, on n'a rien de spécial." In *Chez-soi. Objets et décors: des créations familiales?* edited by Martine Segalen and Béatrix Le Wita, 86–101. Paris: Autrement.

———. 1994. "Au-delà d'une apparente banalité et d'un standard: des décors domestiques particuliers." *Archives suisses des traditions populaires* 90: 165–85.

Cieraad, Irene. 1988. *De elitaire verbeelding van volk en massa; een studie over cultuur* (On the influence of the imagery of rural folk and urban masses in present-day culture). Muiderberg: Coutinho.

_____. 1991a. "Traditional Folk and Industrial Masses." In *Alterity, Identity, Image: Selves and Others in Society and Scholarship,* edited by Raymond Corbey and Joep Th. Leerssen, 17–36. Atlanta: Editions Rodopi.

_____. 1991b. "Ethnographic Research Project on Dutch Cultural Identity." Synthesis reports I and II. RISC (France) in cooperation with the Univ. of Amsterdam.

_____. 1993. "The Material World of Five Dutch Households." Paper presented at the SISWO conference, The Global and the Local: Consumption and European Identity, Amsterdam.

_____. 1994. "Een eigen huis, een plek onder de zon" (On the cultural history of "having a place of your own"). *Rooilijn; Tijdschrift voor wetenschap en beleid in de ruimtelijke ordening* 27, no. 10: 456–61.

_____. 1995. "A Celebration of Differences: An Analysis of the Decor of Boys' and Girls' Bedrooms." *Vrijetijd en Samenleving: Tijdschrift voor de studie van vrijetijd* 13, no. 3–4: 63–79.

Clarijs, Petra. 1941. *Een eeuw Nederlandse woning* (A century of Dutch living). Amsterdam: N.V. Querido's Uitgevers-maatschappij.

Clark, Clifford E. 1986. *The American Family Home, 1800–1960.* Chapel Hill: Univ. of North Carolina Press.

Cohen, Anthony P. 1986. "Of Symbols and Boundaries, or Does Ertie's Greatcoat Hold the Key?" In *Symbolising Boundaries: Identity and Diversity in British Cultures,* edited by Anthony P. Cohen, 1–19. Manchester: Manchester Univ. Press.

Cohen, Lizabeth A. 1984. "Embellishing a Life of Labor: An Interpretation of the Material Culture of American Working-Class Homes, 1885–1915." In *Material Culture Studies in America,* edited by Thomas J. Schlereth, 289–305. Nashville: American Association for State and Local History.

Cohn, Jan. 1979. *The Palace or the Poorhouse: The American House as a Cultural Symbol.* East Lansing: Michigan State Univ. Press.

Coontz, Stephanie. 1988. *The Social Origins of Private Life: A History of American Families, 1600–1900.* London: Verso.

Cooper, Clare. 1974. "The House as Symbol of the Self." In *Designing for Human Behavior: Architecture and the Behavioral Sciences,* edited by Jon Lang et al., 130–46. Stroudsburg, Pa.: Dowden, Hutchingson & Ross.

Cowan, Ruth Schwartz. 1974. "A Case Study of Technological and Social Change: The Washing Machine and the Working Wife." In *Clio's Consciousness Raised: New Perspectives on the History of Women,* edited by Mary Hartman and Lois Banner, 245–53. New York: Harper & Row.

_____. 1983. *More Work for Mother: The Ironies of Household Technology from the Open Hearth to the Microwave.* New York: Basic Books.

_____. 1985. "The Industrial Revolution in the Home." In *The Social Shaping of Technology,* edited by Donald Mackenzie and Judy Wajcman, 181–201. Milton Keynes: Open Univ. Press.

Coward, Rosalind. 1984. *Female Desire.* London: Paladin.

Cowburn, William. 1966. "Popular Housing." *Arena: The Journal of the Architectural Association* 86, no. 905: 76–82.

Cox, Ian. 1951. *The South Bank Exhibition: A Guide to the Story It Tells.* London: HMSO.

Crow, Graham. 1989. "The Post-War Development of the Modern Domestic Ideal." In *Home and Family: Creating the Domestic Sphere,* edited by Graham Allen and Graham Crow, 14–32. London: Macmillan.

Csikszentmihalyi, Mihaly, and Eugene Rochberg-Halton. 1981. *The Meaning of Things: Domestic Symbols and the Self.* Cambridge: Cambridge Univ. Press.

Cunningham, Clark E. 1973. "Order in the Atoni House." In *Right and Left: Essays on Dual Symbolic Classification,* edited by Rodney Needham, 204–38. Chicago: Univ. of Chicago Press.

Damsma, Dirk. 1993. *Het Hollandse huisgezin; 1560–heden* (Dutch family life from 1560 till the present). Utrecht: Kosmos.

Darke, Jane. 1994. "Women and the Meaning of the Home." In *Housing Women,* edited by Rose Gilroy and Roberta Woods, 11–30. London: Routledge.

Daunton, Martin J. 1983. *House and Home in the Victorian City: Working-Class Housing, 1850–1914.* London: Edward Arnold.

Davidoff, Leonore, and Catherine Hall. 1987. *Family Fortunes.* London: Hutchinson.

Davidoff, Leonore, Jean L'Esperance, and Howard Newby. 1983. "Landscape with Figure: Home and Community in English Society." In *The Rights and Wrongs of Women,* edited by Ann Oakley and Juliet Mitchell, 139–75. Harmondsworth: Penguin.

De Amicis, Edmondo. [1876] 1990. *Nederland en zijn bewoners* (The Netherlands and its inhabitants). Utrecht: Uitgeverij L. J. Veen.

de Jager, Jos L. 1981. *Volksgebruiken in Nederland. Een nieuwe kijk op traditie* (Folk rituals in the Netherlands: A new approach). Utrecht: Het Spectrum.

de Jonge, Derk. 1960. *Moderne woonidealen en woonwensen in Nederland* (Modern living in the Netherlands: Ideals and wishes). Arnhem: Vuga-boekerij.

de Jongh, Eddy. 1986. *Portretten van echt en trouw; huwelijk en gezin in de Nederlandse kunst van de zeventiende eeuw* (Dutch seventeenth-century family portraits). Zwolle: Uitgeverij Waanders.

Delaunay, Quynh. 1994. *Histoire de la machine à laver: un objet technique dans la société française.* Rennes: Presses Universitaires de Rennes.

de Leenheer, Joannes. 1681. *Maria, virgo, mystica sub solis imagine. Emblematice expressa. Opusculum votivum.* Antwerpen.

de Mare, Heidi. 1992. "Twee viercanten hooch. Een plananalyse van enkele tekeningen van Simon Stevin" (An analysis of Stevin's architectural drawings). Discussion paper, Univ. of Delft (English translation forthcoming).

———. 1993. "The Domestic Boundary as Ritual Area in Seventeenth-Century Holland." In *Urban Rituals in Italy and the Netherlands: Historical Contrast in the Use of Public Space, Architecture and the Urban Environment,* edited by Heidi de Mare and Anna Vos, 108–31. Assen: Van Gorcum.

———. 1994a. "A Rule Worth Following in Architecture? The Significance of Gender in Simon Stevin's Architectural Knowledge System (1548–1620)." In *Women of the*

Golden Age: An International Debate on Women in Seventeenth-Century Holland, England, and Italy, edited by Els Kloek et al., 103–20. Hilversum: Verloren.

———. 1994b. "De keuken als voorstelling in het werk van Stevin en Cats" (The role of the kitchen in the works of Stevin and Cats). In *Van alle markten thuis. Vrouwen- en genderstudies in Nederland,* edited by Carolien Bouw et al., 185–230. Amsterdam: Uitgeverij Babylon-De Geus.

———. 1997a. "Räumliche Markierungen als holländischer Identität. Das grenzenlose Interesse von Simon Stevin (1548–1620) und Jacob Cats (1577–1660) in Grenzen und Grenzübergängen." In *Die Grenze. Begriff und Inszenierung,* edited by Markus Bauer and Thomas Rahn, 103–129. Berlin: Akademie Verlag.

———. 1997b. "De verbeelding onder vuur. Het realisme-debat der Nederlandse kunsthistorici" (On the realism debate in Dutch art history). *Theoretische Geschiedenis* 24, no. 2: 113–37.

———. 1998 (forthcoming). "Architectonische 'ghedachtenissen'. De huistekening als geheugensysteem in Stevins architectonisch denken" (Stevin's architectural drawings as a system of memory). In *Maatschappij en geheugen,* edited by Willem Frijhoff. Rotterdam.

Denby, Elizabeth. 1942. "Using Space to Advantage." In *The Post-War Home: Its Interior and Equipment,* edited by Oliver Lyttelton, 13–20. London: Studio.

———. 1944. *Europe Rehoused.* 2d ed. London: Allen & Unwin.

Depaule, Jean-Charles. 1985. *A travers le mur.* Paris: Éditions du Centre Georges Pompidou, CCI.

de Regt, Ali. 1984. *Arbeidersgezinnen en beschavingsarbeid: ontwikkelingen in Nederland, 1870–1940. Een historisch-sociologische studie* (On social education of Dutch working-class families). Amsterdam: Boom.

Design of Dwellings (Dudley Report). 1944. London: HMSO.

de Swaan, Abram. 1988. *In Care of the State: Health, Education, and Welfare in Europe and America.* Cambridge: Polity Press.

de Vrankrijker, Adrianus C. J. 1969. *Geschiedenis van de belastingen* (Tax history). Bussum: Fibula-Van Dishoeck.

de Weert, A. A. G. M., ed. 1981. *Beleving en gebruik van ramen in woningen; verslag van een onderzoek naar belevings-en gebruiksaspecten van ramen in voornamelijk de woonkamer en keuken in een en meergezinshuizen* (Report on the experience and use of front windows in the Netherlands). Almere: Nationale Woningraad.

Dittmar, Helga. 1992. *The Social Psychology of Material Possessions.* Hemel Hempstead: Harvester Wheatsheaf.

Donzelot, Jacques. 1979. *The Policing of Families.* New York: Pantheon Books.

Douglas, Mary. 1972. "Symbolic Orders in the Use of Domestic Space." In *Man, Settlement, and Urbanism,* edited by Peter J. Ucko, Ruth Tringham, and G. W. Dimbleby, 513–22. London: Duckworth.

———. 1979. *Purity and Danger: An Analysis of Concepts of Pollution and Taboo.* London: Routledge & Kegan Paul.

Works Cited

Douglas, Mary, and Baron Isherwood. 1979. *The World of Goods: Towards an Anthropology of Consumption.* New York: Basic Books.

Duncan, James S., ed. 1981. *Housing and Identity: Cross-Cultural Perspectives.* London: Croom Helm.

Duncan, James S., and Nancy G. Duncan. 1976. "Housing as Presentation of Self and the Structure of Social Networks." In *Environmental Knowing, Theories, Research, and Methods,* edited by Gary T. Moore and Reginald G. Colledge, 247–53. Stroudsburg, Pa.: Dowden, Hutchingson & Ross.

Duruz, Jean. 1992. "Laminex Dreams." Unpublished paper, Univ. of South Australia.

Dyos, Harold J., and Michael Wolf, eds. 1973. *The Victorian City: Images and Realities.* London: Routledge & Kegan Paul.

Ehrensperger, Ingrid. 1988. *Waschstag; Linge, lessive, labeur.* Biel: Museum Neuhaus.

Eleb-Vidal, Monique, and Anne Debarre-Blanchard. 1989. *Architectures de la vie privée. Maisons et mentalités XVIIe–XIXe siècles.* Bruxelles: Archives d'Architecture Moderne.

———. 1995. *L'invention de l'habitation moderne: Paris 1880–1914. Architectures de la vie privée, suite.* Paris: Éditions Hazan et Archives d'Architecture Moderne.

Elias, Norbert. [1939] 1978. *The Civilizing Process. Vol. 1: The History of Manners.* Oxford: Basil Blackwell.

———. [1939] 1982. *The Civilizing Process. Vol. 2: State Formation and Civilization.* Oxford: Basil Blackwell.

———. 1983. *Die höfische Gesellschaft. Untersuchungen zur Soziologie des Königtums und der höfischen Aristokratie.* Frankfurt: Suhrkamp.

Featherstone, Mike. 1991. *Consumer Culture and Postmodernism.* London: Sage.

Felson, Marcus. 1976. "The Differentiation of Material Life Styles: 1925 to 1966." *Social Indicators Research,* no. 3: 397–421.

Fortes, Meyer. 1949. *The Web of Kinship among Tallensi.* London: Oxford Univ. Press.

Forty, Adrian. 1986. *Objects of Desire: Design and Society since 1750.* London: Thames & Hudson.

Fox, Kenneth. 1985. *Metropolitan America: Urban Life and Urban Policy in the United States, 1940–1980.* London: Macmillan.

Foy, Jessica H., and Thomas J. Schlereth, eds. 1992. *American Home Life, 1880–1930: A Social History of Spaces and Services.* Knoxville: Univ. of Tennessee Press.

Franits, Wayne E. 1993. *Paragons of Virtue: Women and Domesticity in Seventeenth-Century Dutch Art.* Cambridge: Cambridge Univ. Press.

Franklin, Adrian. 1990. "Variations in Marital Relations and the Implications for Women's Experience of the Home." In *Household Choices,* edited by Tim Putnam and Charles Newton, 57–65. London: Futures Publications.

Frazer, William Hamisch. 1981. *The Coming of the Mass-Market, 1850–1914.* London: Macmillan.

Frederick, Christine. 1914. *The New Housekeeping: Efficiency Studies in the Home Management.* New York: Doubleday.

_____. 1920. *Household Engineering: Scientific Management in the Home*. Chicago: American School of Home Economics.

Frykman, Jonas, and Orvar Löfgren. 1987. *Culture Builders: A Historical Anthropology of Middle-Class Life*. New Brunswick: Rutgers Univ. Press.

Gans, Herbert. 1972. *People and Plans: Essays on Urban Problems and Solutions*. Harmondsworth: Penguin.

Gibberd, Frederick. 1953. *Town Design*. London: Architectural Press.

Giddens, Anthony. 1984. *The Constitution of Society*. Cambridge: Polity.

Giedion, Siegfried. 1969. *Mechanization Takes Command: A Contribution to Anonymous History*. 3d ed. New York: Norton.

Gittens, Diane. 1993. *The Family in Question*. Basingstoke: Macmillan.

Glaser, Barney G., and Anselm L. Strauss. 1967. *The Discovery of Grounded Theory: Strategies for Qualitative Research*. New York: Aidinc.

Goffman, Erving. 1959. *The Presentation of Self in Everyday Life*. New York: Doubleday.

_____. 1967. *Interaction Ritual: Essays on Face-to-Face Behavior*. Chicago: Aldine Publishing Company.

Goldthwaite, Richard A. 1972. "The Florentine Palace as Domestic Architecture." *American Historical Review* 77: 977–1012.

Gottlieb, Carla. 1981. *The Window in Art: From the Window of God to the Vanity of Man. A Survey of Window Symbolism in Western Painting*. New York: Abaris Books.

Goubert, Jean-Pierre. 1989. *The Conquest of Water: The Advent of Health in the Industrial Age*. Oxford: Polity.

Gould, Richard A., and Michael B. Schiffer, eds. 1981. *Modern Material Culture: The Archeology of Us*. New York: Academic.

Greenhalgh, Peter, ed. 1990. *Modernism in Design*. London: Reaktion Books.

Grijzenhout, Frans, and Henk van Veen, eds. 1992. *De Gouden Eeuw in perspectief. Het beeld van de Nederlandse zeventiende-eeuwse schilderkunst in later tijd* (On the imagery of Dutch seventeenth-century painting). Nijmegen: SUN.

Grünn, Helene. 1978. *Wäsche Waschen. Volkskunde aus dem Lebensraum der Donau*. Vienna: Niederösterreichischen Heimatwerkes.

Guardian. 1992. 22 April.

Gullestad, Marion. 1984. *Kitchen-Table Society: A Case Study of the Family Life and Friendships of Young Working-Class Mothers in Urban Norway*. Oslo: Universitetsforlaget.

_____. 1992. *The Art of Social Relations: Essays on Culture, Social Action, and Everyday Life in Modern Norway*. Oslo: Scandinavian Univ. Press.

Haak, Bob. 1984. *The Golden Age: Dutch Painters of the Seventeenth Century*. New York: Stewart, Tabori & Chang.

Hall, Edward T. 1966. *The Hidden Dimension: Man's Use of Space in Public and Private*. New York: Doubleday.

Halle, David. 1993. *Inside Culture: Art and Class in the American Home*. Chicago: Univ. of Chicago Press.

Handlin, David P. 1979. *The American Home: Architecture and Society, 1815–1915.* Boston: Little, Brown.

Harris, Neil. 1990. *Cultural Excursions.* Chicago: Univ. of Chicago Press.

Hart, Beatrice. 1992. "Meanings of a Shared Space." Master's thesis, Middlesex Univ.

Haudricourt, André-Georges. 1987. *La technologie science humaine.* Paris: Maison des Sciences de l'Homme.

Hausen, Karin. 1987. "Grosse Wäsche; technischer Fortschritt und sozialer Wandel in Deutschland vom 18. bis ins 20. Jahrhundert." *Geschichte und Gesellschaft* 13, no. 3: 273–303.

Hayden, Dolores. 1981. *The Grand Domestic Revolution: A History of Feminist Designs for American Homes, Neighborhoods, and Cities.* Cambridge, Mass.: MIT Press.

———. 1984. *Redesigning the American Dream: The Future of Housing, Work, and Family Life.* New York: W. W. Norton & Co.

Heller, Geneviève. 1979. *Propre en ordre. Habitation et vie domestique, 1850–1930: l'example Vaudois.* Lausanne: Ed. d'en bas.

Helming, Elisabeth, and Barbara Scheffran, eds. 1988. *Die Grosse Wasche.* Bonn: Rheinland Verlag.

Hollander, Anne. 1991. *Moving Pictures.* Cambridge, Mass.: Harvard Univ. Press.

Hunt, Pauline. 1989. "Gender and the Construction of Home Life." In *Home and Family: Creating the Domestic Sphere,* edited by Graham Allan and Graham Crow, 66–81. Basingstoke: Macmillan.

Inman, Marjorie, and Charlan Graff. 1984. "Effects of House-Style and Life-Style Stage on Family Social Climate." In *Man-Environment, Qualitative Aspects. 7th International Conference on People and Their Physical Surroundings,* edited by Enric Pol, Josep Muntanola, and Montserrat Morales, 240–50. Barcelona: Ed. Universitat de Barcelona.

Karn, Valerie. 1993. "The Control and Promotion of the Quality of New Housing in Britain." Paper presented at the European Network for Housing Research, Budapest.

Kaufmann, Jean-Claude. 1988. *La chaleur du foyer. Analyse du repli domestique.* Paris: Méridiens-Klincksieck.

———. 1992. *La trame conjugale. Analyse du couple par son linge.* Paris: Nathan (English translation forthcoming from Middlesex Univ. Press, London).

Kent, Susan, ed. 1990. *Domestic Architecture and the Use of Space: An Interdisciplinary Cross-Cultural Study.* London: Cambridge Univ. Press.

Kidder, Tracy. 1986. *House.* London: Pan Books.

King, Anthony D. 1984. *The Bungalow: The Production of a Global Culture.* London: Routledge & Kegan Paul.

Kopytoff, Igor. 1986. "The Cultural Biography of Things: Commoditization as Process." In *The Social Meaning of Things: Commodities in Cultural Perspective,* edited by Arjun Appadurai, 64–91. Cambridge: Cambridge Univ. Press.

Korosec-Serfaty, Perla. 1984. "The Home from Attic to Cellar." *Journal of Environmental Psychology* 4: 303–21.

Koumans, Madeline M. C. 1930. *La Hollande et les Hollandais du 19e siècle vus par les Francais*. Maastricht: Van Aalst.

Kron, Joan. 1983. *Home-Psych: The Social Psychology of Home and Decoration*. New York: Clarkson N. Potter, Inc.

Kruizinga, Jacobus H. 1962. *Nederland door vreemde bril* (The Netherlands through foreign eyes). Assen: Uitgeverij de Torenlaan.

Kruse, Lenelis. 1974. *Räumliche Umwelt, die Phänomenologie des räumlichen Verhaltens als Beitrag zu einer psychologischen Umwelttheorie*. Berlin: Walter de Gruyter.

Kurita, Yasuyuki. 1993. "Ordre et désordre domestique." In *Chez-soi. Objets et décors: des créations familiales?* edited by Martine Segalen and Béatrix Le Wita, 164–79. Paris: Autrement.

Laermans, Rudi. 1990. "De mannequin-maatschappij. Over look, lijfstijl en lichamelijkheid" (On looks and corporality). *De Gids* 153, no. 4: 265–74.

———. 1993. "Learning to Consume: Early Department Stores and the Shaping of the Modern Consumer Culture." *Theory, Culture, and Society* 10, no. 4: 79–102.

Laermans, Rudi, and Carine Meulders. 1993. "Gezond Wonen: de woning als lichaams-machine" (On well-being in the home). In *Wegwijs Wonen*, edited by André Loeckx, Herman Neuckermans, and Roger Dillemans, 47–50. Leuven: Davidsfonds.

Latour, Bruno. 1988. *The Pasteurization of France*. London: Harvard Univ. Press.

Lawrence, Roderick J. 1983. "The Comparative Analyses of Homes: Research Method and Application." *Social Science Information* 22, no. 3: 461–85.

———. 1986. *Le seuil franchi*. Geneva: Georg.

———. 1987. "What Makes a House a Home?" *Environment and Behavior* 19, no. 2: 154–68.

Le Corbusier and François de Pierrefeu. 1958. *The Home of Man*. London: Architectural Press.

Leroi-Gourhan, André. 1965. *Le geste et la parole*. Paris: Albin-Michel.

———. 1973. *Evolution et technique*. Paris: Albin-Michel.

Leuker, Maria-Theresia. 1991. "Widerspenstige und Tugenthafte Gattinnen. Das Bild der Ehefrau in niederländische Texten aus dem 17. Jahrhundert." In *Ordnung und Lust. Bilder von Liebe, Ehe und Sexualität in Spätmittelalter und früher Neuzeit*, edited by Hans Jürgen Bachorski, 99–122. Trier: Wissenschaftliche Verlag.

Levie, Tirtsah, and Henk Zantkuijl. n.d. *Wonen in Amsterdam in de 17de en 18de eeuw* (Living in Amsterdam in the seventeenth and eighteenth century). Purmerend: Muusses.

Lewis, Ben W. 1952. *British Planning and Nationalization*. London: Allen & Unwin.

Löfgren, Orvar. 1993a. "Le foyer suedois: un projet national." In *Chez-soi. Objets et décors: des créations familiales?* edited by Martine Segalen and Béatrix Le Wita, 51–67. Paris: Éditions Autrement.

———. 1993b. "Swedish Modern: Nationalizing Consumption and Aesthetics in the Welfare State." Paper presented at the SISWO conference, The Global and the Local: Consumption and European Identity, Amsterdam.

Londos, Eva. 1993. *Uppat vaggarna i svenska hem* (What's upon the wall in the Swedish home). Stockholm: Carlssons.

Lukacs, John. 1970. "The Bourgeois Interior." *American Scholar* 39, no. 4: 616–30.

Lunt, Peter, and Sonia Livingstone. 1992. *Mass Consumption and Personal Identity*. Buckingham: Open Univ.

Lupton, Ellen. 1993. *Mechanical Brides: Women and Machines from Home to Office*. New York: Cooper-Hewitt National Museum of Design, Smithsonian Institution, and Princeton Architectural Press.

McCracken, Grant. 1988. *Culture and Consumption: New Approaches to the Symbolic Character of Consumer Goods and Activities*. Bloomington: Univ. of Indiana Press.

_____. 1989. "'Homeyness': A Cultural Account of One Constellation of Consumer Goods and Meanings." In *Interpretative Consumer Research*, edited by Elizabeth Hirschman, 168–83. Provo, Utah: Association for Consumer Research.

Macdonald, Keith M. 1989. "Building Respectability." *Sociology* 23, no. 1: 55–80.

McDowell, Linda. 1983a. "City and Home: Urban Housing and the Sexual Division of Space." In *Sexual Divisions: Patterns and Processes*, edited by Mary Evans and Clare Ungerson, 142–63. London: Tavistock.

_____. 1983b. "Towards an Understanding of the Gender Divisions of Urban Space." *Environment and Planning D: Society and Space* 1, no. 2: 59–72.

McKenna, Madeline. 1991. "The Suburbanization of the Working-Class Population of Liverpool." *Social History* 16: 173–89.

MacPherson, James C. 1984. "Environments and Interaction in Row-and-Column Classrooms." *Environment and Behavior* 16, no. 4: 481–502.

Madigan, Ruth, and Moira Munro. 1991. "Gender, House, and 'Home': Social Meanings and Domestic Architecture in Britain." *Journal of Architecture and Planning Research* 8, no. 2: 116–32.

Madigan, Ruth, Moira Monro, and Susan J. Smith. 1990. "Gender and the Meaning of Home." *International Journal of Urban and Regional Research* 14: 625–47.

Malcolmson, Patricia. 1986. *English Laundresses: A Social History, 1850–1930*. Chicago: Univ. of Illinois Press.

Mårtenson, Rita. 1981. "Innovations in Multinational Retailing: IKEA on the Swedish, Swiss, German and Austrian Furniture Market." Ph.D. diss., Univ. of Gothenburg, Sweden.

Martin, Bernice. 1984. "'Mother Wouldn't Like It!': Housework as Magic." *Theory, Culture, and Society* 2, no. 2: 19–36.

Matrix. 1984. *Making Space: Women and the Man-Made Environment*. London: Pluto.

Mauss, Marcel. [1923] 1990. *The Gift: The Form and Reason for Exchange in Archaic Societies*. Translated by W. D. Halls. London: Routledge.

Messerschmidt, Donald A., ed. 1981. *Anthropology at Home in North America: Methods and Issues in the Study of One's Own Society*. Cambridge: Cambridge Univ. Press.

Meulders, Carine. 1992. "The Struggle for Cleanliness: 1750–1950." Research report, Univ. of Leuven, Department of Sociology of Religion and Culture.

Meulders, Carine, and Rudi Laermans. 1993. "Aan gene zijde van de reinheid. Over de geschiedenis van het wassen en de verschuivende grenzen tussen 'vuil' en 'proper'" (On the history of laundering and standards of cleanliness). In *De kern van het verschil. Culturen en identiteiten,* edited by Carolien Bouw and Bernard Kruithof, 59–77. Amsterdam: Amsterdam Univ. Press.

Meyer, Erna. 1926. *Der neue Haushalt. Ein Wegweiser zur wirtschaftlicher Hausführung.* Stuttgart.

Miller, Daniel. 1987. *Material Culture and Mass Consumption.* Oxford: Basil Blackwell.

_____. 1990. "Appropriating the State on the Council Estate." In *Household Choices,* edited by Tim Putnam and Charles Newton, 43–55. London: Futures Publications.

_____. 1994. *Modernity: An Ethnographic Approach. Dualism and Mass Consumption in Trinidad.* Oxford: Berg.

_____, ed. 1995. *Acknowledging Consumption.* London: Routledge.

Miner, Horace. 1956. "Body Ritual among the Nacirema." *American Anthropologist* 58: 503–7.

Moore, Jeanne. 1994. "Home: Image or Reality? The Meaning of Home to Homeless People." Paper presented at Ideal Homes? conference, Teesside Univ.

Morley, Christine. 1990. "Homemakers and Design Advice in the Postwar Period." In *Household Choices,* edited by Tim Putnam and Charles Newton, 89–97. London: Futures Publications.

_____. 1996. *The Three-Piece Suite.* London: Middlesex Univ. Press.

Motz, Marilyn Ferris, and Pat Browne, eds. 1988. *Making the American Home: Middle-Class Women and Domestic Material Culture, 1840–1940.* Bowling Green, Ohio: Bowling Green State Univ. Popular Press.

Mount, Ferdinand. 1982. *The Subversive Family.* London: Allen and Unwin.

Muchembled, Robert. 1978. *Culture populaire et culture des élites dans la France moderne (XVe–XVIIIe siècle).* Paris: Flammarion.

_____. 1988. *L'invention de l'homme moderne.* Paris: Fayard.

Munro, Moira, and Ruth Madigan. 1993. "Privacy in the Private Sphere." *Housing Studies* 8, no. 1: 29–45.

Murray, Charles. 1994. *Underclass: The Crisis Deepens.* London: Institute of Economic Affairs.

Muthesius, Hermann. 1910. *Das englische Haus. Band II: Anlage und Aufbau.* Berlin: Ernst Wasmuth.

Muthesius, Stefan. 1982. *The English Terraced House.* New Haven: Yale Univ. Press.

Nairn, Tom. 1983. "Britain's Living Legacy." In *The Politics of Thatcherism,* edited by Stuart Hall and Martin Jacques, 281–90. London: Lawrence & Wishart.

Nasar, Jack L. 1989a. "Symbolic Meanings of House Styles." *Environment and Behavior* 21, no. 3: 235–57.

_____. 1989b. "Perception, Cognition, and Evaluation of Urban Places." In *Public Places and Spaces,* edited by Irwin Altman and Ervin H. Zube, 31–56. New York: Plenum .

Nederlandse. 1966. *De Nederlandse huisvrouw* (The Dutch housewife). Eindhoven: Philips Nederland N.V.

———. 1984. *De Nederlandse huisvrouw op weg naar het jaar 2000* (The Dutch housewife on her way to the year 2000). Amsterdam: Aselect.

Niemeyer, Jan W. 1973. *Cornelis Troost, 1696–1750.* Assen: Van Gorcum.

Nippert-Eng, Christina E. 1996. *Home and Work.* Chicago: Univ. of Chicago Press.

Norberg-Schulz, Christian. 1971. *Existence, Space, and Architecture.* New York: Praeger.

———. 1980. *Genius Loci: Towards a Phenomenology of Architecture.* London: Academy Editions.

Olson, Clark D. 1985. "Materialism in the Home: The Impact of Artifacts on Dyadic Communication." In *Advances in Consumer Research, Vol. 12,* edited by Elizabeth C. Hirschman and Morris B. Holbrook, 388–93. Provo, Utah: Association for Consumer Research.

Orland, Barbara. 1991. *Wäsche Waschen. Technik und Sozialgeschichte der häuslichen Wäschepflege.* Hamburg: Rowohlt.

Pahl, Ray. 1984. *Divisions of Labour.* Oxford: Basil Blackwell.

Paravicini, Ursula. 1990. *Habitat au feminin.* Lausanne: Presses Universitaires et Polytechniques Romandes.

Paul-Lévy, Françoise, and Marion Segaud. 1983. *Anthropologie de l'espace.* Paris: Éditions du Centre Georges Pompidou, CCI.

Pellegrino, Pierre. 1994. "Introduction: Styles de vie et modes d'habiter." *Espaces et Sociétés: Espaces et styles de vie,* no. 73: 9–12.

Pennartz, Paul J. J. 1989. "Semiotic Theory and Environmental Evaluation: A Proposal for a New Approach and a New Method." *Symbolic Interaction* 12, no. 2: 231–49.

———. 1990. "Adults, Adolescents, and Architects: Differences in Perception of the Urban Environment." *Environment and Behavior* 22, no. 5: 675–714.

Perrot, Michelle. 1979. "Femmes au lavoir." *Sorcières* 19: 128–33.

———. 1980. "La ménagère dans l'espace Parisien au XIXe siècle." *Les annales de la recherche urbaine* 9, no. 3: 3–22.

Perrot, Philippe. 1984. *Les dessus et les dessous de la bourgeoisie. Une histoire du vêtement au XIXe siècle.* Bruxelles: Ed. Complexe.

Pinçon, Michel, and Monique Pinçon-Charlot. 1989. *Dans les beaux quartiers.* Paris: Seuil.

Porteous, J. Douglas. 1976. "Home: The Territorial Core." *Geographical Review* 66: 383–90.

Prak, Niels L. 1991. *Het Nederlandse woonhuis: 1800–1940* (The Dutch house: 1800–1940). Delft: Delftse Universitaire Pers.

Pratt, Gerry. 1981. "The House as an Expression of Social Worlds." In *Housing and Identity: Cross-Cultural Perspectives,* edited by James S. Duncan, 135–80. London: Croom Helm.

Praz, Mario. 1994. *An Illustrated History of Interior Decoration from Pompeii to Art Nouveau.* 1964. Reprint, London: Thames and Hudson.

Programme Observation du Changement Social. 1986. *L'Esprit des lieux.* Paris: Centre Nationale des Recherches Scientifiques.

Putnam, Tim. 1993. "Beyond the Modern Home." In *Mapping the Futures: Local Cultures, Global Change,* edited by Jon Bird et al., 150–65. London: Routledge.

———. 1995. "Between Taste and Tradition: Decorative Order in the Modern Home." *Journal of the John Rylands University Library of Manchester* 77, no. 1: 91–108.

Putnam, Tim, and Charles Newton, eds. 1990. *Household Choices.* London: Futures Publications.

Rakoff, Robert M. 1977. "Ideology in Everyday Life: The Meaning of the House." *Politics and Society* 7: 85–104.

Rapoport, Amos. 1969. *House Form and Culture.* London: Prentice-Hall.

Relph, Edward. 1976. *Place and Placeness.* London: Pion.

Rex, John, and Robert Moore. 1967. *Race, Community, and Conflict: A Study of Sparbrook.* Oxford: Oxford Univ. Press.

Riffault, Marie Cécile. 1980. "De Chaptal à la mère Denis: Histoire de l'entretien du linge domestique." *Culture Technique,* no. 3: 257–63.

Roberts, Marion. 1991. *Living in a Man-Made World: Gender Assumptions in Modern Housing Design.* London: Routledge.

Robinson, Franklin W. 1974. *Gabriel Metsu (1629–1667): A Study of His Place in Dutch Genre Painting of the Golden Age.* New York: Abner Schram.

Rochberg-Halton, Eugene. 1984. "Object Relations, Role Models, and Cultivation of the Self." *Environment and Behavior* 16, no. 3: 335–68.

Rosenfeld, Myra N. 1978. *Sebastiano Serlio on Domestic Architecture: Different Dwellings from the Meanest Hovel to the Most Ornate Palace.* Cambridge, Mass.: MIT Press.

Rullo, Giuseppina. 1987. "People and Home Interiors: A Bibliography of Recent Psychological Research." *Environment and Behavior* 19, no. 2: 250–59.

Russell, Gordon. 1959. "Focus on British Design." *Design,* no. 112: 20–64.

Rutherford, Jonathan. 1990. "A Place Called Home: Identity and the Cultural Politics of Difference." In *Identity: Community, Culture, Difference,* edited by Jonathan Rutherford, 9–29. London: Lawrence & Wishart.

Rybczynski, Witold. 1987. *Home: A Short History of an Idea.* Harmondsworth: Penguin.

Sadalla, Edward K., and Virgil L. Sheets. 1993. "Symbolism in Building Materials: Self-Presentational and Cognitive Components." *Environment and Behavior* 25, no. 2: 155–80.

Sadalla, Edward K., Beth Vershure, and Jeffrey Burroughs. 1987. "Identity Symbolism in Housing." *Environment and Behavior* 19, no. 5: 569–87.

Sadooghi, Marzi. 1989. "De magische functie van de open-raamcultuur; een studie naar de culturele betekenis van het open-raampatroon in Nederland" (The magical function of the Dutch window). Master's thesis, Univ. of Amsterdam.

Sanchez-Robles, J. Cecilio. 1980. "The Social Conceptualization of Home." In *Meaning and Behaviour in the Built Environment,* edited by Geoffrey Broadbent, Richard Bunt, and Tomas Llorens, 113–33. New York: John Wiley.

Saunders, Peter. 1990. *A Nation of Home Owners*. London: Unwin Hyman.

Saunders, Peter, and Peter Williams. 1988. "The Constitution of the Home: Towards a Research Agenda." *Housing Studies* 3, no. 2: 81–93.

Schaffer, Frank. 1972. *The New Town Story*. London: Paladin.

Schäffer, Jacob Christiaan. 1766. *De gemakkelyke en in de huishouding alleszins ten hoogsten voordeelige wasch-machine* (On the practical and profitable domestic washing machine). Amsterdam: J. C. Sepp.

Schama, Simon. 1979. "The Unruly Realm: Appetite and Restraint in Seventeenth-Century Holland." *Daedalus, Journal of the American Academy of Arts and Sciences* 108, no. 3: 103–23.

———. 1987. *The Embarrassment of Riches: An Interpretation of Dutch Culture in the Golden Age*. London: Collins.

Schlereth, Thomas J., ed. 1982. *Material Culture Studies in America*. Nashville: American Association for State and Local History.

———. 1992. "Conduits and Conduct: Home Utilities in Victorian America, 1876–1915." In *American Home Life, 1880–1930: A Social History of Spaces and Services,* edited by Jessica H. Foy and Thomas J. Schlereth, 225–41. Knoxville: Univ. of Tennessee Press.

Schotel, G. D. J. 1867. *Het oud-hollands huisgezin der zeventiende eeuw* (On Dutch family life in the seventeenth century). Haarlem: A. C. Kruseman.

Schuurman, Anton. 1989. "Materiële cultuur en levensstijl. Een onderzoek naar de taal der dingen op het Nederlandse platteland in de 19e eeuw: de Zaanstreek, Oost-Groningen, Oost-Brabant" (On Dutch regional material culture of the nineteenth century). Ph.D. diss., Univ. of Wageningen.

Segalen, Martine, et al. 1990. *"Etre bien dans ses meubles." Une enquête sur les normes et les pratiques de "consommation" du meuble*. Paris: Centre d'Ethnologie Française.

Segalen, Martine, and Béatrix Le Wita, eds. 1993. *Chez-soi. Objets et décors: des créations familiales?* Paris: Éditions Autrement.

Sèze, Claudette. 1994. *Confort moderne*. Paris: Éditions Autrement.

Shove, Elizabeth. 1986. "Domestic Decision Making: A Question of Power." Ph.D. diss., Univ. of York.

———. 1994. "Four Walls, Three Pieces, and Two Patterns." Paper presented at the Ideal Homes? conference, Teesside Univ.

———. 1995. "The Division and Integration of Building Professional Knowledge." End of Award Report to the Economic and Social Research Council. Project no. R000221106.

Shove, Elizabeth, and John Connaughton. 1990. "Investigating the Feasiblity of Implementing Low-Energy Housing at No Extra Cost." Report for the Building Research Establishment Energy Conservation Support Unit, Davis Langdon and Everest Consultancy Group.

Silberzahn-Jandt, Gudrun. 1991. *Wasch-maschine. Zum Wandel vom Frauenarbeit im Haushalt*. Marburg: Jonas.

Silverstone, Roger, and Eric Hirsch, eds. 1992. *Consuming Technologies: Media and Information in Domestic Spaces.* London: Routledge.

Simmel, Georg. 1980. *La philosophie de la monnaie.* Paris: Presses Universitaires de France.

Skelton, Peter. 1971. "The Dutch Window Puzzle." *Holland Herald* 12, no. 6: 25–26.

Spain, Daphne. 1992. *Gendered Spaces.* Chapel Hill: Univ. of North Carolina Press.

Spradley, James. 1979. *The Ethnographic Interview.* New York: Holt, Rinehart, and Winston.

Stalleybrass, Peter, and Allon White. 1986. *The Politics and the Poetics of Transgression.* London: Methuen.

Stamp, Gavin, and André Goulancourt. 1986. *The English House, 1860–1914: The Flowering of English Domestic Architecture.* London: Faber and Faber.

Stevin, Simon. [1590] 1939. *Het Burgherlick Leven* (On burgher's life). Reprint, Amsterdam: N. V. De Wereldbibliotheek.

———. 1649. "Vande oirdeningh der steden" (On town planning) and "Byvough der Stedenoirdening, vande oirdening der deelen eens huis Met 't gheene daer ancleeft" (On domestic architecture). In *Materiae Politicae,* edited by Hendrick Stevin, 3–128. Leiden.

Stewart, Ann, and Roger Burridge. 1989. "Housing Tales of Law and Space." *Journal of Law and Society* 16: 65–82.

Strasser, Susan. 1982. *Never Done: A History of American Housework.* New York: Pantheon Books.

Sutton, Peter C. 1984. *Masters of Seventeenth-Century Dutch Genre Painting.* Philadelphia: Philadelphia Museum of Art.

Swales, Valerie M. 1990. "Making Yourself at Home: A Study in Discourse." In *Household Choices,* edited by Tim Putnam and Charles Newton, 103–18. London: Futures Publications.

Swenarton, Mark. 1981. *Houses Fit for Heroes: The Politics and Architecture of Early State Housing in Britain.* London: Heinemann Educational Books.

Synnott, Anthony. 1990. "Pink Flamingoes: Symbols and Symbolism in Yard Art." In *Dominant Symbols in Popular Culture,* edited by Ray B. Browne, Marshall W. Fishwick, and Kevin O. Browne, 96–127. Bowling Green, Ohio: Bowling Green State Univ. Popular Press.

t'Amsterdamsch hoerdom. 1684. *t'Amsterdamsch hoerdom* (Amsterdam's whores). t'Amsterdam: Elias logchemse van Rijn.

Tardieu, Suzanne. 1976. *Le mobilier rural traditionnel français.* Paris: Aubier-Flammarion.

Taverne, Ed R. M. 1984. "Architecturae domesticae Stevini synopsis." In *Bouwen in Nederland, Leids Kunsthistorisch Jaarboek Vol. 3,* edited by Jacobus J. Terwen, 441–56. Delft: Delftsche Uitgevers Maatschappij.

Thompson, Francis M. L. 1982. *The Rise of Suburbia.* Leicester: Leicester Univ. Press.

Thornton, Peter. 1978. *Seventeenth-Century Interior Decoration in England, France, and Holland.* New Haven: Yale Univ. Press.

————. 1985. *Authentic Decor: The Domestic Interior, 1620–1920.* London: Weidenfeld and Nicholson.

Townsend, Peter. 1977. *Family Life of Old People.* London: Penguin Books.

Tuan, Yi-Fu. 1971. *Man and Nature.* Washington: Association of American Geographers.

Tubbs, Ralph. 1942. *Living in Cities.* Harmondsworth: Penguin.

Turner, Victor W. 1969. *The Ritual Process: Structure and Anti-structure.* Chicago: Aldine Publishing Company.

Tzonis, Alexander. 1972. *Towards a Non-Oppressive Environment.* Press Series on the Human Environment. New York: Braziller.

Ungerer, Catherine. 1986. "Les valeurs urbaines du propre. Blanchissage et hygiène à Paris au XVIIIe siècle." *Ethnologie Française* 16, no. 3: 295–98.

Van Braam, Aris. 1966. *Verhuld en onthuld; sociologische beschouwingen over privacy en deprivatisering* (Veiled and revealed: On the sociology of privacy and deprivatization). Assen: Van Gorcum.

Van den Heuvel, Charles. 1995. "De Huysbou, De Crychconst en de Wysentijt. Stevins teksten over architectuur, stede- en vestingbouw in het licht van zijn wetenschappelijke oeuvre" (On Stevin's scientific works). In *Spiegheling en Daet. Simon Stevin van Brugghe (1548–1620). Exhibition's catalogue,* edited by Valerie Logghe, 44–69. Brugge: Centrale Openbare Bibliotheek.

Van de Ven, Cornelis J. M. 1981. "Toekomstvisie op het raam (1)" (The future of the window). In *Het raam: raakvlak van techniek en beleving van het gebouw,* edited by H. L. Leebeek et al., 79–80. Delft: TH Delft.

Van Gennep, Arnold. [1909] 1981. *Les rites de passage.* Paris: Éditions Picard.

Van Moorsel, Wies. 1987. "Wonen: meer dan een dak boven je hoofd?" (On Dutch postwar architectural reform). In *Inrichten,* edited by Hetty Berens et al., 5–13. Groningen: Zomeruniversiteit Vrouwenstudies Groningen.

————. 1992. *Contact en controle; over het vrouwbeeld van de Stichting Goed Wonen* (On the gender image of postwar Dutch domestic reform). Amsterdam: SUA.

Van Oostrom, Frits P. 1992. *Court and Culture: Dutch Literature, 1350–1450.* Berkeley: Univ. of California Press.

Van Setten, Hendrik. 1986. "In de schoot van het gezin. Opvoedingscondities in Nederlandse gezinnen in de twintigste eeuw" (In the heart of the family: Child rearing conditions in Dutch families in the twentieth century). Ph.D. diss., Univ. of Nijmegen.

Veblen, Thorstein. [1899] 1945. *The Theory of the Leisure Class: An Economic Study of Institutions.* New York: Viking Press.

Vera, Hernan. 1989. "On Dutch Windows." *Qualitative Sociology* 12, no. 2: 215–40.

Verdier, Yvonne. 1979. *Façons de faire, façons de dire. La laveuse, la couturière, la cuisinière.* Paris: Gallimard.

Vigarello, Georges. 1988. *Concepts of Cleanliness: Changing Attitudes in France since the Middle Ages.* Cambridge: Cambridge Univ. Press.

Ward, Colin. 1993. *New Town, Home Town: The Lessons of Experience.* London: Calouste Gulbenkian Foundation.

Warner, W. Lloyd. 1960. *Social Class in America: A Manual of Procedure for the Measurement of Social Status.* New York: Harper & Row.

Warnier, Jean-Pierre, ed. 1994. *La paradoxe de la marchandise authentique: Imaginaire et consommation de masse.* Paris: L'Harmattan.

Wasserman, Françoise. 1989. *Blanchisseuse, laveuse, repasseuse. La femme, le linge, et l'eau.* Fresnes: Ecomusée.

Watson, Sophie. 1986. "Housing and the Family." *International Journal of Urban and Regional Research* 10, no. 1: 8–28.

Weber, Eugene. 1976. *Peasants into Frenchmen: The Modernization of Rural France, 1870–1914.* Stanford: Stanford Univ. Press.

Weiner, Annette B. 1985. "Inalienable Wealth." *American Ethnologist* 12, no. 12: 210–27.

Wheelock, Arthur K., Jr., ed. 1995. *Johannes Vermeer.* Zwolle: Waanders.

Whitehead, Christine M. E. 1990. "Housing Policy in the 1980s." *Economics* 26: 151–55.

Whiteley, Nigel. 1993. *Design for Society.* London: Reaktion Books.

_____. 1994. "High Art and the High Street." In *The Authority of the Consumer,* edited by Russell Keat, Nigel Whiteley, and Nicholas Abercrombie, 119–37. London: Routledge.

Williams, Raymond. 1977. *Marxism and Literature.* Oxford: Oxford Univ. Press.

Wilson, Elizabeth. 1985. *Adorned in Dreams.* London: Virago.

Woodham, Jonathan. 1995. "Resisting Colonization: Design History Has Its Own Identity." *Design Issues* 11, no. 1: 22–37.

Wright, Gwendolyn. 1980. *Moralism and the Model Home: Domestic Architecture and Cultural Conflict in Chicago, 1873–1913.* Chicago: Univ. of Chicago Press.

_____. 1981. *Building the Dream: A Social History of Housing in America.* New York: Pantheon Books.

Wright, Patrick. 1985. *On Living in an Old Country: The National Past in Contemporary Britain.* London: Verso.

_____. 1991. *A Journey through Ruins: The Last Days of London.* London: Radius.

Young, Michael, and Peter Willmott. 1957. *Family and Kinship in East London.* Harmondsworth: Penguin.

_____. 1960. *Family and Class in a London Suburb.* London: Routledge & Kegan Paul.

Zantkuijl, Henk J. 1993. *Bouwen in Amsterdam; het woonhuis in de stad* (Domestic architecture in Amsterdam). Amsterdam: Poortpers B. V.

Zeldenrust-Noordanus, Mary. 1956. "Onderzoek naar enige psychologische aspecten van de woninginrichting" (On psychological aspects of furnishings). Ph.D. diss., Univ. of Amsterdam.

Zola, Emile. [1876] 1969. *L'Assomoir.* Paris: Flammarion.

Zukin, Sharon. 1982. *Loft Living: Culture and Capital in Urban Change.* Baltimore: Johns Hopkins Univ. Press.

Index

McCracken, Grant, 90n. 7, 95n. 1, 140
Maids. *See* Servants
Manchester Guardian (newspaper), 63
Mantelpieces, 40n. 4, 79, 146
Maori, 6, 83, 93, 94
Marginal zones, 54, 58
Market and Opinion Research International
    Ltd. (MORI), 60n. 1
Market traders (homeowners), 70, *71,* 72
Marriage: Cats on, 14, 18–20; companionate,
    107, 111; early stages of, 149; home-related
    decisions and, 132; premarital independ-
    ence and, 148; secrets of, 123. *See also* Fam-
    ilies; Newlyweds; Weddings
Marx, Karl, x
Marxism, 6, 8n. 9
Mary, Virgin, 40
Masonry, 75
Mass Observation (1937), 146, 150
Mass-produced housing, 82, 108, 109, 117. *See
    also* Preconstructed parts
Mass-produced objects, 144; "alienation" of,
    83, 84; as heirlooms, 91, 94; at Les
    Fontenelles, 88; personalization of, 86–87
Master bedrooms, 10, 111–12
Material culture: British studies of, 2; design
    history and, 74n. 3; family lineage and, 92;
    French studies of, 1, 83; housing and, 143;
    Miller on, 6; personalization and, 149
Mauss, Marcel, 58, 93
Mealtimes, 110–11, 151. *See also* Dining rooms
Mechanized housework, 118. *See also* Appli-
    ances
Mechanized laundering, 125, 128
Mechanized window cleaning, 43
Medical-hygienic discourse, 120–21, 125–26
Men: blinds symbolic of, 49; in coffeehouse,
    46; exterior decoration and, 71; family
    identity and, 82; financial responsibilities
    of, 126; home improvement by, 60; honor
    and, 20; interior decoration and, 139, 140,
    148; keys of, 18; laundering and, 123; light
    symbolic of, 40; prostitutes and, 31n. 1, *37;*
    public careers of, 30; visits with, 56, 114;
    window cleaning by, 43, 47, 50, 51; window
    climbing by, 32, 47. *See also* Patriarchy
Mennonites, 44
Messerschmidt, Donald A., 3n. 2
Messiness. *See* Disorderliness
Metsu, Gabriel, 33, 44; *Man Writing a Letter, 42,*
    43; *Woman Reading a Letter, 34,* 39–40, 43
Meyer, Erna, 126

Mezuzas, 55
Microbes, 8, 120
Middle classes: cleanliness and, 119, 120;
    Dutch, 44; family boundaries in, 107;
    French, 84, 88; furniture decisions of,
    139–40, 141; gender division in, 126; house
    buying by, 136, 141
Middle-class housing: American, 145n. 1;
    British, 109, 150; Dutch, 13–30, 36, 49;
    halls of, 54; parlors of (*See* Parlors)
Middle-class women, 7, 10, 46, 51, 127
Midlands, The, 64–72
Migrants, 50
Military laundries, 124
Military operations, 119
Miller, Daniel, 6, 11n. 13, 74
Miner, Horace, 4
Mirrors, 36–37, 51, 58, 146
Model cottages, 77
Modernity: contradiction and, 11n. 13; Dutch
    housing and, *38–39;* infrastructure for,
    145–46, 151; laundering and, 121n. 1, 124,
    128; mass consumption and, 84n. 1; open
    plan and, 6, 73–82; resistance to, 146;
    showcase mentality and, 51. *See also* Post-
    modern home life
Morality, 14, 21n. 4, 30, 46–47, 120
More Beautiful Everyday Living movement,
    9n. 11
Morley, Christine, 150–51
Mortgages, 60n. 1
Mothers. *See* Women
Motor vehicles, 70. *See also* Traffic
Moucharabiehs, 55
Mourning, 46n. 6
Munch, Edvard, 140
Municipal housing estates. *See* Local authority
    housing estates
Museum of Popular Arts and Traditions
    (Paris), 83
Music, 98
Musical apparatus, 40, 151

Nairn, Tom, 63
Nameplates, 66
Nanterre, 85–92
Napoleon III, Emperor of the French, 123
Narrative practices, 6, 87n. 4, 92, 94
National Association of Estate Agents, 70
Nature, 75, 84. *See also* Green zones; Land-
    scapes
Nazi Germany, 48

Professional window cleaners, 43, 47, 50, 51
Professional women, 126
Prostitution, 4, 52; dishonor of, 20; in 1930s, *37;* sexual liberation and, 39; "showcase mentality" and, 31, 32. *See also* Brothels
Psychology. *See* Environmental psychology; Sociopsychological elements
Public housing, 95–106, 145n. 1. *See also* Local authority housing estates
Public infrastructure. *See* Infrastructure
Public-private boundary, 12; artistic symbols of, 43; atmosphere and, 7; Dutch domesticity and, 3, 30, 36; female domestication and, 3–4; halls and, 54, 55, 56, 59; honor and, 19–20; house exteriors and, 62; interior decor and, 132; in nineteenth century, 7–8; porches and, 67; in postmodern era, 146; raised ground floors and, 35; vertical blinds and, 50; visitors and, 4; windows and, 32, 38, 43, 47, 48, 51
Public space: burgher halls and, 18; conceptual evolution of, 3; defilement by, 58; Dutch working class and, 36, 48; empirical study of, 96; female entrance into, 51; infection risk in, 8, 125–26; interiors as, 19; withdrawal from, 147, 149. *See also* Streets
Public washhouses, 8, 123–24, 128
Putnam, Tim, 74n. 5

Quarrels, 19
Quimper, 88

Radio, 98
Rainwater, 16, 17, 18
Rakoff, Robert M., 5n. 6
Ranch fencing, 68
Rape, 52
Rational housekeeping, 126, 127
Reading, 39, 99, 114–15
Reconstruction (post-WWII era), 73, 75, 76, 81, 145
Recreation, 101, 146, 148. *See also* Broadcast media; Games
Rectangularity, 105
Rectilinearity, 105
Reform movements: British, 5, 6, 73n. 1, 74; domestic, 9, 77, 82, 145
Relaxation, 7, 115; disorder and, 103; in parlors, 146; pleasantness and, 99–100, 101, 104; in postmodern home, 150; tidiness and, 116
Religious calendar, 122

Religious paintings, 20n. 3
Religious symbols, 55, 123
Relph, Edward, 96
Renaissance, 15
Rental housing, 5, 60, 62, 74. *See also* Apartment buildings
"Repro-contemporary" style, 81
"Right to buy" legislation, 5, 63, 66
Rituals, 4. *See also* Passage rites
Roller blinds, 47
Rome, 90
Roofs, 15, 105
Royal College of Surgeons of England, 63
Rufin family, 87–89
Rural residences, 6, *69;* Dutch, 48; French, 54, 83–85, 92–93. *See also* "Cottage" style; Farmhouses
Rural washing places, 8, 121–24, 128
Russell, Gordon, 79–80
Rustic furniture, 81
Rustic objects, 49
Rutherford, Jonathan, 68
Rybczynski, Witold, 13, 14, 30

Sadalla, Edward K., 62
Sanitary facilities, 16, 18. *See also* Bathrooms; Hygiene; Plumbing
Sash windows, 33, 35, 36, 44, 49
Saxmundham, 134
Scandinavian furniture, 81
Scandinavian social studies, 2
Schäffer, Jacob Christiaan, 124
Schama, Simon, 3, 11n. 13, 13, 14, 30
Schlereth, Thomas J., 145n. 1
Schoolchildren. *See* Children
Scientific discourse, 120–21, 125–26
Scientific planning, 75
Sculleries, 18, 127
Seasons, 122
Segaud, Marion, 56
Seine River, 123
Self-identity, 108, 140
Serlio, 15
Servants: in art, 33, 39; in brothels, 44; cleaning by, 43, 47; dining spaces and, 150; disorder before, 19; in Dutch homes, 14, 35–36; laundering by, 124, 125, 128; modern planning and, 146; quarters for, 76
Settees, 139, 141. *See also* Sofas
Sewer systems, 126
Sewing, 39, 44